This Land

AMERICA, LOST AND FOUND

This Land

AMERICA,
LOST AND FOUND

Dan Barry

BLACK DOG
& LEVENTHAL
PUBLISHERS
NEW YORK

Black Dog & Leventhal Publishers
Hachette Book Group
1290 Avenue of the Americas
New York, NY 10104

www.hachettebookgroup.com
www.blackdogandleventhal.com

First Edition: September 2018

Black Dog & Leventhal Publishers is an imprint of Running Press, a division of Hachette Book Group. The Black Dog & Leventhal Publishers name and logo are trademarks of Hachette Book Group, Inc.

The publisher is not responsible for websites (or their content) that are not owned by the publisher.

The Hachette Speakers Bureau provides a wide range of authors for speaking events. To find out more, go to www.HachetteSpeakersBureau.com or call (866) 376-6591.

Additional copyright/credits information is on page 391.

Print book interior design by Kris Tobiassen of Matchbook Digital

Library of Congress Cataloging-in-Publication Data

Names: Barry, Dan, 1958– author.
Title: This land : dispatches from real America / Dan Barry.
Description: First edition. | New York, NY : Black Dog & Leventhal Publishers, [2018] | Includes index.
Identifiers: LCCN 2018011819| ISBN 9780316415514 (hardcover) | ISBN 9781549141973 (audio download) | ISBN 9780316415484 (ebook)
Subjects: LCSH: United States—Social conditions—21st century. | United States—Civilization—21st century.
Classification: LCC HN59.2 .B365 2018 | DDC 306.0973—dc23
LC record available at https://lccn.loc.gov/2018011819

ISBNs: 978-0-316-41551-4 (hardcover); 978-0-316-41548-4 (ebook)

Printed in China

APS

10 9 8 7 6 5 4 3 2 1

Contents

Part Three: Misdeeds

HERE YOU HAVE YOUR MORNING PAPERS, ALL ABOUT THE CRIMES

Part Four: Intolerance

I'M ALWAYS CHASING RAINBOWS

Part Five: Hard Times
HARD TIMES, HARD TIMES, COME AGAIN NO MORE

Part Six: Nature
THE BEAUTIFUL, THE BEAUTIFUL RIVER

Part Seven: Grace
AH! SWEET MYSTERY OF LIFE

Part Eight: The Ever-Present Past

SHINE LITTLE GLOW-WORM, GLIMMER, GLIMMER

Epilogue: In the Middle of Nowhere, a Nation's Center ·

Introduction

If I'm in Illinois, the rental is from Texas; if I'm in Texas, it is Wyoming; if I'm in Wyoming, Florida. The license plate alone marks me as someone not from here, wherever here is. And yet here I am.

In a small sedan considered mid-size only in Avis-speak, I adjust the mirrors and the driver's seat to fit my lanky, question-mark frame. I make musical scat of the syndicated radio provocateurs before choosing a local station on the inferior AM bandwidth, where every sound seems to pass through the filter of an indefinable past. Depending on mood and place, I might absorb the aching wails of Hank Williams, the fire-next-time portents of some storefront preacher, or the folksy reassurance of an avuncular DJ who once was God in times of weather-related school closings.

With any luck I might find a program called *Tradio*, or *Swap Shop*, through which callers engage in a sort of on-air eBay. Once, while driving through West Virginia, I heard a woman announce that she was looking to sell a house, 16 acres, a bowling ball, and a sequin dress slit up the side.

Seat; check. Mirrors; check. Radio; check. The steering wheel carries the trace of drivers before me, their commingled scent on the wheel and now on my palms, faintly, until I reach the hotel. Have I booked a hotel? This is a serious matter. I have slept on the floors of airports; in condemnation-worthy motels with scorched electrical outlets; in a bed-and-breakfast whose proprietor offered the use of her absent husband's bathrobe, hanging there on a treadmill; in an unsupervised, nearly deserted Old West hotel haunted by Molly, a maid who ended it all with poison and alcohol a century ago.

I usually wind up in the soothing sameness of a Hampton Inn or Holiday Inn Express, places I recommend for their pliant pillows and welcome absence of any personal touch. They are also often within walking distance of a roadside chain restaurant, where I can consider the angles of the story before me while drinking table wine and eating freshly nuked salmon.

And now I am driving away from the city, along an interstate that leads to a secondary road that leads to a tertiary road that might very well be unpaved, my lunch some truck-stop trail mix washed down with a Coke. In more than a decade, I have been pulled over only twice: once on a remote road along the Mexican border, by a deputy sheriff who didn't recognize the car and wanted reassurance that I wasn't smuggling undocumented immigrants; and once in Kansas, because I was speeding while singing backup for the Moody Blues on "Nights in White Satin." I accepted the ticket I so richly deserved—for singing, if not for speeding—and dutifully signaled as I pulled away.

Where I was headed then is so different from where I am headed now, no matter the dulling uniformity of the rental cars and hotels and chain restaurants. I am driving and driving to some American somewhere, confident only in the revelations that await.

The idea was mad, farcical, quixotic, so I agreed to do it.

For the last three years I had been happily roaming Gotham while writing a twice-weekly column for *The New York Times* called "About New York." But a temporary assignment to cover the aftermath of Hurricane Katrina in 2005 had given me a glimpse of the larger American story. I chronicled the Gulf Coast communities immersed in mucky black waters; the roads scarred by the hulls of ships storm-muscled onto land; the telltale markings on shotgun-house doors, indicating date of search and number of bodies found. (I had seen these somber symbols before, on Lower Manhattan brick and steel.)

A defining moment came when *The Times* photographer Nicole Bengiveno and I spotted a dead body on a downtown New Orleans street, its feet jutting from a wet blue tarp surrounded by traffic cones. We watched as six National Guardsmen strode up to the corpse. Two blessed themselves, one took a snapshot, and all walked away.

Shaken by what we had seen, Nicole and I drove on to record other dystopian moments under the hot September sun. With the body still there when we returned in the evening, I reported the situation to a Louisiana state trooper. He explained that he was the one who had placed those traffic cones around the body—to keep some news truck from running over it.

The next morning, the corpse still lay on the pavement, where it would remain through another hot day and into the dusk of another curfew. How could a corpse be left to decompose, like carrion, on a downtown street in a major American city? Would this dead black son of New Orleans have been left there for days if he had been white? Hunched over my laptop in the rental car, I wrote what I saw, and felt.

This was the moment that sparked the idea of a wandering national column. Mad, farcical, quixotic: Let's do it.

Over a few drinks, a couple of national editors and I struck upon the name of this proposed column: "This Land." I'd been raised on the words and music of Woody Guthrie—mostly through the muse of Pete Seeger, a secular saint in my boyhood home—and was perhaps a bit too proud that I knew the lesser-known lyrics to Guthrie's subversive masterwork, "This Land Is Your Land." You know, about the other side of that No Trespassing sign saying nothing—that side that "was made for you and me."

So began more than a decade on the other side of that sign. Spurred by curiosity and, occasionally, the news, I have crisscrossed the country in a mostly whimsical endeavor that started toward the end of the presidency of Bush the Younger, spanned the entirety of Obama's eight-year presidency, and has dipped now into the startling era of Trump. The many dozens of columns I've written, some of which are included in this collection, have explored American moments small and profound, fleeting and enduring: columns about a county fair bake-off in Marquette, Michigan, and a bullet fired through the living room window of a black mayor in Greenwood, Louisiana; about the larger meaning of a knocked-down telephone booth in Prairie Grove, Arkansas, and the economic struggles of a dairy farmer in Ferndale, California; about a gathering of a group of retired burlesque queens in Baraboo, Wisconsin, and the execution by electric chair of a man in Nashville, Tennessee—a death I witnessed. Filed from every one of the 50 states, these stand-alone dispatches also fit together, jigsaw-like, into an epic larger than their individual selves.

But when combined, what were they telling me?

What was The Story?

In my travels, I am rarely alone and thank God for that, since I find myself to be miserable company. Sometimes I am with Todd Heisler, a revered *Times* photographer who covers wars and parades with the same intense dedication of purpose, or Kassie Bracken, an exceptional *Times* videographer with a flair for visual storytelling. Often the person beside me is Nicole Bengiveno, whose empathy is evident with every click of her camera, and who deserves national commendation for having put up with my road-weary crankiness. But the first photographer to work with me on "This Land" was Ángel Franco, of Harlem and the Bronx, whose mild learning issue as a child was misdiagnosed as intellectual disability. Having never forgotten the stigma, he has used his photography ever since to dignify the lives of the misunderstood, the disenfranchised, the underestimated.

For our inaugural column, in January 2007, Franco and I went to Logan, a small West Virginia city grappling with a fatal mine disaster and the decline of King Coal. At first we did nothing more than walk the quiet streets, noticing: the coal train snaking and squealing through the city's core; the ashen dust settling on buildings along the tracks; the shop-window display featuring a Jesus Christ figurine carved from anthracite. Just—noticing.

In trying to file a column a week in those first years, our adventures would often begin Monday morning at Newark International Airport and end on Friday, or Saturday, even Sunday, with frantic efforts to figure out where to go next. Louisiana? Montana? Maine? Helping to ease the madness of this misbegotten venture was our colleague Cate Doty, who often handled everything from story ideas and travel logistics to dinner recommendations.

Kalispell, Montana. Lake Mead, Nevada. Ainsworth, Nebraska. Newport, Indiana. Pascagoula, Mississippi. Greensburg, Kansas. Hollywood, Maryland. Sylva, North Carolina. The datelines blur into one.

We went to a retirement home in Jacksonville, Florida, to visit the coroner in *The Wizard of Oz*. To Havana, Illinois, to report on the Asian carp infesting the Illinois River. To Kalaupapa, Hawaii, to meet the last residents of a colony to which those with Hansen's disease (also known as leprosy) were once relegated. To Bethel, Alaska, to explore the cat-and-mouse games of bootleggers. To Bill, Wyoming— population 5, maybe—to stay in a new hotel catering to railway workers. To Cottage Grove, Wisconsin, to meet the pastor who baptized Jeffrey Dahmer in a prison whirlpool. To Denver, to cover the annual convention of the Sovereign Grand Lodge of the Independent Order of Odd Fellows, where I felt oddly at home.

I often had no idea what the next column would be. One Saturday morning, while scanning online newspapers for ideas, I noticed a community news item about a farewell breakfast in a V.F.W. hall in Mohave Valley, Arizona, for a high school graduate named Resha Kane. After the meal, she was to be taken by motorcycle escort to Las Vegas, to catch a flight to Fort Hood, where she would begin her Army career in exchange for college tuition.

I called Franco, who, of course, got it immediately. We flew out the next day, and were present for the send-off of Ms. Kane, who looked much younger than her 18 years. Franco's memorable photograph of this small young woman in fatigues, gazing up at her father while saying goodbye—the fear of her unknown, of ours, expressed in her eyes—hangs in the newsroom.

Here was a part of The Story, no? Touched by geopolitical forces far removed from this remote corner of southwest Arizona, an 18-year-old girl-woman was leaving family and home to give her service and perhaps her life to her country. To represent and defend the Odd Fellows and their wives, those railroad workers in Wyoming, that prison pastor in Wisconsin, the coroner of Munchkinland. Franco. Me.

Given our fractured and fractious times, you could argue that this country has no center; that what exists instead is an ever-widening chasm between the reds and blues, the haves and have-nots, the rural and urban, us and them. At times it seems as though the United States of America is less one country than a collection of distinctly different countries, connected more by geographic happenstance than by a shared embrace of ideals.

In the days and weeks after the 2016 election, the pundits who inhabit cable television spoke often of no longer recognizing their own country. Some of them could not imagine who out there, beyond the hushed confines of a television studio in Manhattan or Washington or Atlanta, would ever dream of electing yet another professional politician, particularly one with the surname of Clinton? Others could not abide the notion of voting for a real-estate developer and reality-television star who trafficked in race-tinged conspiracy theories, misogyny, and the celebration of the Trump brand.

But as I traveled the country for a decade, from 2007 to 2017, politics rarely entered my mind. With no campaign events to attend, no polling data to interpret, I lingered and listened, following the advice of Tom Heslin, a good friend and my editor long ago at the *Providence Journal*, who told me once:

Slow it down.

The men and women I encountered were not numbers to be tallied in yet another political survey; they were individuals, trying to get through another day in

America. By slowing it down, I witnessed their wills being tested by crime, by fates, by natural disaster. I watched them struggle and tumble, laugh and cry, pause to take a breath or whisper a prayer. To echo Faulkner, I saw them endure. And that is what, I think, this volume of columns and stories conveys: the American endurance that transcends politics, and is ever-present no matter the presidential era.

If a tornado tears through our city, we clean up. If a new highway bypasses our town, we erect a roadside monument to declare our defiant continuance. If society mistakenly relegates us to sheltered workshops and group homes, we learn to drive. If the Mississippi threatens once again to overflow its banks, we work side-by-side to erect a sandbag wall. And if racists burn down our church, we rebuild.

For me, it all goes back to that first visit for that first column—to Logan, West Virginia.

After Franco and I had taken our maiden walk down the streets of this distressed coal town—after we had dodged the coal train and reflected before that anthracite Jesus—we went in search of a late lunch or early dinner. We slid into a booth in a narrow, downtown diner and studied what was left of the daily specials.

The waitress, smiling through her late-day weariness, pulled out her pad, poised her pen in anticipation, and asked the eternal question:

"Are we ready yet, children?"

PART ONE

Change

After the ball is over,
after the break of dawn

A Way of Life, Seen Through Coal-Tinted Glasses

LOGAN, W.VA. — JANUARY 14, 2007

That daily reminder of coal's dominion courses again through this small town of a city, stopping traffic, giving pause. It is a coal train, maybe 90 open cars long, creaking and groaning and coating the old brick buildings hard against the tracks with a fine, black dust.

And as a cold dusk settles like more dust on Logan's tired streets, Chuck Gunnoe sits in an unheated launderette and explains how coal runs through veins beyond those in the surrounding hills. He is a coal miner seeking work, and he yearns to have his boots muddied, his face blackened—to be swallowed again by the Appalachian earth.

The mines received him two days after he turned 18. Now 24, and between mines, he takes pride in doing the same crazy-dangerous work that his grandfather did. But the primary draw has always been the money, and with his girlfriend two months pregnant, he says he needs the $20 an hour he can earn by toiling miles removed from natural light.

"It's the best-paying job in this state," says Mr. Gunnoe, who hours earlier filled out an application with a local mine. "Unless you're college-educated."

And yes, he knows, the burly man says softly. He knows what happened to the two miners in the Aracoma coal mine not five miles down the road. Who here doesn't.

Downtown Logan has changed a lot, its people say, for so many reasons: the mechanization of mining, leading to fewer jobs; many young people seeking opportunity elsewhere; a Walmart replacing a nearby mountaintop. A walk down once-bustling Stratton Street, past the closed Capitol movie theater, the closed City Florist, the closed G. C. Murphy dime store, can be a walk through stillness.

But in certain profound ways, Logan has not changed at all, and not just because warm apple pies sell for $5.99 at the Nu-Era Bakery, or because the waitress at Yesterday's Diner refills coffee cups with maternal affection. ("Are we ready yet, children?")

For one, the city of 1,600 remains the West Virginia template for public corruption, with election fraud a local specialty. Not long ago, investigators caught the former mayor in some wrongdoing, and soon he was wearing a wire; down went the police chief, the county sheriff and the county clerk, among others. Now the former mayor sits behind the large glass window of his law office on Stratton Street, disbarred, on probation, on display.

For another, Logan remains the coal-field capital. This means that a figurine made of coal in a pawnshop window depicts Jesus comforting a miner. It means that schoolchildren learn about the 1921 armed uprising called the Battle of Blair Mountain, when more than 10,000 miners wanting to unionize squared off against state and federal troops. That you are a friend of coal, or you are not. That miners die.

Almost exactly a year ago, a fire broke out in that nonunion mine down the road, the Aracoma Alma Mine No. 1, owned by the state's dominant coal company, Massey Energy. Every employee escaped, save two: Don Israel Bragg, 33, and Elvis Hatfield, 46.

Months later, two reports—one by the state's mining-regulatory office, the other by J. Davitt McAteer, a veteran mine-safety consultant—shed light on what had happened in the Aracoma darkness. In Mr. McAteer's words, the evidence suggested that the fire had "erupted at the lethal intersection of human error and negligent mining practices."

A misaligned conveyor belt ignited and spilled coal that should not have been there. A fire hose contained no water. A missing ventilation wall allowed smoke to seep into a primary escapeway meant to provide fresh air to miners.

A crew of a dozen escaping miners hit that smoke and began to panic. In blinding, nauseating clouds of black, they grabbed one another's shirts and tried to feel their way to a door leading to fresh air. Ten made it to the other side; two did not.

One more thing, the reports said: the maps of the mazelike mine given to the would-be rescuers were inaccurate—a cardinal sin in the land of coal.

The deaths of Mr. Bragg and Mr. Hatfield provided an unnecessary reminder of how dangerous coal mining can be. In all, 24 miners died on the job in West

Virginia last year, with this year's first fatalities coming on Saturday, when two miners died in a partial tunnel collapse inside a mine about 75 miles south of here.

Massey Energy, which employs more than 4,000 in West Virginia, has declined detailed comment about the two reports, other than to say that some conditions in the mine had not met its standards, and that "deficiencies were not fully recognized by mine personnel or by state or federal inspectors."

Chuck Gunnoe

Few in Logan criticize Massey publicly. The closest they come is to say that the widows have sued, and to smile when recalling how the company's president, Don L. Blankenship, spent more than $3 million trying to wrest control of the Legislature from Democrats last year. He called it his "And for the Sake of the Kids" campaign, and he lost.

Instead, people like the mayor, Claude Ellis, known as Big Daddy, point out that Massey gives a big employee party in the center of the city every summer, attracting tens of thousands. Last year people had to wear a company-issued T-shirt to hear Hank Williams Jr. and other entertainers sing. Mr. Ellis says the company gave him 100 or so of those shirts.

"Without coal, we'd be in a bad state," Mr. Ellis explains, as if to concede that coal is the true Big Daddy.

Back in the cold of that launderette, Mr. Gunnoe proudly displays photographs of himself in the mines: on his knees, unable to stand, soot-covered, one with coal. In one photo, he and other miners are hunched around pizza boxes. Christmas present from the boss, he explains.

A Teenage Soldier's Goodbyes
on the Road to Over There

MOHAVE VALLEY, ARIZ. — MARCH 4, 2007

It is time. The fresh young soldier has a plane to catch.

People file out of the dimness of V.F.W. Post 404 and into the morning light. They chat and smoke and mill about on the parking lot gravel, then come together to form a ragged circle of support.

The dozen motorcyclists among them finalize plans to escort the soldier for most of the two-hour ride to the airport in Las Vegas. Just before raising voices and fists to a recording of the country-western anthem "God Bless the U.S.A.," the crowd bows its collective head and asks God for another favor: to keep safe this soldier, just 10 months removed from her senior prom.

That night she wore a gown the color of valentines; this morning she wears fatigues the color of mud. The uniform has a name patch, KANE, for Pvt. Resha Kane. Eighteen years old and five feet tall. Of Needles High School, Class of 2006, and, lately, of the United States Army, Fourth Infantry Division.

Earlier this morning, Private Kane walked out of her family home in Needles, a small railroad city in California just across the Colorado River. Before her, the family van, packed with two Army duffel bags. Behind her, a living room decorated with family portraits and a large mock check from her current employer.

"Reserved in the name of Resha Kane," the check reads, $37,200 from the Army College Fund and the Montgomery G.I. Bill. It represents her partial compensation for enlisting for three years and 22 weeks. She plans to study biochemistry someday.

At the moment, though, she stands outside this club for veterans of foreign wars, where a bar sign advertises Sunday bloody marys, a buck apiece, 10 to noon.

Former soldiers tell her to keep her nose clean over there. Her father, Wesley Kane, has to leave soon for his job as a car dealership's lot manager, but he holds her tight and asks, again and again, do you know how to clean your weapon?

"Yes, Daddy," she says.

The motorcyclists, including some from a group called the Patriot Guard Riders, mount their bikes. Among them is Rich Poliska, a gray-bearded Air Force veteran who lives nearby, in Bullhead City. A Route 66 earring dangles from his left earlobe.

Several months ago Mr. Poliska and his daughter, Heather Ching, heard about a local soldier who had returned from Iraq to no welcome home. They decided to form the Bullhead Patriots, dedicated to honoring soldiers going off to war, or returning from it. This is the group's first deployment effort, he says. "But I've done six funerals and two homecomings."

The Bullhead Patriots had heard of Private Kane's imminent deployment from a veteran who knows a woman who works at the Family Dollar store with the soldier's mother, Patricia Kane. First a surprise potluck supper—the soldier left church on Sunday to find a limousine waiting to whisk her away to the V.F.W.— and now this: an escort to the airport.

Bike engines growl, signaling that it is time. Private Kane climbs into the family van, which features rear-window decals for Jesus and for the Army ("My Daughter Is Serving"). She sits in the back, surrounded by her three younger siblings and a sister's boyfriend. Her quiet mother takes the driver's seat.

Soon the caravan is crossing the Colorado River. It passes a man sitting on the back of a parked pickup, his fist raised in the air: the soldier's father.

This mobile honor guard continues on, heading north on Highway 95, into a desolate, arid stretch of southern Nevada. Motorcycles in front, motorcycles behind, and in the middle, a white van containing a young soldier with just-polished fingernails.

She took care of her siblings while her parents worked, and learned to make a mean baked chicken. She graduated in the upper ranks in a class of about 60. She was honored for her grades and for her abstract artwork of flowers and butterflies. She has yet to learn to drive.

She enlisted in April, the same month as her prom, because she saw the military as a way to further her education. Right after graduation she went through boot

camp and some extra training, before coming home a couple of weeks ago to talk up the Army at her alma mater.

"Hometown recruiting," the Army calls it.

"Everyone knows me there," Private Kane says of Needles High School, home of the Mustangs.

Now, riding in the midst of this caravan of protection and respect, she is bound for Fort Hood in Texas to await deployment—probably to Iraq, she says.

"Nobody wants to go, but it's our job," she said the other day, her tone all business. "That's what we're trained for. We'll go over, do our job and come back."

The motorcade stops briefly in the old gold-mining town of Searchlight, and a few bikers say goodbye. Then it continues on, across the nothingness, through spits of rain, before stopping again in Railroad Pass, about 20 miles south of the airport. The Bullhead Patriots say farewell to Private Kane.

"Best of luck to you," Mr. Poliska says.

A lone biker continues to lead the Kanes toward Las Vegas, a large American flag flapping from the rear of his motorcycle. He rumbles into the city of gamblers, past drivers oblivious to the now-common moment of a wartime soldier leaving home.

At the last moment the biker peels off. And the white family van follows the signs that say Departures.

In a Town Called Bill,
a Boomlet of Sorts

BILL, WYO. — MARCH 3, 2008

For decades this speck of a place called Bill had one, two or five residents, depending on whether you counted pets. But recent developments have increased the population to at least 11, so that now Bill is more a dot than a speck, and could be justified if one day it started to call itself William.

In mid-December those developments appeared like some Christmas mirage: a 112-room hotel and a 24-hour diner. Here. In Bill. Amid the swallowing nothingness of grasslands, where all that moves are the wind, the antelope, the cars speeding to someplace else—and those ever-slithering trains.

Day and night the trains, each one well more than a mile long, rattling north with dozens of empty cars to the coal mines of the Powder River Basin, then groaning south with thousands of tons of coal. They clink and clank behind the cramped general store and shuttered post office to create the soundtrack of Bill.

But Bill is also a crew-change station for the Union Pacific railroad company, which means that dozens of conductors, engineers and other railroaders on the coal line take their mandatory rest here. Few of them want to be in Bill, but in Bill they must stay. They are its transients, forever lugging their lanterns, gloves and gear.

For many years the railroaders stayed in what they called, without affection, the Bill Hilton, a tired, 58-room dormitory near the rail yard with thin walls and, lately, not enough beds, as the booming coal business has increased the demand for trains. At 2 in the morning or 2 in the afternoon, bone-tired workers just off their shift would wait for a bed to open up, and then hope for sleep to come.

Union Pacific addressed the situation by working with a hotel company called Lodging Enterprises. The company agreed to build a hotel and diner in, essentially, nowhere, and Union Pacific guaranteed most of the rooms for its weary railroaders.

This is why, one day last August, a woman named Deloris Renteria found herself driving up desolate Highway 59, having just accepted a job as general manager of a yet-to-be-built Oak Tree Inn and Penny's Diner in some place called Bill. But she drove right past Bill, missing it entirely. And when she turned around to face the remoteness, she had one thought:

Oh my God. This is Bill.

The history of Bill is recorded in age-brittled papers and newspaper articles kept behind the bar at the back of Bill's general store. It seems that a doctor settled here during World War I, and that his wife came up with the town's name after observing that several area men were all called Bill.

There came a small post office, and a small store selling sandwiches to truckers, and a small school for children from surrounding ranches, and little else, except for those trains. At one point the owner of the general store established the Bill Yacht Club: no boats, no water, no costly boating accidents. He sold hats and T-shirts to tourists who felt in on the joke.

At first Ms. Renteria thought the joke was on her. She is 50, the single mother of four adult children; seeking isolation was not her life's goal. But she had a job to do, with a steady stream of clients, almost all of them railroaders passing through, stepping up to the counter at the diner, signing in, signing out.

Now, she says, she likes Bill. When she steps out a back door for a cigarette, she sees nothing but beautiful nothingness.

The hotel in Bill—some call it the Bill Ritz-Carlton—is open to everyone, but is especially designed to accommodate these railroaders. For example, in keeping with a contractual agreement between the railroad company and the unions, it must have a break room, an exercise room and, very importantly, a card table.

Because railroading is hardly a 9-to-5 profession, each room has window shades designed to thwart any peek of daylight and thick walls to snuff out sounds like vacuuming. The hotel also has a "guest finder" system that uses heat sensors to signal if someone is in a room, possibly resting, almost certainly uninterested in a cheery call of "Housekeeping!"

The Ritz of Bill still has its growing pains, its clash between two cultures— hotels and railroads—as evidenced by a slightly misspelled sign on the diner's door: "Union Pacific Guest: Please remove kleats before entering building. Automatic $50 fine for violation!!!!!! Thank you for your cooperation."

Providing mild counterpoint is Jarod Lessert, 35, a train engineer and one of Bill's longtime transients, who has just checked out of the hotel. He is sipping a Diet Coke at the general store's back bar while waiting for midnight, when he will drive a coal-loaded train the 12 hours back to South Morrill, Neb., where he lives and prefers to sleep.

He says the new hotel is far better than the old dormitory, but adds that some of the hotel's rules are plainly ridiculous. He also expresses shock at the prices in the diner: "Nine dollars for an omelet?"

Actually, an omelet costs $7.99, plus tax, with meat, hash browns, toast and drink. But at least now you can have an omelet here.

At least Greg Mueller, a manager of train operations, can eat a hot roast beef sandwich ($7.49) while thinking about a hill nearby where he can see the crisscross of trains below and the constellation of stars above. At least Marty Castrogiovanni, another manager, can sip a coffee ($1.46) while marveling that Bill, tiny Bill, is part of what may be the busiest train line in the world, in terms of tonnage.

At least now you can look up from your omelet, overpriced or not, and see through the window another train carting part of Wyoming away.

Day and night, those trains, creating a consuming sound undeterred by special curtains and thick walls. It is a sound of money being made, lights turning on and the disturbed earth rumbling at your feet. It is the sound of a dot called Bill, too busy to sleep.

Silence Replaces Bids and Moos at Stockyards in Suburbs

SOUTH ST. PAUL, MINN. — APRIL 14, 2008

In a place that no longer belongs where it has always been, there rises from wood-slat pens the farewell lows and bellows of cold, wet cows. So long, so long, they call out to the oblivious human bustle. The stockyards of South St. Paul say goodbye.

The cattle adieu has been years in the planning, but now it is time. No longer can the end be forestalled by milk-and-meat memories of 122 years; by the boast that these trampled grounds once constituted the largest stockyards in the world; by the vital daily ritual of muck-flecked yardmen coaxing muck-flecked cows into the sales barn, where the auctioneer's sweet serenade only hardens those bovine expressions of uh-oh.

Times have overtaken the stockyards, for reasons too obvious to dispute. Higher costs. Farms lost to suburban sprawl. The increasingly awkward presence of livestock in the Twin Cities metropolitan area, accustomed now to more sophisticated aromas than what wafts from the pens.

Punctuation to this reality came in January, when yet another animal escaped from the stockyards. A bull weighing nearly a ton apparently did not like what it had been sold for and wound up for a while on Interstate 494 during the morning rush hour. A police officer's shotgun blast soon freed the animal from worrying about the evening commute.

So this day—Friday, April 11, 2008—is the last day, closing a deal struck over a year ago when the owner of the stockyards, the Central Livestock Association, sold off the last 27 acres of what was once 166 acres of mooing, bleating, undulating commerce. The new owners will soon bulldoze everything to make room for more buildings of light industry—pens for people.

Stockyard denizens in blue blazers and in Carhartt overalls, in fine cowboy hats and in cheap baseball caps, pause in the gray morning cold to talk memories and to sell memorabilia. They assure one another that they'll soon be catching up at Minnesota auctions in Albany and Zumbrota. But mostly they just wait to buy and sell and ship and talk and do the business of livestock.

Here is John Barber, big and strong and 69, the yard's main auctioneer for nearly four decades. What a voice he has, so deep and soothing that you want to bid on something, anything: Would there be room for a heifer in the apartment? He lubricates his throat with apple juice and Halls cough drops and says he doesn't use a lot of filler words when singing his auction song because he doesn't want to confuse people.

John Barber

But that voice breaks a bit when he talks about this day. His wife, Toots, works here as a clerk, and so did his three daughters, and so did his father, Bob, hauling livestock. When Mr. Barber was a boy, he would ride in the cab of his father's Mack truck for those 150-mile night rides from Milroy—and then they were here, father and son, in the roiling, toiling, raucous yards.

His father died not long ago at 93, he says. "You have to think about him" on this day, he says. And the slightest drop in that mellifluous voice tells you it's time to talk about something else.

And here is David Krueger, 50, in bib overalls, and his son, Paul, 27, in bib overalls, two farmers who know the stockyards as well as they know their own spread in nearby Hastings. The Krueger name goes back a long ways here, so much so that when they're selling their livestock, Mr. Barber always calls it "reputation cattle," and people know what that means.

The Kruegers have donated a 900-pound heifer to be the last cow auctioned at the stockyards, with the sale proceeds going to an agricultural scholarship fund. Its father was a Simmental named Red Rock, and its mother was a Black Angus named, simply, N501 Commercial. As for its own name, chosen well before its historical role was determined: Timeless.

Why the donation? Simple, says David Krueger: "To say we had the last one."

To understand their desire to claim this honor, you need only walk up the 18 rusty steps to the catwalk that stretches over acres of open-air pens brimming with snorting, urinating, defecating cattle—a black-white-brown sea surrendering puffs of steam from wet hides, and the occasional yardman shout of Hey! Hey! Hey!

Hands inside his overalls, the elder Krueger wonders aloud about fortunes made and lost on these grounds, the packing companies come and gone, the characters who haunted Hog Alley and Sheep Alley. He wonders how many animals have moved through here since the yards opened.

A mind-twisting sort of answer is contained in a stockyard brochure commemorating the end of this era: "If the 300 million head of livestock that came to the South St. Paul Stockyards since its opening in 1887 were placed head-to-tail, they would form a line 248,560 miles long that would extend around the earth at the equator more than 10 times."

Yes, but who would clean up afterward?

The catwalk leads for the last time this gray day to the sales barn, a half-arena facing a ring covered with wood shavings as fine as beach sand. For the first part of the morning the stockyards have been auctioning off memorabilia to a standing-room-only crowd. A Ziploc bag of 10 pencils bearing the names of livestock-broker companies long gone goes for $180.

"Folks, if you have a question, just raise your hand," one of the auctioneers, Lyle Bostrom, jokes. "We'll get right to ya."

After a while Mr. Barber reclaims his seat, signaling that the final cattle auction is about to begin. All that livestock from Minnesota and Wisconsin, unloaded from trucks and herded into pens, now to be rushed into the arena for some momentary preening, bought, rushed out, loaded up and carted away.

At the same time there comes the smell of cooking beef—free hamburgers!— to settle over the arena and pens, and to underscore the fate of at least some of those gathered here.

Mr. Barber gives a verbal tip of the Stetson to the Minnesota Beef Council, and to Barb, the owner of the stockyards cafe: "Stop in there, and Barb'll fix ya up." Then, with nothing else to say, he begins his auction song, a tongue-dancing scat of words and numbers that thwarts translation.

He sings to the cattle trotting into the arena 10 and 20 at a time, many of them relieving themselves to convey what they think of the honor. He sings to the audience, from the old farmhand who keeps his callused hands down to the rich buyer who bids with mere flicks of a finger.

He sings to the Kruegers in the pens, to Barb in the cafe, to Toots in the back and his girls far away. To his father. He sings with a voice steady and strong, as if he's afraid to stop. As if the sheer force of his song can hold off the entrance of the final cow, the one called Timeless.

Far Removed and Struggling, but Still a Piece of America

AKIACHAK, ALASKA — OCTOBER 6, 2008

The bush plane glides over the tundra in autumn, descending slowly into the green and orange with avian grace. Soon its wheels kiss a spit of an airstrip in a western Alaska place where senators and governors rarely visit, a Yup'ik Eskimo village called Akiachak.

Its tribal police chief, John Snyder, waits in a white pickup at the end of the gravel runway, wrapped in a maturity beyond his 23 years. He introduces himself with a gentle joke, then begins down the rutted road to his community of 700.

25

A veteran of the Iraq war lives here. An Obama campaign worker arrived not long ago to shake hands, a rare moment of political recognition. A local elder is part of a federal lawsuit demanding that election ballots and referendum questions also be provided in the language of Yup'ik. Through an interpreter she says: I want to know what I am voting on.

And here, tribal customs and the Internet vie for the attention of the young. People live on the salmon they've caught, the moose they've killed and the box of Cheerios that costs them double what you pay. The rising prices of gasoline and heating fuel have forced some families to double up or move away, and about a third of them have no running water.

"Welcome to Akiachak," the police chief says, in surplus-rich Alaska.

With a cold rain falling, the truck bangs along a gray road past weather-beaten houses raised on stilts. A few years ago, two-thirds of the village was finally connected to water and sewer lines; this is the one-third still waiting. Many residents, including Mr. Snyder, bathe with water retrieved from the Kuskokwim River and use honey buckets as latrines. Some of these malodorous buckets sit like garbage cans along the roadside.

Past the paint-peeled Moravian Christian church, in need of new windows and containing small black books from 1945 that say "Liturgy and Hymns in the Eskimo Language of the Kuskokwim District, Alaska."

Past one of the two general stores, where the crazy-high cost of living is stamped on the cans and boxes arranged under the dull light. A 12-ounce bag of Lay's potato chips: $7.39. A 19-ounce can of Progresso beef barley soup: $4.29. A 20-ounce box of Cheerios: $8.29.

Mr. Snyder pulls up to an office building where three tribal leaders offer greetings. Between private consultations in Yup'ik, they explain how Akiachak replaced its city form of government two decades ago with a tribal council. They say they work hard to maintain native customs: the language, the care and respect for elders, the refusal to waste food like salmon.

"If you do," the tribal administrator, George Peter, says, "the abundance of salmon will go down."

The keen national interest in Alaska's governor, Sarah Palin, the Republican candidate for vice president, is not shared in this outpost of the state. At the mention of her name, the elders say nothing but look at one another with half-smiles.

Instead, they cite another Alaska Republican, Senator Lisa Murkowski, who recently held a hearing in the small city of Bethel—a 15-minute flight from here—to discuss how some people can no longer afford to live in the villages of their ancestors and are leaving for Anchorage. The elders say she is on to something.

Although the population in Akiachak has risen slightly in recent years, they say, young people seem more interested in iPods than in Yup'ik. And while every eligible Alaskan will receive more than $3,200 in oil rebates and dividends this year, they say, gas here costs $6.59 a gallon, and heating oil $7.06 a gallon.

"Yesterday our village police officer told us two families just moved to Anchorage," Daniel George, the tribal council chairman, says. "Even my nephew and niece have moved to Anchorage."

Anchorage, the Oz of Alaska. Natalie Landreth, a lawyer with the Native American Rights Fund, recalls that when the local elder, Anna Nick, 70, was summoned to Anchorage last year to be deposed in her voting rights lawsuit—which so far has prompted a preliminary injunction requiring that Yup'ik translations be made available at the polls—the tiny woman arrived with a wish list of things needed by people in her village.

Ms. Landreth drove her to a Walmart at 8 in the morning and asked her when she wanted to be picked up.

"When do they close?" Ms. Nick asked.

The rain has stopped but the cold has not. With work to do, the tribal elders return to their trucks and desktop computers. Police Chief Snyder drives on.

Past a fish camp at the river bank, where caught salmon are cleaned and smoked, with carcasses saved for mush dogs. Past the boat he uses to travel hundreds of miles in search of moose and bear and caribou. Past small ducks that he says make for good soup.

People on all-terrain vehicles wave to Mr. Snyder as they drive past. He is well-known here, the son of a former police chief, a law enforcement officer who carries no gun and rarely uses handcuffs. For one thing, if his boat were to tip in the Kuskokwim while taking suspects to jail in Bethel, anyone in shackles could drown.

"You cooperate with me, I'll cooperate with you," he says.

The village is safe. But six months ago it experienced its first murder in anyone's memory when, the police say, a man ended a bootleg whiskey night by shooting his female companion. Mr. Snyder answered that call and does not want to discuss it; too close.

His truck wends past the village's sprawling school, built a few years ago to resemble a traditional community house for elders. It has a room lined with Mac computers, a library with expansive windows and a cafeteria that serves as the village's only luncheonette. In one kindergarten class, children are learning the Yup'ik word for star.

"Agyaq," they say together. "Agyaq."

Mr. Snyder continues on to accommodate a request to visit the village cemetery—clearly not something he wants to do. He walks along a boardwalk above the mud-topped permafrost to where white wooden crosses rise like too many candles on a birthday cake. Some crosses are fresh, their bone-whiteness stark against the

brown-green weeds. Others are collapsing into gray rot, returning to the earth.

"My buddy's down here somewhere," Mr. Snyder says, tramping through the weeds and crosses. A buddy who committed suicide at 18.

There are more: here lie three relatives, dead before 40 from alcohol; another school friend lost to suicide; another relative. Although alcohol is banned in many rural villages, including Akiachak, it remains the scourge of native life. Mr. Snyder walks downhill, head bowed.

Driving toward the airstrip, passing high school athletes on a late-afternoon run, he says he could never live in a place as crowded as Anchorage. He says he prefers rainwater to any other drink, enjoys the taste of bear, whether barbecued or in a pot roast, and plans to teach his two young sons to speak Yup'ik.

The dot of a bush plane skims the horizon. It lands, and eight passengers board. The pilot asks each one how much they weigh.

Three small children and a lame dog watch from a safe distance. Then, as the whining plane pulls away, these Yup'ik children, these American children, wave goodbye.

At a School in Kansas, a Moment Resonates

JUNCTION CITY, KAN. — JANUARY 21, 2009

Shortly before lunchtime on Tuesday, a strange quiet settled over Junction City Middle School. Strange because quiet does not come naturally to a collection of 875 students in the full throes of adolescence. But this clearly was a moment, a time to set aside childish things.

The sixth and eighth graders had shuffled into the auditorium of the year-old school, past the signs saying no gum, drinks or food, while the seventh graders took seats in the adjacent cafeteria, redolent of chicken patties frying. All were silent, and not only because the expressions of the adults hovering about signaled the need for communal reverence.

They gazed up at large screens to watch the presidential inauguration in Washington, nearly 1,100 miles away, though the distance sometimes seemed even farther. While the audio feed remained steady, the video stream stopped and stuttered, like old NASA images from space, so much so that Aretha Franklin seemed to start singing "My Country 'Tis of Thee" before opening her mouth.

But this glitch only added to the moment's import, as if to echo other firsts—sending a man to the moon, say—along the American continuum. And these YouTube-era students never snickered; they only watched, some wide-eyed, some sleepy-eyed, the flickering images of power's formal transfer.

Also watching, also looking up, was Ronald P. Walker, 55, the schools superintendent, from a cafeteria table he was sharing with six seventh-grade girls. He wore a dark suit, a white shirt and a red tie—the same attire as the president-elect now striding across the screen above.

Mr. Walker grew up in an all-black town in Oklahoma, worked his way through the ranks of education, and is now the only black schools superintendent in Kansas. He worries about budget cutbacks as a result of the economic crisis throttling his state and his country, but he saw in the man appearing above him a thinker, a statesman, the embodiment of hope.

"And his emphasis on education is critical for all of us," Mr. Walker said.

One could argue that many of the students in Mr. Walker's charge have more at stake in this far-off Washington ceremony than most. Junction City may be a place of about 20,000 in the flat plains of Kansas, but it is as diverse as any place in the country, mostly because in many ways it serves at the pleasure of Fort Riley, a major military base a few miles away.

Slightly fewer than half the students are white, more than half receive free or discounted lunches—and a full third have some connection to Fort Riley, which adds both a cultural richness and an uncommon kind of stress.

School officials say the students worry less about grades and friends than about when a parent will be deployed, when a parent will return, whether a parent will survive combat.

These are not daydream worries, what with 3,400 soldiers from Fort Riley now in Iraq, and the knowledge that 159 soldiers and airmen from the base had been killed in the wars in Iraq and Afghanistan by the end of last year.

Not too long ago, there was a report of graffiti in the bathroom at the high school. The culprit was a girl, and what she had written, over and over, was: I Miss My Dad.

So here they were, the children of a place called Junction City—a community proud of its distinctive Kansas limestone buildings, struggling still with its honky-tonk, "Junk Town" reputation of long ago—looking up at screens, waiting for a new and different show. Gazing up, too, were many adults, most of whom had thought they would never see the day.

Here was Ferrell Miller, 63, the school's principal, whose father used to say the "N" word as if it were just any other word. Dr. Miller came to Junction City more than 40 years ago as a soldier, met and married a young woman from the Philippines, returned to his Ohio hometown—and then moved back to Junction City because that place in Ohio "didn't have the diversity we were looking for." But Junction City did.

And here were the cafeteria workers, white, Hispanic, black, most of them wearing hairnets, taking a break from food prep to share in the moment. Margaret Langley, 73, a German woman who married a G.I. in the mid-1950s, is proud to be a naturalized citizen; Nellie Vargas, 29, from Houston, married to a soldier stationed at Fort Riley; Phyllis Edwards, 46, of North Carolina, married to a retired soldier and with a son in the eighth grade here.

"I'm just so nervous," said Ms. Edwards, failing to find the words to match her emotions. Finally, the moment. The announcer asked people in Washington to please stand; the students of Junction City remained seated. The chief justice of the United States said, "Congratulations, Mr. President"; those students burst into applause.

As President Obama began his Inaugural Address, the seventh-grade students began their lunch. They filed into the kitchen to collect their trays of chicken-patty sandwiches, fries and chocolate milk. Few opted for the peas.

Kimberlee Muñoz set down her tray and rendered her review of the Inaugural Address—"It was the bomb!"—while at a table nearby, Reggie Campbell ate his lunch in forced exile, having gotten into it with another student who was making fun of him. He said he lived with an uncle who was in Iraq at the moment, and he said he enjoyed watching the inauguration.

"I think it's nice to have a black president for once," he said.

Meanwhile, the adults at the middle school began the orderly transition from historic to mundane. Ms. Edwards took her place behind the buffet table, wishing all the while that she was in Washington. Ms. Vargas left her cafeteria work early to drive her husband to the airport; an emergency leave had ended, and he was returning to Iraq.

And Mr. Walker, in his dark suit, white shirt and red tie, set off for another meeting in another building in Junction City, leaving in his wake one word: Wow.

On the Bow'ry

NEW YORK, N.Y. — MARCH 14, 2010

Open the door to a small hotel on the Bowery.

A small hotel, catering to Asian tourists, that used to be a flophouse that used to be a restaurant. That used to be a raucous music hall owned by a Tammany lackey called Alderman Fleck, whose come-hither dancers were known for their capacious thirsts. That used to be a Yiddish theater, and an Italian theater, and a theater where the melodramatic travails of blind girls and orphans played out. That used to be a beer hall where a man killed another man for walking in public beside his wife. That used to be a liquor store, and a clothing store, and a hosiery store, whose advertisements suggested that the best way to avoid dangerous colds was "to have undergarments that are really and truly protectors."

Climb the faintly familiar stairs, sidestepping ghosts, and pay $138 for a room, plus a $20 cash deposit to dissuade guests from pocketing the television remote. Walk down a hushed hall that appears to be free of any other lodger, and enter Room 207. The desk's broken drawer is tucked behind the bed. Two pairs of plastic slippers face the yellow wall. A curled tube of toothpaste rests on the sink.

Was someone just here? Was it George?

Six years had passed since I was last in this building at 104-106 Bowery. Back then it was a flophouse called the Stevenson Hotel, and I was there to write about its sole remaining tenant, a grizzled holdout named George; toothless, diabetic, not well. He lived in Cubicle 40, about the length and width of a coffin.

All the other tenants, who had paid $5 a night for their cubicles, had moved on or died off, including the man known as the Professor, and Juliano, who used to beat George. The landlord, eager to convert the building into a hotel, a real hotel,

The cubicle of George Skoularikos

had paid some of them to leave. But George had refused, saying the last offer of $75,000 was not enough.

It was as though he belonged to the structure, a human brick, cemented by the mortar of time to the Professor and Alderman Fleck and all the others who gave life to an ancient, ordinary building on the Bowery.

Now the place is the U.S. Pacific Hotel, and George is nowhere to be seen. I dim the lights in my own glorified cubicle, and give in to musings about his whereabouts, and long-ago murders, and the Bowery, where, the old song said, they say such things and they do strange things.

On the Bow'ry. The Bow'ry.

The building at 104-106 Bowery, between Grand and Hester Streets, has been renovated, reconfigured and all but turned upside down over the generations, always to meet the pecuniary aspirations of the owner of the moment. Planted like a mature oak along an old Indian footpath that became the Bowery, it stands in testament to the essential Gotham truth that change is the only constant.

Its footprint dates at least to the early 1850s, when the Bowery was a strutting commercial strip of butchers, clothiers and amusements, with territorial gangs that never tired of thumping one another. Back then the building included the hosiery shop, which promised "all goods shown cheerfully"—although an argument one night between two store clerks, Wiley and Pettigrew, ended only after Wiley "drew a dark knife and stabbed his antagonist sixteen times," as The New York Times reported with italicized outrage.

Over the years the Bowery evolved into a raucous boulevard, shadowed by a cinder-showering elevated train track and peopled by swaggering sailors and hard-working mugs, fresh immigrants and lost veterans of the Civil War. The street was exciting, tawdry and more than a little predatory. The con was always on.

By 1879, 104-106 Bowery had become a theater and beer hall, with a bartender named Shaefer who was arrested twice in two weeks for selling beer on Sunday. The adjacent theater, meanwhile, sold sentiment.

During one Christmas Day performance of "Two Orphans," precisely at the audience-pleasing moment when the blind girl resolves to beg no more, someone shouted "Fire!" A false alarm, it turned out, caused when a cook in the restaurant next door dumped hot ashes onto snow. The crowd returned to rejoice in the blind girl's triumph.

The theater changed names almost as often as plays: the National, Adler's, the Columbia, the Roumanian, the Nickelodeon, the Teatro Italiano. In 1896, when it was known as the Liberty, the police arrested two Italian actors for violating the "theatrical law." He was dressed as a priest, she as a nun.

But the building's dramas were not relegated solely to the stage. One of its theater proprietors skipped to Paris with $1,800 in receipts, leaving behind a destitute wife, six children and many unpaid actors. One of its upstairs lodgers drowned with about 40 others when an overloaded tugboat, chartered by the Herring Fishing Club, capsized off the Jersey coast.

In 1898, two men were laughing and drinking at a vaudeville performance when a third walked up, drew a revolver and shot one of them in the head. Hundreds scrambled for the exits to cries of "Murder!"

The shooter, Thompson, told the police that he had seen the victim, Morrison, on the street with his wife. "He has ruined my life; broken up my home," Thompson said, as he gazed at the man groaning on the floor. "It's a life for a wife."

And the fires, the many fires. The one in 1898 gutted the building and displaced the families of Jennie Goldstein and Sigmund Figman, while the one in 1900 sent 500 theatergoers fleeing into the Christmas night, prompting a singular Times headline: "Audience Gets Out Without Trouble, but the Performers Were Frightened—Mrs. Fleck Wanted Her Poodle Saved."

Mrs. Mabel Fleck, whose poodle survived, was the wife of the proprietor, one Frederick F. Fleck: city alderman, bail bondsman and self-important member of the court to the Bowery king himself, Timothy D. Sullivan—"Big Tim"—a Tammany Hall leader said to control all votes and vice south of 14th Street.

Alderman Fleck was there whenever Big Tim staged another beery steamboat outing for thousands of loyal Democrats, or another Christmas bacchanal for Flim-Flam Flanigan, Rubber-Nose Dick, Tip-Top Moses and hundreds of other Bowery hangers-on. There to provide bail when some Tammany hacks were charged with enticing barflies at McGurk's Suicide Hall to vote the Democratic ticket in exchange for a bed, some booze and five bucks.

When Alderman Fleck was not demonstrating his Tammany fealty, he was managing the Manhattan Music Hall, here at 104-106 Bowery, a preferred place for dose in de know.

But the city's good-government types, the famous goo-goos, hated how the Bowery reveled in its debauchery. In 1901, a reform group called the Committee of Fifteen raided Alderman Fleck's establishment and charged him with maintaining a disorderly house. He responded by calling the arresting officer "a dirty dog."

Undercover agents testified to having witnessed immoral acts on stage and off. One reported seeing a woman lying on a table, moaning; when he asked what was wrong, he was told she had just consumed $60 worth of Champagne, and so was feeling bad.

But this was Big Tim's Bowery. A jury quickly acquitted Fleck, prompting a night of revelry at the music hall. A Times reporter took note:

"Strangers as soon as they entered were piloted in the same old way by a watchful waiter to the gallery and curtained boxes upstairs, and as if by magic women 'performers' in abbreviated costumes appeared on the scene with capacious thirsts, which could be satisfied only with many rounds of drinks at the same music hall—$1 per round."

Soon, Alderman Fleck was competing in the "fat man's race" at one of Big Tim's annual outings, weighing in at 260 pounds. Soon he was back in his rightful place as a minor character along a boulevard so chock-full of characters—the predatory, the dissolute, the tragicomic—that slumming parties of uptown swells would tour the Bowery to gawk and feign allegiance. Some locals were even hired to portray Bowery "characters" to meet tourist expectations.

But denizens who lingered too long on the Bowery often paid a price. A few doors up from Fleck's place was a saloon owned by the famous Steve Brodie, whose survival of a supposed leap from the Brooklyn Bridge earned him the lucrative lifetime job of recounting the tale. After his premature demise at 43, the saloon's new owners hired his son, Young Steve Brodie, as a tough-talking character, but he soon drank himself into the more tragic role of Bowery inebriate.

As he lay dying in the gutter, young Brodie, 27, gazed up at a concerned police officer and whispered: "I'm in, Bill. Git me a drink of booze, quick."

The officer obliged. It was his civic duty.

The downfall of Alderman Fleck, who once sported diamond-encrusted cufflinks, was less dramatic. First the city marshal came after him for not paying for 281 chickens he had ordered for yet another Tammany dinner. Then his poodle-loving wife sued for divorce. Then he wound up spending a night in jail, following a row with a butcher over another unpaid bill.

His obituary a quarter-century later made no reference to goo-goo raids or fat men's races, to precious poodles, Big Tim Sullivan or a street called the Bowery. It described him instead as having been in the theatrical business for many years, which seems close enough.

The theaters and music halls, the museums for suckers and the likes of Steve Brodie—they all gradually faded from the Bowery. Big Tim Sullivan, who in later years championed women's suffrage and labor law reform after the Triangle Shirtwaist fire of 1911, was seen less and less, in part because disease, probably syphilis, had rendered him mentally incompetent.

One afternoon in 1913, Sullivan escaped from his handlers, only to be struck and killed by a freight train in the Bronx. His body lay unclaimed in the morgue for 13 days, until a police officer, glancing at yet another corpse bound for potter's field, did a double take and shouted: "Why, it's Tim! Big Tim!"

More and more, the Bowery became the place for men with nowhere else to go: thousands and thousands of them, from war veterans to would-be masters of the universe, often seeking the deadening effects of alcohol and, later, drugs. They found cheap beds and brotherhood in flophouses that fancied themselves as hotels.

After housing a variety of passing ventures—a moving-picture theater, a rag-sorting operation, a penny arcade—the building at 104-106 Bowery became the Comet Hotel, a flophouse. And it remained a flophouse for decades, as wholesale restaurant suppliers and lighting-fixture stores moved onto the street; as many other flophouses disappeared; as the fits and starts of gentrification claimed loft space.

In the late 1970s, the Comet's lodgers would trudge up the 17 steps to the lobby, where a television hung from the wall and a proprietor in a cagelike office collected the fee—slightly less than $3 a night—slipped under a grate. One of the floors upstairs was an open room, with 65 beds and 65 lockers. The other two floors had 100 cubicles combined, each one measuring 4 feet by 6 feet, with partitions 7 feet high and a ceiling of chicken wire.

Cubicle No. 40 was home to a Greek immigrant named George Skoularikos. A sometime poet, he moved here in 1980 and stayed, and stayed. As it became the Stevenson Hotel. As the other men left or died. As the current owners, Chun Kien Realty, tried to entice him with money to move.

By 2004, when I visited George, he was 74 and this flophouse's last lodger, sleeping in a cramped, green-painted cubicle that he secured with a loop of wire. A Housing Court judge and a Legal Aid lawyer were advising him to take the landlord's offer of $75,000. Looking with exasperation upon this frail, sick man, the judge had said, "And who do you think will last the longest?"

But George would not, perhaps could not, leave.

Today, at 104-106 Bowery, what used to be a hosiery store and a beer hall and a theater and a penny arcade and a flophouse is now a hotel of less than luxurious means. Tucked between a Vietnamese restaurant and the Healthy Pharmacy, it has a blue marquee in English and Chinese. The cubicles and chicken wire are gone, as is George.

I found him, eventually, in court files. In late 2004, a few months after my column about him, a city-appointed psychiatrist came calling to the squalid and all-but-deserted flophouse. She later wrote that George was delusional, paranoid and in need of a guardian who could help move him to "more amenable accommodations."

But George refused to go. At one point a social worker tried to take him to a hospital, but George barricaded himself on the flophouse's second floor. Police officers eventually forced open the door to conduct a search by flashlight. And there they found him, hiding in a cubicle, a Bowery holdout.

In late 2005, the matter of George Skoularikos was adjudicated in State Supreme Court in Manhattan.

> ORDERED, that the landlord pay George's court-appointed guardian the sum of $80,000; ORDERED, that the guardian arrange for "an appropriate place of abode" for George in Greece, and set up a mechanism for payment of his bills; ORDERED, that a caseworker accompany George to Greece to make sure his new residence is properly established.

In a sense, this Bowery building that once received George had returned him to his native Greece, where he would die a few months later, in April 2006. There was enough money from his settlement with the landlord to pay for his funeral and marble tomb.

Screams at the bottom of the night disrupt a Bowery sleep. A woman on the other side of the hotel is crying, "I love you, I love you," to someone who seems not to love her back. Her wails last an hour, unleashing into the pitch a swirl of imagined sounds and whispers.

The glass shimmers of a million beer mugs. The faint strains of a thousand vaudeville ditties. The entwined polyglot murmurs, of English and German and Yiddish and Italian and Mandarin—and Bowery. The stentorian blather of a Tammany blowhard. The final exhalation of a dying inebriate. A weepy farewell toast to Big Tim. The shouts of "Fire!" The bark of a poodle.

The echoing clatters of a lone man building a barricade.

At morning's light, the sounds recede into the walls. It's a new day on the Bowery.

Annie and Gloria

NEW YORK, N.Y. — OCTOBER 17, 2010

The fish men see her still, their Annie, in the hide-and-seek shadows of South Street. She's telling her dirty jokes and doing anything for a buck: hustling newspapers, untaxed cigarettes, favors, those pairs of irregular socks she'd buy cheap on Canal. She's submitting to the elements, calling out "Yoo-hoo" to the snow and the rain and her boys.

For several decades, Annie was the profane mother of the old Fulton Fish Market, that pungent Lower Manhattan place fast becoming a mirage of memory. Making her rounds, running errands, holding her own in the blue banter, she was as much a part of this gruff place as the waxed fish boxes, the forklift-rocking cobblestones, and the cocktail aroma of gasoline, cigarettes and the sea.

Some ridiculed and abused her; others honored and protected her. Young men new to the market were occasionally advised to make acquaintance with Annie's prodigious breasts; kiss them for good luck. And the veterans, young men once, often slipped her a dollar, maybe five, for a copy of a fresh tabloid; pay her for good luck.

Young and old, they all had heard that the faded color photograph on display at Steve DeLuca's coffee truck—of a striking young woman, a raven-haired knockout in a two-piece bathing suit, running barefoot against a glorious sky—was of Annie in her younger days, decades before her dark fish-market terminus. But some could not see the coffee-truck goddess in this bent woman at shadow's edge, clutching the handle of the shopping cart she used to hold wares and provide balance, wearing a baseball cap, layers of sweaters, and men's pants, navy blue, into which she had sewn deep, leg-long pockets to keep safe her hard-earned rolls of bills.

The supposed link between pinup and bag lady sounded too much like an O. Henry tale of Old New York, and begged too many questions.

Who are you, really, Annie? How did you wind up here, at the fish market, receiving your boys, their taunts, the slaps of the East River winds? Where does all your money go? What is the larger meaning of your life's arc?

Never asked; never answered.

Annie was just there, always, as rooted to the market as the cobblestones.

Five years ago, when the city pried the 175-year-old fish market from Lower Manhattan and moved it to Hunts Point in the Bronx, Annie came with it, at first, often paying for a ride from her home, somewhere in Manhattan. She was in her 80s by then, and she struggled to find warmth in the new market's chilled air. The men would sometimes see her in a corner, huddled against herself, sleeping.

Annie at the fish market

So maybe it was for the best when the city regulators at Hunts Point told Annie she could no longer hawk her best seller, her untaxed cigarettes—an order that would have been laughable in the old market's wide-open days. Soon the raucous market chorus, of curses and price calls and forklift beeps, was missing the occasional, punctuating "Yoo-hoo."

Then again, maybe the market was her life's oxygen. A few weeks ago, word spread among the fishmongers: South Street Annie, also known as Shopping Cart Annie, also known as their Annie, had died. She was 85. Her given name was Gloria Wasserman. And the larger meaning of her journey's arc was this: Life is a wondrous gray.

When someone dies, the rest of us cobble together old photographs, faint remembrances and snippets of things once said to make sense of the life lived. It is folly, but it is what we do. So here is Annie, incomplete, partially hidden still in the market's eternal dusk cast by the Franklin Delano Roosevelt Drive above.

According to one of her two daughters, Barbara Fleck, Gloria Wasserman's parents were Polish immigrants who tried to make a living as egg farmers in rural New Jersey before settling in Crown Heights, Brooklyn. The father, Pincus, found work as a tailor; the mother, Sadie, was a homemaker. Together they fretted over their only daughter.

"She was almost too beautiful, which caused her to—well," Ms. Fleck said. "She had a lively spirit, which was almost frightening for these poor Jewish immigrants. Very beautiful and very spunky."

A portrait from the mid-1940s shows Ms. Wasserman in pearls, her dark hair swept up and sculpted, her expression that of a confident starlet waiting to be discovered. "I think in her heart she would have wanted to have been an actress," Ms. Fleck said. "She didn't make it to the screen, but she acted in real life."

While working in Manhattan's jewelry district, Ms. Wasserman met an ex-soldier named Fred Fleck, who planned to bicycle to Alaska, where he would attend college on the G.I. Bill. He suggested that she accompany him. "And she did," Ms. Fleck said. "A free-spirited woman."

The front page of the Sept. 5, 1947, edition of The Fairbanks Daily News-Miner featured an article with the headline: "'Bike-Hikers' Reach City 83 Days Out of New York."

"Clad in clean white duck slacks, faded colored wool shirts and moccasins, the young couple, deeply tanned, looked as though they had been on an afternoon's jaunt. Gloria's nut-brown shoulder-length hair glistened in the sun. . . . Glowing with enthusiasm, Gloria left her job as a manufacturer's model and amateur entertainer, bought a bicycle, and came along. She plans to get a job in Fairbanks, possibly as an entertainer."

She was 22.

After that, details get blurry. Ms. Wasserman married Mr. Fleck, gave birth to Barbara in 1950, and broke up with Mr. Fleck. She lived a bicoastal life, it seems, working in Alaska and the Pacific Northwest—running a bar, then a record store—but returning to New York often to visit and provide financial support for her widowed mother, who by now was raising Barbara.

"She had a knack," Ms. Fleck said. "She could make money."

Ms. Wasserman married a second time, to a man named Grinols, and gave birth to two sons. Then, after this marriage broke down, she had a relationship that produced another daughter, Robin, in 1964. During these years, and in the many that followed, Ms. Fleck often had no idea what her mother did for a living.

"I don't know how you could put it nicely," said Ms. Fleck, who lives in Los Angeles. "But she had a flamboyant life."

At some point, Ms. Wasserman returned to New York for good. And, at some point, she assumed the role of Annie and began appearing at the Fulton Fish Market, selling her wares and, her close friends at the market gently say, herself. Exactly when is lost to time, but far enough in the past that it seemed as though she was as permanent as the skyscrapers, as permanent as the river, calling out to the late-night fishmongers and early-morning Wall Street suits. When Frank Minio, an erudite, reflective man, joined the market in 1978, she was already a fixture.

No matter the weather, he said, "She was always there."

What a brutal way to live. She cleaned the market's offices and locker rooms and bathrooms. She collected the men's "fish clothes" on Friday and had them washed and ready for Monday. She ran errands for Mr. DeLuca, known as Stevie Coffee Truck, hustling to Chinatown to pick up, say, some ginseng tea. She accepted the early-morning delivery of bagels. She tried to anticipate the men's needs—towels, bandannas, candy—and had these items available for sale.

"If the Brooklyn Bridge could fit in her shopping cart, she would have sold it," Ms. Fleck said.

Since all this hustling meant carrying around a lot of cash, she tucked away wads of bills in those deep-pocketed pants and other hiding places, including her brassiere. "She tried to look shabby so people wouldn't give her a hard time" when she left the market, recalled one of her protectors, Joe Centrone, better known as Joe Tuna. "But she was regularly robbed."

Away from the market, Annie lived as Gloria Wasserman, in the East Village, in a city-owned apartment building that later became part of the Cooper Square Mutual Housing Association. She found joy in her family—a grandson, Travis, in California, and a granddaughter, Chelsea, in New Hampshire—but also sorrow. One of her sons, Kenneth Grinols, died in a fire while squatting in a building in the city. The other, Karl Grinols, struggling with drugs, moved into her apartment at one point, while she slept in a room at the market—"between the mackerel and the salmon," Ms. Fleck said. But he died young, too, hit by a car in the East Village.

All the while, Annie kept working, rarely missing a day, and gave nearly everything she had to others.

Barbara Grinols, Karl's ex-wife, who lives in New Hampshire, said that Ms. Wasserman often sent as much as $4,000 a month, usually through money orders, to her relations on both coasts. She also routinely sent along boxes of used clothing that she had culled from places like the Catholic Worker's Mary House, on East Third Street, where she was known as that rare visitor who searched for items that fit others, and who had a gift for using humor and kindness to deflate the tensions arising from hardship.

"She became like a grandmother to dozens of women on the street who had nobody," said Felton Davis, a full-time Catholic Worker volunteer. Sensing the lack of esteem in a woman beside her, he said, "She would say: 'I have just the shirt that you need. I'll get it for you.'"

Meanwhile, up in New Hampshire, the clothes kept coming. "The boxes would be opened, and it would be like: 'Who wants this T-shirt?' 'Who wants this sweatshirt?'" Ms. Grinols recalled. "So many people in this area got gifts from her."

In 1999, Ms. Wasserman decided to retire as Annie, telling the men at the fish market that she had health problems—circulation problems in her legs, Ms. Fleck said, related to years of working in the wet and cold. Joe Tuna and Stevie Coffee Truck raised $3,000 for her by hitting up all the hardened fishmongers. Off she went, to live with her daughter Robin in California, and then with Ms. Grinols and Chelsea in New Hampshire. After nine months in the country, though, Annie was back at the market, calling yoo-hoo and forcing Joe Tuna and Stevie Coffee Truck to do some explaining.

With the money she earned by working in all weather, in the hours when the rest of us slept, Annie bought Chelsea a used Toyota Tercel. She paid for Chelsea's tuition at the University of New Hampshire, and provided financial support to a ballet school in Los Angeles. Whatever money she took in, she sent out, while owning little more than a bed and a radio. Her relatives, in turn, regularly visited her in New York, where she would always tell them, "If we see anyone, I'm Annie." They called her often, sent her gifts that she probably gave away, and constantly begged her to retire from a job whose parameters were left vague, but whose pull for her was undeniable. "She would always say, 'We'll see,'" Chelsea recalled. "She never wanted to leave New York and stop doing what she was doing."

About 10 years ago, Joe Tuna and Stevie Coffee Truck heard that Annie had been hospitalized. They went to New York Downtown Hospital and asked to see—actually, they didn't know whom to ask for. "Annie?" they volunteered. "Shopping Cart Annie?"

"Gloria Wasserman," the clerk said, and directed them to her room, where their tough, tough Annie now seemed so vulnerable.

"That was the first time I ever saw her with her hair down," Joe Tuna said. "You could see the remnants of a beautiful woman."

Then Annie got out of the hospital, and went back to work. She continued to flash her breasts, more for the shock and a laugh than for anything else. She sold her goods, ripped into those who owed her money, accepted a hot cup of coffee when offered, and slipped away now and then to read from one of the books she always carried, like a stage actress resting between scenes.

She also continued her other life, as Gloria Wasserman, traveling to New Hampshire to attend Chelsea's wedding, in 2006. There she is in the photographs, smiling with the bride and groom, a proud, beloved grandmother.

For the last year of her life, the reluctantly retired Gloria Wasserman spent her days charming the East Village and her nights sharing dinner at Mary House. In spirit, she remained defiantly independent. In truth, she needed help: with her hygiene, with her apartment, with climbing the stairs.

She suffered a stroke in the brutal August heat and was admitted to Bellevue Hospital Center, where Mr. Davis, from the Catholic Worker, visited nearly every day. She was released after a month, spent a couple of weeks in New Hampshire, and then a couple more in California, with her daughter Barbara. But she refused to eat or to take her medication, and died in her sleep, 2,800 miles from the fish market.

"New York was her life," her daughter said. "Work was her life."

Word of Annie's death gave pause to the fish men. Mr. Minio reflected on that space between black and white where all of us reside. And Joe Tuna has discovered that whenever someone in a crowd calls out, "Yoo-hoo," his head jerks up and he is instantly back on South Street, amid the beds of glassine ice, and the dead-eyed fish, and here she comes.

The impressions and old photographs that Ms. Wasserman left behind are, in the end, only impressions and old photographs. In fact, whenever reporters, including this one, referred to her in a news story, she would always complain that they had failed to capture her "essence"—which may, again, be true.

A Bypassed Small Town Makes
a Visual Statement: Here We Are

HOOPER, NEB. — DECEMBER 8, 2010

A few years ago, the Nebraska Department of Roads rolled out a highway bypass to hasten the already-hurried everyday pace. Motorists rushing north to Norfolk, or south to Omaha, no longer had to slow to 40 miles an hour through a blink-and-miss-it place called Hooper.

No longer did travelers have to pass the Hooper ice cream parlor, or the Hooper grain elevator, or the ancient railroad cars sitting on discontinued tracks,

47

or the decades-old neon marquee, long past glowing, that welcomed travelers to a downtown from the late 19th century.

The people of Hooper—population 827, more or less—knew what this meant. The small green sign planted beside the new highway barely whispered their town's name. And in the flat terrain of rural Nebraska, the eye can see far into the distance, yet miss so much. They feared being missed. Bypassed.

Another community might have resigned itself to this subtle humiliation, enduring the slight on behalf of rural America as just one more nudge toward oblivion. But Hooper was determined to raise its collective hand somehow, and say to the busy world:

We are still here.

"We kind of lost our identity now that the highway didn't go through town," said David Hingst, 58, the general manager of Hoegemeyer Hybrids, a local seed company. "We needed our identity brought back."

But how?

You pronounce Hooper not with a HOO, but with a kind of HUH. Its name derives either from an otherwise forgotten railroad official or from a man who won an uphill wagon race, and, with it, naming rights. Founded as a railroad depot in 1876, it grew to become a hub for farmers raising corn, soybeans and livestock—a point of interest along U.S. 275.

Gone, now, are many of the businesses that once defined its Main Street: the Studebaker dealership, the furniture store, the three groceries. The Lions Club, which donated that neon marquee, no longer roars, and the Hooper Commercial Club, once thriving, is taking a protracted rest. The population is older, the children leaving once they come of age.

"We have a hard time keeping young people," said Joel Hargens, 59, a Hooper native who, like his father before him, runs the town's bank, now known as the First National Bank Northeast. "This is rural America. You could go 200 miles in any direction, talk to a banker, and he'd tell you the same."

But Hooper is hardly asleep. It has the bank, a small market, a library, a couple of insurance offices and the office of an ancient newspaper, where printed memories sit in a vault, fragile to the touch. But you can still buy ads in the paper to thank people for remembering your 90th birthday or for providing all those 50-mile rides to doctor's appointments in Omaha.

You can shoot pool at the Iron Horse. You can get your hair cut at Don's barber shop, where the Farm Journal—or is that Playboy?—is made available. And if you don't get to The Office restaurant by 6:30 on a weekend night, you can use the long wait for prime rib to admire the Hooper memorabilia on the walls, from the signs for out-of-business businesses to the H.H.S. pennants for the long-gone high school.

This is what was being passed by. Customers from Fremont were walking into The Office to say that they had driven all the way to Scribner, seven miles to the north, before realizing they had missed the turn-off for Hooper.

So, when some local people created the Hooper Area Community Foundation two years ago, its first order of business was to address the real and psychic impact of the bypass. True, the bypass had its benefits; at least now, with old Highway 275 suddenly quiet, you could cross the road without fear for life.

Still.

"Hooper was just missed completely," Mr. Hargens said. "Unnoticed. Unknown. We just felt we had to make a statement."

The foundation's handful of members—Mr. Hingst and Mr. Hargens, a dentist, a housewife, a feed salesman and a couple of others—began meeting in the bank's small conference room. There, under the gaze of a mounted white-tailed deer and a few University of Nebraska toy animals, they resolved to erect a sign beside the bypass to remind people of Hooper. Not just a sign, but a SIGN.

They took road trips to photograph and study the signs of other towns. Then they asked a contractor, Ronnie Fauss, to sketch out a few designs for their consideration.

Mr. Fauss, 76, was a good choice. He grew up in town, and remembers when it had a blacksmith and a harness shop. At 4:30 every morning, he takes a two-mile meditative walk through the dark and quiet, passing houses that evoke certain surnames. He knows Hooper.

Mr. Fauss came back with several sketches, the foundation asked for a few tweaks, and, finally, two designs were chosen: one horizontal, one vertical. The foundation displayed these options at the front of Mr. Hargens's bank—next to the popcorn machine that pops on Fridays—and asked people to write their preference on pieces of paper.

"It was almost split in half," said Mr. Hargens, the foundation's vice president.

"But there were no hanging chads," said Mr. Hingst, its president.

The foundation made the final pick: a tapered, 24-foot tower that would spell "Hooper" in 18-inch-high letters down two of its three sides. This way, the sign would rise above the fertile flatness.

Fund-raising letters went out in the fall of 2009. Quickly, the foundation surpassed its $18,000 goal, thanks to several thousand dollars from the old Commercial Club and to the many, many checks written out for amounts closer to $25.

Mr. Fauss arranged to buy a small corner of a cornfield from a cousin who happened to own land at the intersection of the new U.S. 275 and a county road leading into town. But wet weather in the spring delayed the project, as did some business commitments that Mr. Fauss simply had to meet.

Finally, right about harvest season, a brick-and-concrete base was built upon a concrete foundation. Then the three precast concrete sides were raised and secured to form the tapered tower, on top of which was placed a cap adorned with a large concrete ball.

Some finishing touches were still needed. The police chief, Matt Schott, used his excavator to dig a shallow trench for a retaining wall, after which a landscaping firm came in to plant some shrubs and make the ground look like an inviting garden, planted in a cornfield.

The project's completion prompted no fanfare. The foundation's members doubted that many people would gather beside a highway to celebrate a concrete tower. Besides, the sign was its own celebration.

Now, as the endless horizon along U.S. 275 surrenders to the wintry dusk, the beams of two spotlights sprout from the ground to illuminate the name of a place you might otherwise miss. A place where people say thank you through the newspaper, where the restaurant has prime rib on weekends, and where a white-haired native son takes predawn walks, taking it all in.

Sewers, Curfews and
a Ban on Gay Bias

In a former pool hall that is now the municipal building for a coal smudge of a place in eastern Kentucky called Vicco, population 335, the January meeting of the City Commission came to order. Commissioners and guests settled into patio chairs, bought at a discount and arranged around a long conference table. Those who smoked did.

The Commission approved the minutes from its December meeting, hired a local construction company to repair the run-down sewer plant and tinkered with the wording for the local curfew. Oh, and it voted to ban discrimination against anyone based on sexual orientation or gender identity—making Vicco the smallest municipality in Kentucky, and possibly the country, to enact such an ordinance.

After that, the Commission approved a couple of invoices. Then, according to a clerk's notes, "Jimmy made a motion to adjourn and Claude seconded the motion. All voted yes."

Admit it: The Commission's anti-discrimination vote seems at odds with knee-jerk assumptions about a map dot in the Appalachian coal fields, tucked between Sassafras and Happy. For one thing, Vicco embraces its raucous country-boy reputation—home to countless brawls and a dozen or so unsolved murders, people here say. For another, it is in Perry County, where four of every five voters rejected President Obama in the November election.

But the Vicco Commission's 3-to-1 vote this month not only anticipated a central theme in the president's second inaugural speech ("Our journey is not complete until our gay brothers and sisters are treated like anyone else under the law . . ."), it also presented a legislative model to the nation's partisan-paralyzed Capitol, 460 miles away.

You discuss, you find consensus, you vote, and you move on, explained the mayor, Johnny Cummings. "You have to get along."

Mr. Cummings, 50, runs a hair salon three doors down from the City Hall storefront. He spends his days hustling between the two operations, often wearing a black smock adorned with hair clips. One moment this wiry chain-smoker is applying dye to a client's hair; the next, he's dealing with potholes and water lines.

Now back to assumptions.

For a good chunk of the last century, Vicco was the local coal miner's Vegas, its narrow streets lined with bars and attractions that ran on money earned the hard way in the subterranean dank. The city's very name derives from the initials for the Virginia Iron Coal and Coke Company.

But as the coal camps folded, Vicco emptied out. Away went the car dealerships, the schools, the department store, the A&P, and even the Pastime theater, whose farewell film is said to have been "10," with Bo Derek. In 1979.

Into the Vicco void came abandonment, drug abuse and budget deficits so dire that the city could not afford a police officer. There was also the requisite touch of public corruption. A few years ago, a mayor and his son, a city commissioner, were charged with using thousands of dollars in city money for their personal use. They both entered Alford pleas, in which they did not admit guilt but conceded that the case against them was pretty darn good.

The next mayor stepped down last year for health reasons and was replaced by one of the city commissioners, the hairstylist down the street, Mr. Cummings.

Cummings is a longtime Vicco surname. Johnny Cummings's mother, Betty, was a schoolteacher; she has some dementia now and spends most days in his salon, telling him she loves him. His father, John, ran several businesses, including a bar; he died from a blow to the back of the head in 1990. One of those unsolved Vicco murders.

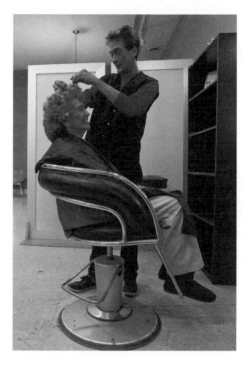

Mr. Cummings is gay, an identity he has never hidden, and the occasional rude encounter while growing up was nothing that he and his protective friends couldn't handle. After high school, he was offered a scholarship to a beauty academy in California, but he returned after two months. Other than a brief spell in South Carolina, he has been planted here in Vicco, where, for the last quarter-century, he has co-owned a salon called Scissors.

"I make 20 trips a day" between Scissors and City Hall, he said recently. "Right now I have a lady with color in her hair."

As mayor, Mr. Cummings inherited a skeleton-crew city that could not afford to keep all the office lights on. What's more, the creaky pipes in its water system, which generates money for the city through sales to area customers, were leaking more than 40 percent of the water, or revenue.

"How do you fix this?" Mr. Cummings remembers thinking. "I'm just a hairdresser."

He began by making amends with government agencies that had long since written off Vicco, hiring back the maintenance whiz who knew the city's pipes better than anyone and securing public grants to pay for the work. Now, he says, the repaired pipes are creating enough revenue to hire more workers and restore some color to Vicco's dreary black-and-white.

For example, he paid $600 for the bold blue metal bench that now sits in front of City Hall, emblazoned with the city's name. He also hired the city's first police officer in years: Tony Vaughn, a former detective and one of Mr. Cummings's protectors back in high school.

"We have five drug dealers here, and everyone knows it," said the barrel-chested Mr. Vaughn. "I'll ask 'em nicely to stop, and then I'll put 'em in jail."

This place-in-progress called Vicco was one of a handful of municipalities to receive a request last year from the Fairness Coalition, a Kentucky-based advocacy group for people who are gay, lesbian, bisexual or transgender. Mr. Cummings happens to have a sister, Lee Etta, who is active in the coalition.

The coalition's request: to consider adopting an anti-discrimination ordinance.

The city's forward-thinking attorney, Eric Ashley, trimmed the coalition's 28-page ordinance proposal down to a couple of pages. Then the mayor and the four-member Commission, all heterosexual men, met in December for a first reading and a discussion that ended with a 4-to-0 vote in favor of adoption.

The Commission's agenda for its January meeting, two weeks ago, included the second reading and the formal vote on the anti-discrimination proposal. This time, representatives of the Fairness Coalition took patio seats in the smoke-filled room.

The commissioners hashed through their questions and doubts, which Mr. Ashley did his best to answer and allay. But one commissioner, Tim Engle, who has known Johnny Cummings since forever, said he needed to change his vote.

"Tim stated that due to his religion, that he had to vote no to the above-mentioned ordinance," a clerk's notes of the meeting said.

"There are things we're not going to agree on, and that's perfectly fine with me," Mr. Engle said, according to the local newspaper, The Hazard Herald. "That's what the debates are for . . . that's what this group's here for. I want them to do what they think's right and what they think they need to do."

Because the mayor votes only to break a tie, Mr. Cummings mostly just listened to the discussion. Yes, it was a little shocking to hear an old friend change his vote on grounds of religion. But it was also gratifying, even crystallizing, to hear another commissioner say simply: Everyone should be treated fairly.

Claude Branson Jr., 56, a retired coal miner who sits on the Commission—and the only commissioner, he proudly notes, with a mullet haircut—said recently that

Mr. Cummings's presence had not played as much of a factor in the vote as had "the whole broad perspective of the world."

"We want everyone to be treated fair and just," he explained.

In Vicco, at least, officials just assumed that such a belief is self-evident and therefore not that big of a deal. Besides, this tough little city has other matters on its collective mind.

The maintenance supervisor is tackling problems with the sewage plant. The new police chief wants to revisit some of those unsolved murders. And the mayor is planning to transform an empty lot into a park, open to all.

EPILOGUE

Johnny Cummings remains the mayor of Vicco.

After he and Vicco were featured in the This Land column, a segment about Mr. Cummings appeared on "The Colbert Report" television program. That, in turn, prompted Max Mutchnick, a co-creator of the "Will and Grace" television show, and his husband, Erik Hyman, to build a children's park for the community.

"All that was fun," Mr. Cummings said. "It took about a year for my 15 minutes of fame to die down."

Storied Providence Skyscraper, Now Empty, Seeks a Future

PROVIDENCE, R.I. — NOVEMBER 13, 2013

The last full-time employee in the tallest building in Rhode Island has grown accustomed to the 26 stories of emptiness. He doesn't even hear the absence anymore—that silent roar of business not transacted.

"At first it was very weird," says Paul Almeida, the chief engineer and resident optimist for a 428-foot Art Deco skyscraper that has defined the Providence cityscape since 1928. "Then, all of a sudden, it was nothing."

Just another job. Single-handedly maintaining a skyscraper that once announced Providence as a Gotham of industry, but whose soaring hollowness today only nags at the city's sense of self-worth. Like a chastened Ozymandias, it whispers: Now what?

Until that vexing question is answered, Mr. Almeida, 48, continues his rounds, hands shoved in a 2004 World Series Champions Boston Red Sox sweatshirt. His work boots echo as he walks across the marbled lobby, where the last day of public business for the last tenant, Bank of America, remains set in metal calendars beside pens chained to counters: FRI APR 12.

Mr. Almeida began as a porter right out of high school nearly 30 years ago, after submitting an application to Human Resources, Third Floor. Back then, hundreds tended to the financial needs of thousands, as money was deposited, withdrawn, made. Now, the Greek gods adorning the lobby ceiling preen in vain.

A button's push in a golden elevator sends Mr. Almeida rocketing through floors of office vacancy hinting of former purpose, like window lettering announcing "Commercial Real Estate Group." A former porter ascends, up, up, up.

When it opened, this steel-frame structure sheathed in Indiana limestone rose in sleek contrast to the Colonial-style buildings at its feet. Winning hopeful huzzahs and inspiring advertising Babbittry—"A Business Building for Building Business"—the skyscraper welcomed Providence to tomorrow.

"This was a really bold statement that said, 'We are going somewhere—we are charging forward,'" says Matthew Bird, an associate professor of industrial design at the Rhode Island School of Design who has studied the building's history.

From a top-floor perch, the masters of Rhode Island industry could admire their domain spread out before them: the jewelry factories and textile mills, the Narragansett Bay shimmer, the Providence bustle. They might then repair to a prefabricated, leather-upholstered dining room—said by some to resemble an airship's gondola—plopped near the apex of the building.

"All designed for party time," Mr. Bird says. "There's absolutely nothing public about that space."

Built as the Industrial Trust building, the structure became known as the "Superman building," in the mistaken belief that it had appeared in an establishing shot for the Superman television series of the 1950s. Set aglow by floodlights, it was the beacon of the capital, signaling to Rhode Islanders coming south from Massachusetts that they were home.

But nearly all those mills once seen from above closed down, and Providence's role as a financial center came and went. The building slipped into economic irrelevance, its ownership changing hands, until a Massachusetts company called High Rock Development bought it for more than $33 million in 2008.

The owner's timing has been exquisitely bad. Not long ago, for example, it announced a plan to carve the building into 280 rental apartments—though, to do so, it would need tens of millions of dollars in tax credits and tax breaks. But the state was still reeling from its backing of a spectacularly unwise loan to a failed video game company owned by the former Red Sox pitcher Curt Schilling.

On the hook now for $100 million, the taxpayers of Rhode Island are not feeling generous.

David Ortiz, a spokesman for Providence's mayor, Angel Taveras, says the mayor did not think helping to convert the building into pricey apartments "was the wisest use of taxpayer dollars." But he says that city officials are trying to work with the developers to find a viable plan.

"It's a beautiful and iconic building," Mr. Ortiz says. "And we're doing everything we can to find a solution."

But High Rock is pressing on, saying the days of one company's occupying a skyscraper are over. It argues that the redevelopment will create hundreds of jobs and address the growing trend of young professionals' wanting to live in downtown environments.

"We have a vacant 428-foot symbol of Rhode Island's economic challenges sitting in downtown Providence," says Bill Fischer, a spokesman for the owner. "We're fully prepared to re-engage."

Private dining car in the sky

But the building no longer glows at night. Although a bluish green continues to beam from its very top, the rest of the skyscraper now disappears into the daily dusk. Perhaps to save $30,000 a year or, perhaps, to make a point.

"Lighting up the entire exterior of the building every night and saying everything is O.K. is not right," Mr. Fischer says. "Everything is not O.K. with the Superman building."

Mr. Almeida, its last and lonely employee, is not more powerful than a locomotive, but he does his best to keep the building fit for its next purpose. "I guess somebody's got to do it," he says.

And why not a man who linked together tables for meetings of the board of directors? Who knows that this empty room was known as the "dish room," because of the valuable china once on display, and that this empty conference room was called "green acres," because of a carpet the color of money?

The ascending elevator stops at the 26th floor, formerly the bank president's preserve. "His secretaries would sit here," Mr. Almeida says, nodding at some carpet space. "I would come up here, but not very often. I'd do whatever needed to be done. Furniture moved. . . ."

He takes in a panoramic view once reserved for industrialists, and now at his feet. Then he heads out a side door to a stairwell, where a red Superman cape, the vestige of a recent catered party, dangles from a sprinkler-system pipe. Mr. Almeida ignores it.

He climbs a staircase to reach the private dining car, where the wine closet is empty and the dark leather cracked. Just outside one window is a birdhouse for a peregrine falcon.

"The only tenant we have," he says.

Soon he is plummeting to the basement, to a series of vaults that look like stainless-steel props from the Chaplin classic "Modern Times."

Rows of gaping safe-deposit boxes, some containing metal shavings from having been drilled open. Huge cages that once contained Persian rugs and other bulk items of value. Vacuum tubes that sent cash zipping from the bank lobby to the counting room—at one time, $2.3 billion in deposits was stored right here.

Mr. Almeida seems unimpressed. He turns out some lights and heads down one more flight, to the very bottom, to his office in the boiler room, where, somewhere, water is dripping.

He sits at his tidy desk, upon which the red leather work diary, the glass mug filled with pens and the stack of Bank of America Post-it notes are arranged just so.

He worked his way up—or down—to this position. After years as a porter, he studied hard to earn certification as a boiler operator. He studied some more to become a stationary engineer. Then he looked up one day and someone said, "You're the only one here. I think you're in charge."

Mr. Almeida gets up from his desk. He has things to do. And soon he'll be turning on the heat so that no pipes burst in the tallest building in Rhode Island.

EPILOGUE

Paul Almeida, the chief engineer and true superman of the Superman building, died unexpectedly in 2015. He was 49.

And, as of this writing, the tallest building in Rhode Island remains vacant. Potential tenants have expressed interest over the past few years, but hopes have, like the building's elevators, rarely soared beyond the first floor.

Then again, "Hope" is the motto of Rhode Island.

At the End, Divide Between Clinton and Trump Is Only a Manhattan Mile

NEW YORK, N.Y. — NOVEMBER 10, 2016

Just one mile. That was all.

After the most divisive presidential campaign in living memory, a cross-country melee for the ages, the two warring camps pitched their election night tents and waited to hear the nation's agonized decision. All that separated them, as the bird flies, was a single mile across the midsection of Manhattan.

The Republican Party of Donald J. Trump prepared to cheer or cry at the New York Hilton Midtown, a spacious establishment along the Avenue of the Americas, between 53rd and 54th Streets. Meanwhile, to the southwest, the Democratic Party of Hillary Clinton braced to celebrate or concede at the glass-encased Jacob K. Javits Convention Center, on 11th Avenue and 34th Street.

And geographically, at least, only a mile of New York City pavement divided them.

It seemed odd at first, even tone deaf, for the two candidates to have chosen to end their races in Manhattan. This was, after all, evil Gotham, supposed home of liberal elites so out of touch with "real" Americans everywhere else.

The easy explanation is that Mr. Trump is a born New Yorker, while Mrs. Clinton is a former United States senator from New York who has adopted the Westchester County town of Chappaqua as her home. They are the first New Yorkers to represent the two major parties in a presidential election since Franklin D. Roosevelt (D) defeated Thomas E. Dewey (R) in 1944.

But back to that mile of pavement. Suppose a line were drawn between the Javits Center and the Midtown Hilton on a map of Manhattan. What would be seen? What would it say about a country on the cusp of new leadership? And what would be found in the exact middle, between Mrs. Clinton and Mr. Trump?

The Javits Center gleamed a frozen-blue in the distance, a cube-stacked glass structure that conveyed the proverbial ceiling that Mrs. Clinton intended to smash. It seemed unattainable—the building, at least—given the many police barricades. At every turn, it seemed, a police officer holding a cup of Dunkin' Donuts coffee pointed to a distant entrance, on 40th Street.

Here, a stencil in the street of a Clinton silhouette, accompanied by the words "Madam President." There, a street vendor, selling red-white-and-blue Clinton flags to be worn like shawls, or superhero capes. ("Big flags are $20, little flags are $10.") And above it all, a billboard for an Amazon program called "Good Girls Revolt."

Meanwhile, at the Midtown Hilton a mile away, security was looser, as hotel guests tried to wheel their luggage past the formally dressed Trump supporters gathering on the lobby's marble floor. If some women heading for the Clinton party wore white, to honor suffragists, some women bound for the Trump gathering were wearing fire-red, the chosen color of the "Make America Great Again" movement.

Heightened security also tied the two camps together. Orange sanitation trucks filled with sand served as barricades, while police officers with "Counterterrorism" emblazoned on the backs of their blue shirts kept watch. It was one of many reminders of the America that the night's president-elect would be inheriting.

Heading northeast from the Javits Center, that diagonal path passed Clyde Frazier's Wine and Dine, where the many televisions meant for sporting events now displayed the slow tally of electoral votes—a scene that recalled how the three presidential debates were often promoted with the hyperventilated fervor of a football game.

It passed the concrete road loops leading to the Lincoln Tunnel, leaving the Empire State Building—aglow in lights of red, white and blue—in the small of many rearview mirrors. And, in the shadows of the underpass, stood an unkempt man with a thin mattress at his feet, carrying on a solitary conversation.

The complex issues of the homeless and mentally ill—this too shall be inherited.

The path also crossed Covenant House, an eight-story shelter for homeless youth that was a polling place for the night. Busy, the poll workers said. Very busy.

Now, heading southwest from the Midtown Hilton, the diagonal path cut across restaurants rare and routine, Le Bernardin and Sbarro's, the Capital Grille and TGI Friday's. It sliced across the eternal brightness of Times Square and past a homeless man who pitched for donations—"My name is William and I'm a good guy, not a bad guy"—while a tourist recorded the desperate street performance without reaching into his own pocket.

It passed, too, the Engine Company 54/Ladder Company 4 firehouse on Eighth Avenue that lost 15 firefighters in the World Trade Center attacks. Their names and photographs are on display, but a sign says, "Please No Photos." The raw aftermath of that day will also be passed on to the new president.

So where, then, do these two paths meet? The one coming from the Hilton Midtown to the north and the other from the Javits Center to the south? The meeting point is, roughly, at El Rancho Burritos, a small Mexican restaurant near the corner of Ninth Avenue and 45th Street, between the Westside Deli and Cleantopia Cleaners.

There, the owner, Manuel Gil, was working the counter, taking orders for burritos and enchiladas

and steak ranchero. A short man of 54, wearing a white paper hat and a white apron over a dark T-shirt, he agreed to sit for a minute and tell his story.

Mr. Gil came to New York from the Mexican city of Puebla more than 30 years ago, joining his father. He worked as a dishwasher at a fancy restaurant, a worker in a garment factory, and an assistant in a burrito restaurant, all the while saving his money for one day.

That day came 20 years ago, when he rented out this cramped space and opened his restaurant. It has room enough for only five tables, each adorned with a small vase of plastic tulips. Stacks of Jarritos soda, mango and lime, take up what little room is left. On the far wall hangs an oval portrait of the Virgin Mary, a poster providing instructions for the Heimlich maneuver ("Choking Victim"), and a television that on this night was broadcasting election coverage in Spanish.

Mr. Gil, who lives in Queens and works 60 hours a week, became a citizen 15 years ago. He and his wife, Carmen, who often works beside him, have four children: an accountant, a photographer, a student at Ithaca College and a student at the High School of Fashion Industries.

In the late 1940s, shortly after Mr. Trump and Mrs. Clinton were born, this part of Manhattan, called Hell's Kitchen, was mostly Irish and Italian. But now here was Mr. Gil, representing the ever-changing city, the ever-changing country.

This flow of change will also be inherited.

Mr. Gil removed his white apron to reveal a Hillary Clinton shirt that his daughter Leslie, the photographer, had bought him. He had voted for Mrs. Clinton, he said, because she was more capable. Mr. Trump, he said after a long pause, was not yet ready to be president.

The reports in Spanish that emanated from the television behind him were suggesting that the rest of the country disagreed. But this is how it goes. And no matter who won, come late morning he'd be back behind the counter of his restaurant, greeting the new, uncertain day.

Another Day at a
Monument to Democracy

WASHINGTON, D.C. — JANUARY 21, 2017

The glorious Lincoln Memorial was closed on Inauguration Day, leaving its white marble inhabitant to inspire from a distance. The monument had served as a backdrop for an inaugural concert the night before, and now, in the late morning, construction workers were methodically removing the silvery bars of scaffolding that imprisoned it.

Even so, its sole resident could still be seen behind the Doric columns, his gaze trained on the far-off domed Capitol, where a peaceful transfer of power was about to take place. And people still came to be in his presence, some to remind themselves that a country riven by dissent can come together. It has before.

No matter that the sky was as gray as the Potomac, or that the cold air felt like a wet sweater. Here they were, from the North and South, East and West, in red Trump hats and blue Hillary T-shirts, jubilant, distressed, feeling a part and apart. They stood in admiration of Lincoln, as workers tore down and cleaned up, including a man collecting debris with a hand-held picker, his dog tag laced securely into one of his military-issue boots.

Ed Rich, he said his name was, while taking a Camel break. Forty-four years old. A mortgage broker from Annapolis, trying to ride out a slow period. So it's $12 an hour working for the inauguration, putting up fencing, laying down flooring, snapping up cigarette butts with a metal picker.

"I voted for him," Mr. Rich said of Donald J. Trump, at this point still the president-elect. "I think he could make a mess of it, but it could be cleaned up easily. People seem to forget there's a House and a Senate."

Mr. Rich tossed his spent cigarette into the box of garbage he was carrying and returned to collecting butts and paper bits, his words nowhere near as eloquent as those of Lincoln, carved into the memorial's walls, yet in the same vein: the belief—often tested, including on this day—in the country's democratic system of governance.

Generations have come to the Lincoln Memorial to reassure themselves—or to remind the rest of the nation—of this foundational belief. The African-American contralto, Marian Anderson, sang here in 1939, after the Daughters of the American Revolution had barred her from another Washington venue; she began with "My country 'tis of thee, sweet land of liberty."

The Rev. Dr. Martin Luther King Jr., of course, delivered his "I Have a Dream" speech here in 1963, after Mahalia Jackson called out, "Tell them about the dream, Martin."

Even Richard M. Nixon, during a dark moment of his presidency (and that is saying something), came here on a very early May morning in 1970, valet in tow; he wound up in profoundly strange conversations with some Vietnam War protesters, his disjointed message: Don't give up on this country.

In their footsteps came others on this inaugural morning.

Jerry Naradzay, 56, a physician from Henderson, N.C., cycled up to the monument with his 13-year-old son, Sammy, the father's broad smile explained by his red "Make America Great Again" cap.

He noted that the memorial's stone had come from both the North and the South to convey unity after division. He then said he had goose bumps just thinking of more than two centuries of peaceful transfers of power.

Nodding toward the memorial, Dr. Naradzay said, "This monument represents how the country is bigger than one man."

Standing nearby in full agreement were four Hillary Clinton supporters from Wisconsin's North Country. They had made plans for this Washington visit in expectation of a different result, but decided to come anyway, in part to participate in the women's march on Saturday.

So: How did they feel?

"Hollow," said Jackie Moore, 33, a member of the Ashland City Council. Several awkward seconds of silence followed.

When conversation resumed, another Ashland council member, David Mettille, 32, and his partner, Teege Mettille, 36, recounted how their blue Hillary shirts had spurred some heckling, but they didn't mind. It was their way of saying: We're still here.

"We will remember this," David Mettille said. "We will remember how painful today is, so that four years from now—we work to win."

Then Teege Mettille noted that they had about a half-hour left of President Obama, and off the visitors from Ashland went.

It was true: Time was winding down, or winding up. From the swearing-in ceremony in the distance, beyond the reflecting pool's greenish waters, came the echoes of ministers beseeching God for guidance, the raised voices of the Missouri State University Chorale, the somber tones of imminent transition.

All the while, others came to be in Lincoln's presence.

A retired civil engineer from Virginia who said he had voted for Mr. Trump because a relative is a heroin addict, and because the Mexican border is a sieve. A couple from Utah who voted for Mr. Trump because their community depends on natural gas and oil. Mothers and their adult daughters from Texas and New Mexico, so dismayed that Mr. Trump would soon be their president that they kept their backs to the inauguration.

Soon the Mormon Tabernacle Choir could be heard singing "America the Beautiful." Then came the distinctive voice of the new president, his assertions of a restored American greatness in all things floating through the gray noon and up the four score and seven steps leading from the reflecting pool to the memorial.

No longer president-elect, he was now President Trump.

While the pageantry unfolded, Mr. Rich, the debris collector, kept working. A former Marine, he said he spent six months in Iraq with a mortuary affairs unit, collecting bodies and body parts from the front.

Sometimes there wasn't enough for certain identification, he said, "so you'd write, 'Believed to be.'"

He said he was making plans to succeed again in the mortgage business, in a country whose balanced-power form of government he trusts. But for now Mr. Rich had what he called his mission, which was to keep the plaza beneath Lincoln's gaze clean.

PART TWO

Hope

Meet me tonight in Dreamland

Planning a Path Through
Life on the Walk to School

ST. LOUIS, MO. — APRIL 22, 2007

Under a dreary sky the color of uncertainty, on a city block pocked by abandonment, a door opens and a girl of 15 steps out. With a black-and-blue book bag slung across her back, she starts walking to school, a high school sophomore of this country.

Her name is Janay Truitt, and she lives on the crime-rich and money-poor north side of St. Louis. She shares an apartment above a dry-cleaning store with two grandparents, two sisters, a brother and her mother, who leaves at 4:30 in the morning to drive a school bus. Her father lives elsewhere.

Janay sets out at 7:05 today for a city school system in which poverty, politics and mismanagement so closely conspire against the likes of her that the state recently decided to take it over. But who knows what that takeover means for this lanky girl with braids, now lugging gym clothes, math homework and a world history textbook the size and weight of a slate slab you'd find along a footpath.

Wearing a thin blue sweatshirt over a T-shirt that says "Purrfect," she moves through the St. Louis gloom, past the dry cleaners' trellised gates of security, past an alley where no child should play, past buildings that are well kept and buildings that are vacant, their window frames like empty eye sockets.

A man in an old green Volvo passing by beeps his horn. He is Travis L. Brown Sr., the principal of her high school, Beaumont. He grew up near here, one of 10 children. Enforcer and guardian, he drives the streets before the morning bell to signal that school matters, that he cares. I've been there and now I'm here, his actions say.

Janay continues on, aware that she must pass through the school's metal detector before the 7:20 bell or else be marked again as absent, and be subjected again to a Mr. Brown lecture. She is not a morning person, does not even eat breakfast, but she has a plan for her life that begins with a first-period literature class.

She thinks as she walks. She thinks about keeping her grades up; she had five A's and two B's last marking period, and those two B's, in world literature and biology, vex her.

She thinks about learning long ago how to toss balls into a milk crate nailed to a post, and about starting as a guard on the girls' varsity basketball team this fall. When asked whether she's a point guard or a shooting guard, she does not hesitate to answer: "Both."

She thinks, she hopes, that with her high grades and honed basketball skills, she might one day attend the University of North Carolina, or Duke, or Tennessee. That one day she can become an anesthesiologist and make a lot of money.

"I'm thinking, probably, about trying to get out of the neighborhood," Janay says later, explaining that at the moment she has to walk a mile to buy a decent ice cream cone, and take two buses and a light-rail train to see a movie.

She walks under a liquor store's red-and-white beer sign and stops in front of the Upper Room Fire Christian Assembly to meet two other Beaumont students: LuCretia Scott, who wants to be a fashion designer, and Dominique Taylor, who says she might become a psychiatrist because she gives good advice.

It is 7:11, nine minutes until the bell. They push on toward Beaumont.

Beaumont High School, built in the 1920s, looms over the troubled neighborhood like a castle of trapdoors and passageways. With high student turnover and a low graduation rate, it reflects an urban system plagued by poverty and homelessness. Nearly 80 percent of the school's 1,200 students receive free or discounted lunches.

Still, Beaumont tries. Mr. Brown, the principal, and his top assistant, Pamela Hendricks, walk the grounds so much—cajoling, disciplining, and, when necessary, hugging—that they wear sneakers with their suits. If he sees a boy wearing a hood, he shouts the school slogan, "Not at Beaumont!" If she sees a girl dawdling, she bellows, "Hurry up! Come on! What's the problem?"

Mr. Brown says he emphasizes the possible by celebrating every success: school T-shirts one day, pizza the next. The students know that achieving a perfect average of 4.0 means they and their parents will be taken by limousine to lunch in a restaurant. The limo is a donated service, and the restaurant, of course, is several miles from here.

"You look for ways to keep the students engaged," says Mr. Brown, enthusiastic still after 10 years at Beaumont.

Janay and her two friends rush across Vandeventer Avenue and follow a concrete path around the building, opting not to cut across the school's wet grass. They make it to the metal detector just as the maternal Ms. Hendricks is calling, "You have 30 seconds! Everybody needs to be in class!"

A dozen hours from now, Janay will travel to a nice gymnasium in a nice suburb to practice with other young women on a traveling team called the St. Louis Queens. She will demonstrate her crossover dribble and her sweet jump shot. An accidental hit to the mouth will bloody her lip and chip a tooth; it does not stop her from playing in a scrimmage.

But that is later. For now, she settles into a small classroom in a challenged high school in the flawed school system of St. Louis, looking forward to sixth period, her favorite class, the history of the world.

Where Little Else Grows, Capitalism Takes Root

LUCIN, UTAH — MAY 13, 2007

Great Location! Rare Parcel! Premium Lot!

Somehow these hoary come-ons still cast their spell, drawing us in, relieving us of that obstacle to suspect acquisition, our disbelief. With words that all but wink in confidence, they slyly suggest that our mothers raised no fools, that we should get while the getting's good—and that desert land in Utah is the next big thing.

"Excellent investment property in high-growth area," reads an eBay advertisement for the sale of 40 acres in a remote part of rural Box Elder County. Good roads (unencumbered by pavement), close to casinos (if 80 miles is close), and, the ad says, "Only one mile away from Lucin Town."

Ah, the lure of Lucin Town.

To reach Lucin from the pleasant county seat, Brigham City, you must drive nearly 150 miles, around the top of the Great Salt Lake and then southwest, along a two-lane road curling past tumbleweeds and the very occasional ranch. After a long while you turn left onto a dirt road, travel six bumpy miles—and there you are, smack in the middle of spectacular nothingness: Lucin.

Lucin is not even a ghost town; it is a ghost junction, where lonely dirt road crosses lonely railroad track, and the most prominent inhabitants are a snake, a beetle and some large ants. Step on the parched earth to examine that toppled Lucin sign, and dust kicks up.

Nearly 1,800 miles away, in Houston, one of the partners in the company selling the land answers his telephone. His name is Sanjit Tayi, and he says he has never set foot on these desolate 40 acres that his company describes as "high growth."

"What's there?" he asks. "Is there a gas station or something there?" Uh, no.

If you've always dreamed of owning parched, inaccessible property in Utah, you may have missed your chance. Essentially to protect people from themselves, Box Elder County officials are cracking down on how remote lands within its sprawling boundaries are misleadingly advertised and illegally subdivided.

The county has notified more than 3,000 people that the property they bought for hundreds or thousands of dollars, often sight unseen, appears to have been carved from much larger parcels in violation of county and state zoning laws. The owners of these illegally subdivided properties were informed that they cannot sell their land, cannot develop their land—and, in many cases, cannot even visit their land, because there is no access.

Other than that, welcome to Box Elder County!

The county plans to file criminal charges against the offending developers. In the meantime, it has hired several temporary workers to handle the flood of calls from landowners who received notices of noncompliance. Some callers say they bought a cheap quarter-acre just for the kick of owning land in Utah; others say that suburban sprawl will reach the desert someday, and when that day comes, oh boy.

"They're calling from all over the world, basically," says LuAnn Adams, the county recorder and clerk. "I know I've had Germany, Australia."

Ms. Adams says she has seen advertisements for desert land that include photographs of the glittery waters of Willard Bay, a mere three hours' drive from the property for sale. She has also fielded calls from people who say they own a lot on Sunset Drive.

Although Sunset Drive does not exist, she readily assures them that "there are beautiful sunsets out there."

Land speculation, of course, is nothing new. What is new is how the Internet has quickened the timing referred to in a familiar saying. Now, it seems, there's a sucker born every second.

Officials say that another run on desert land years ago prompted them to create zoning laws requiring that most lots for sale in the county's western desert be a minimum of 160 acres. Nevertheless, in recent years entrepreneurs have bought, subdivided and sold the parcels, and then have filed deeds with the recorder's office—though, alas, without securing the required approval of zoning officials.

Take, for example, the 160-acre parcel that one of the more active entrepreneurs, Larry Madsen, of Bluffdale, Utah, subdivided in the middle of nowhere, well more than a mile from where unpaved Little Pigeon Road ends. The map of that parcel is now a crazed checkerboard of small boxes, each one bearing the name of a proud owner.

Mr. Madsen declined this week to discuss his real estate business. He wrote in an email message that "I am simply a retired person who purchased some investment land and sold part of it when I retired to help cover living expenses."

One of his customers is Reza Stegamat, a business manager who lives near Pittsburgh. Two years ago Mr. Stegamat saw one of Mr. Madsen's advertisements on eBay, became convinced that Utah land would be a good investment and bought five acres for about $1,500. A year later he made his way to Box Elder County and tried to find his property, somewhere in the vicinity of Little Pigeon Road.

"I kept going back and forth," he recalls. "But there was nothing, really."

Out where Mr. Stegamat once searched in vain, the desert stretches like a dream-swallowing ocean. For all the petty deceit and human folly, it remains the same, hostile and beautiful, daunting and serene.

On this spring evening, a snake slithers, the warm breeze offers a phantom kiss, and unseen birds sing the chuckling, rarely heard song of Lucin Town.

For a Family of
Migrant Farmworkers,
a New Season Is Dawning

BRECKENRIDGE, MINN. — AUGUST 5, 2007

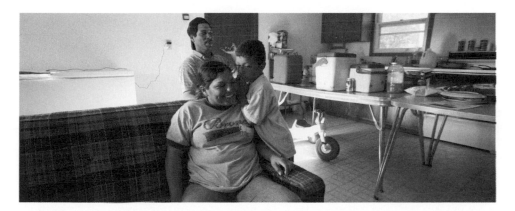

Minerva Hinojosa and her family migrated north again last month, traveling from the Texas bottom of this nation to its Minnesota top to weed the sugar beet fields of a farmer named Blaufuss. Once here, they each claimed the hoe that felt truest in their hands by carving a telltale mark into the wooden handle.

For Ms. Hinojosa, 22, this is how it has always been: the Hinojosas working the Blaufuss fields, following the rows of beets deep into the green distance, then working back down new rows, their hoe blades getting duller with every hack at the black earth. All for about $22 an acre.

But she also knows how profoundly this migrant life is changing. It hit home a couple of weeks ago when her cellphone trilled while she was working in the fields, her long brown hair tucked under a Texas Longhorns cap.

Holding the hoe with one hand, she flipped the phone open with the other. "Hello?"

Three decades ago, well before she was born, some of Ms. Hinojosa's relatives began traveling 1,600 miles north, from Weslaco, Tex., to Breckenridge. Jim Blaufuss needed help with his sugar beets, and so a bond between two families was made.

Among those arriving from Texas every season was Eleuterio Hinojosa, a Mexican-born laborer accustomed to traveling far for work, whether to the fields or to the cotton gins that long ago changed the feel of his handshake by taking three finger tops. His wife, Rachel, and their ever-expanding family would join him on those long trips north, including his daughter Minerva, an American citizen who says she has been migrating "since I was born."

The Blaufuss family eventually built a squat, one-story duplex with air-conditioning on their farm to accommodate the Hinojosas and their many relatives. The workers felt fortunate; not all growers provided housing, and those who did sometimes offered little more than shacks.

The hundreds of migrant families of Breckenridge became a tight but time-sensitive community, here for the sugar beet crop, then gone, some back to Texas, some to Michigan to pick apples. Not all local residents accepted them, that is for sure. But on summer Sunday afternoons, at least, they claimed a town park as their own, for music and barbecues.

"You'd see no white people," Ms. Hinojosa recalls.

Back then, she was just one of many Texan children running about. Every morning she would take a bus to a supplemental education program for migrant children at the elementary school, overseen by a teacher named Bill Mimnaugh. She studied, played, got fed and stayed out of the fields—at least, that is, until she was about 11.

At 13, Ms. Hinojosa became pregnant. She named the boy David, took a hard look at what kind of woman his mother would be, and went back to school. This meant that every summer she would hoe her rows all day, then head off for night classes at Mr. Mimnaugh's education program, determined.

Early last month the Hinojosas returned again to that squat duplex in Breckenridge, where they found a freezer full of meat, courtesy of Mr. Blaufuss. "They're family," he explains.

But this Texas contingent included only Ms. Hinojosa, her parents, her older brother Jay and her son, David—meaning that the many bunk beds in the house would remain empty.

People in Minnesota say that changes in sugar beet farming, including the use of improved herbicides, have reduced the need for migrants; that adequate housing remains a problem; that cuts in the migrant education program have caused child care and schooling problems for migrant families.

At the same time, the children of migrants are finding different paths, says Jay Hinojosa, 36, who has just changed out of jeans that are damp with sweat. "Some of them pursued education," he says. "Some joined the Air Force, the Navy. Other family members decided it wasn't worth it."

Still, the Hinojosas see familiar Texan faces in Breckenridge, including that of Maribell Molina, 35, who migrates now to work for the Tri-Valley Opportunity Council as a family service liaison for the migrant education program. She says that older migrants return because they need the money, they feel loyal to employers, and they want to set an example.

"To show their kids the value of the dollar," she says.

A couple of weeks ago the Hinojosas rose again before dawn. Rachel Hinojosa baked the tortillas and made the beans that would be breakfast and lunch. Eleuterio Hinojosa packed the coolers and sharpened the hoe blades with his metal file. Minerva roused David, now 7, and got him dressed. The family of five drove to the field and began hoeing at 5:30.

While David dozed in the pickup's cab, the Hinojosas hacked at the weeds inhibiting the subterranean growth of the sugar beet, which is used to sweeten your soda, your cookies. After a while, Rachel Hinojosa drove David to the same migrant education program that his mother attended, run by the same Mr. Mimnaugh, who is sometimes called the "Dairy Queen guy" because on Fridays he rewards good students with cool treats.

"The same school!" Ms. Hinojosa exclaims. "I love it!"

The Hinojosas worked their rows, paused to eat, then reached again for their hoes. The sun arced high and hot over the Minnesota flatness. A cellphone rang, and Ms. Hinojosa answered.

"Finally!" she shouted, and the Hinojosas around her immediately knew:

Minerva Hinojosa, daughter of migrants, had graduated with a degree in English from the University of Texas-Pan American, and would be teaching this fall at her alma mater, Weslaco East High School. She is the family's first college graduate.

Her mother said, "Thanks to God." Her father said the family should celebrate by hoeing another row. And so they did.

On the Bottle, Off the Streets, Halfway There

SEATTLE, WASH. — NOVEMBER 11, 2007

The Moocher introduced them years ago down by the ferry terminal, near that "No Loitering" sign scratched up to read "Know Loitering." It was Ed, meet Daryl, Daryl, Ed, between sips and slugs of bottom-shelf whiskey and high-octane beer.

Soon, in the blathering small talk that kills time, Ed Myers and Daryl Jordan identified a bond beyond a shared dislike for the Moocher, who drank but never bought. They both had survived the same firefight in Vietnam, it seemed; brothers now, in blood and booze.

Together they panhandled with Nam Vet Needs Help signs at the highway entrance, converted their proceeds into Icehouse beer and Rich & Rare whiskey, and shared their nights in the perpetual dusk beneath the elevated highway, taking turns seeking the full sleep that never came, so loud was the traffic above, so naked were they below, in addled vulnerability.

Now and then they came in from the elements, sometimes to the same shelter, sometimes to separate shelters, sometimes to the Sobering Support Center on Boren Avenue, where you store your shoes and coat in a black plastic bag, have your vitals checked, accept the soup and juice or not, then fold up on a thin mat over concrete.

If separated, Daryl would spend the early morning pacing the dark streets, until finally here would be Ed, already to drinking to quell those first shakes of the day. And the two would return to Know Loitering.

They came to know the jagged pieces of each other's bottle-shattered past, the broken marriages, the lost jobs, the ghosts. Daryl still sees what he saw in Vietnam. As for Ed, he was working on a fifth one day in his Iowa hometown when suddenly, there before him, stood his father and grandfather, telling him for shame. That both were dead only underscored the point.

Ed dumped the bottle and didn't drink for 12 years—until one day he did. Back he fell to the hard, hard streets, which at least offered up another man who understood. Daryl.

Hell, Daryl was there that Thanksgiving time when a woman slipped Ed two twenties; they gave thanks with two days of beer, whiskey and chicken-fried-steak dinners. And Daryl was there when some young cop poured out most of a fifth and tossed the bottle on the ground, prompting Ed to say he didn't appreciate littering.

Early last year, some people, not cops, tracked Daryl down at the sobering center, where he had slept off a drunk 360 times in one calendar year. They were from a homeless outreach organization and they had some news, good for a change.

The organization had just built a 75-unit residence for homeless chronic alcoholics at 1811 Eastlake Avenue, and was offering rooms to the frailest and costliest to the system, as determined by time spent in the sobering center, the emergency room and jail. The idea: provide them first with housing and meals, gain their trust, then encourage them to partake of the available services, including treatment for chemical dependency.

No mandatory meetings or church-going. And one more thing, crucial to all: You can drink in this place.

Welcome, Daryl. A month later: Welcome, Ed.

"I damn near bawled," Ed recalls.

The $11 million project has endured the angry complaints of some that it uses public money to enable, even reward, chronic inebriates. And Bill Hobson, the director of the Downtown Emergency Service Center, has met that anger with some of his own.

First, he says, the complaints reflect no understanding of the grip of alcoholism: Do you really think these men and women would rather live on the streets? Second, the cost to the public appears to have dropped as the number of visits to the emergency room, jail and the sobering center has plummeted.

1811 Eastlake Avenue

Finally, he asks, what kind of equation of humanity is this: Since you refuse to stop drinking, since you refuse to address your disease, you must die on the streets.

"These guys have nothing going for them," he says. "They could not be more dispossessed." So, welcome. Pay a third of your disability income for rent, and remember to behave; this isn't a party house.

The handsome building at 1811 Eastlake stands on the shores of Interstate 5, a short walk from both the sobering center and a convenience store that sells cheap staples like cans of Icehouse and Midnight Special tobacco. Its first floor includes a laundry, a nurse's office, counseling rooms and a bulletin board adorned with photos of smiling residents.

Captured in those snapshot smiles, evidence of this life: missing teeth, ill-fitting clothes, faces disfigured by subdural hematomas—from beatings and falls to the pavement. Some residents snatch these photos to decorate their rooms, along with the cardboard signs they once used while panhandling.

Above are three floors of studio apartments, including one for Daryl and one for Ed, both immaculately maintained. Daryl, 59 and with a left forefinger burned orange by tobacco, was July's resident of the month. Ed, 61 and with a taste for western-style clothes, was August's. The poster boys for visiting journalists, forever twinned, it seemed.

Then something happened. On July 1, one day not blurred in memory, Ed felt he needed some nutrients, so he fixed himself a tomato beer: tomato juice and a can of Rainier. He took a sip, winced, took another sip, winced, and that was that. He hasn't had a drink since.

"It didn't taste good anymore," Ed says.

Ed has been drinking ginger ale, and Daryl has been struggling. For a long while Daryl would not go to Ed's apartment, with its coffee table and La-Z-Boy, and the occasional sound of a resident falling to the floor upstairs. He didn't want to drink in front of Ed because he didn't want to tempt his friend, and because, because—"I'm done trying," he says, eyes tearing.

The other day Daryl was back in Ed's cozy apartment. Ed was drinking coffee he had just brewed, and Daryl was drinking a can of Rainier from that six-pack Ed never finished. They talked around old and fresh wars for a while, but it was clear that whatever Ed was looking at, Daryl could not yet see.

EPILOGUE

The daily routine at 1811 Eastlake Avenue remains the same. The program continues to demonstrate success in improving lives and saving public funds, with the model attracting the interest of communities across the country.

Ed Myers has since moved, confident that he no longer needed the building's services. His friend Daryl Jordan died in 2017 at the age of 68, leaving behind family members who say that Eastlake extended his life by many years.

Bill Hobson, the longtime advocate for the homeless in Seattle who helped to establish the program, died in 2016; he was 76. In his honor, the street outside the Eastlake residence has been rechristened "Bill Hobson Way."

Amid Ruin of Flint, Seeing Hope in a Garden

FLINT, MICH. — OCTOBER 19, 2009

On one side of the fertile lot stands an abandoned house, stripped long ago for scrap. On the other side, another abandoned house, windows boarded, structure sagging. And diagonally across the street, two more abandoned houses, including one blackened by a fire maybe a year ago, maybe two.

But on this lot, surrounded by desertion in the north end of Flint, the toughest city in America, collard greens sprout in verdant surprise. Although the broccoli and turnips and snap peas have been picked, it is best to wait until deep autumn for the greens, says the garden's keeper, Harry Ryan. The frost lends sweetness to the leaves.

His is not just another tiny community garden growing from a gap in the urban asphalt. This one lot is really 10 contiguous lots where a row of houses once stood. On this spot, the house burned down. ("I was the one who called the fire department.") On that spot, the house was lost to back taxes. ("An older guy; he was trying to fix it up, and he was struggling.")

Garbage and chest-high overgrowth filled the domestic void of these lots on East Piper Avenue until four years ago, when Mr. Ryan decided one day: no. After receiving the proper permission, he began clearing the land.

Rose Barber, 56, a neighbor who keeps a 30-inch Louisville Slugger, a Ryne Sandberg model, by her front door, offered her help. Then came Andre Jones, 40, another neighbor, using his shovel to do the backbreaking work of uncovering long stretches of sidewalk, which had disappeared under inches of soil, weeds and municipal neglect.

East Piper Avenue now has its sidewalk back, along with a vegetable garden, a grassy expanse where a children's playground will be built, and, close to one of those abutting abandoned houses, a mix-and-match orchard of 18 young fruit trees.

"This is a Golden Delicious tree," Mr. Ryan says, reading the tags on the saplings. "This is a Warren pear. That's a McIntosh. This is a Mongolian cherry tree...."

In many ways, this garden on East Piper Avenue reflects all of Flint, a city working hard to re-invent itself, a city so weary of serving as the country's default example of post-industrial decline. Nearly every day its visitors' bureau sends out a "Changing Perceptions of Flint" email message that includes a call to defend the city's honor:

"If a blogger is bashing Flint and Genesee County, go post a positive message. If there is an article about the depressed economy in Flint, go post something uplifting."

But uplifting and depressing both describe Flint, where encouraging development grows beside wholesale abandonment. You can visit one of the first-class museums (at the moment, the Flint Institute of Arts has a music-enhanced exhibit of rock 'n' roll posters), then drive past rows of vacant, vandalized houses that convey a Hurricane Katrina despair—though Flint's hurricane came in the form of the automobile industry's collapse.

No question: Downtown Flint, about five miles from Mr. Ryan's garden, suddenly feels vital. A large civil engineering firm has built an office there, and the headquarters of a second large firm is about to open. New dormitory rooms at the University of Michigan-Flint are full. New restaurants have popped up, including an Irish pub in a long-closed men's clothing store. An old flophouse is now a smart apartment complex. The majestic Durant Hotel, vacant for 35 years, is being transformed into apartments for students and young professionals.

And just last week, General Motors announced a $230 million investment in four local factories as part of its plan to build a new generation of fuel-efficient cars.

But Dayne Walling, the recently elected mayor, says these developments, while exciting, tell but one side of the city's story. The other side: a steep decline in the tax base, an unemployment rate hovering around 25 percent, rising health care and pension costs, drastic cutbacks in municipal services, a legacy of fiscal mismanagement—and, of course, the loss of some 70,000 jobs at General Motors, the industry that defined Flint for nearly a century.

The job loss, compounded by the recession, has led to an astonishing plunge in the city's population—to about 110,000, and falling, from roughly 200,000 in 1960. Thousands of abandoned houses now haunt the 34-square-mile city; one in four houses is said to be vacant.

As a result, Flint finds itself the centerpiece of a national debate about so-called shrinking cities, in which mostly abandoned neighborhoods might become green space, and their residents would be encouraged to live closer to a downtown core.

The matter is being pressed here by the Genesee County Land Bank, which acquires foreclosed properties and works with communities to restore or demolish them. It has been sponsoring a series of forums titled "Strengthening Our Community in the Face of Population Decline."

Mayor Walling, though, prefers to talk about sustainable cities, rather than shrinking cities. He imagines the Flint of 2020 as a city of 100,000, with a vibrant downtown surrounded by greener neighborhoods, in which residents have doubled their lot sizes by acquiring adjacent land where houses once stood.

"We're down, but we're not out," he says. "And that's a classic American story."

Part of that classic story is up in the north end, on East Piper Avenue, where

some people are trying to make use of one of the few abundant resources in Flint: land.

Harry Ryan, 59, the child of auto workers, traveled for years as a rhythm and blues musician before returning to follow his parents into the auto plants. He got laid off, found other employment, and is now retired, with gray in his mustache and a stoop to his walk.

In 2005 he went to the land bank—he is on its advisory board—and received permission to plant a garden on a lot it owns a few yards from the broken side window of an abandoned house. He and some neighbors cleaned brush, removed the remnant pieces of concrete of demolished houses, and planted hardy turnips and greens.

But the garden could not contain their growing sense of pride in their community. Soon they were mowing front lawns all along East Piper Avenue—for free, and without seeking permission. "We just cut everybody's property, even if they were sitting on the porch," he says. "Sometimes they wouldn't say anything, and that would get us mad."

That first year, Mr. Ryan and Ms. Barber, who works nights at the post office, bagged up the greens and gave them away, often by just leaving a bag at the door of someone they suspected could use the food but was too proud to ask for it. But they also ate some of what they harvested; Mr. Ryan still savors that first batch of collard greens he had with some smoked turkey.

Today, the ever-expanding garden continues to feed people. Front lawns are still mowed, though now by neighborhood children paid through a county grant. Ms. Barber still works in the garden, and Mr. Jones has expanded his sidewalk mission to the cross street of Verdun, where he has cleared a path past the shell of a house lost to arson.

When asked why he does the work, he just says, "It needs to be done."

As for Mr. Ryan, he is working on a plan to build a power-generating windmill in the garden on East Piper Avenue in the great Michigan city of Flint. That's right: a windmill.

A Dealer Serving Life Without Having Taken One

GREENVILLE, ILL. — DECEMBER 22, 2013

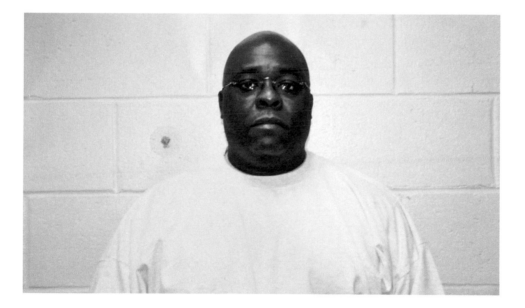

A lifer with a pen sat in the 65-square-foot cell he shares. A calendar taunted from a bulletin board. He began to write.

Dear President Obama.

He acknowledged his criminal past. He expressed remorse. And he pleaded for a second chance, now that he had served 18 years of the worst sentence short of execution: life without parole, for a nonviolent first offense.

Mr. President, he wrote, "you are my final hope."

Sincerely, Jesse Webster.

Eleven hundred men reside in medium security at this remote Greenville federal prison in southern Illinois. Most come and go, sentences served. Others stay, their legal appeals exhausted, their only hope to take up a pen and enter the long-shot lottery of executive clemency with a salutation that begins: Dear President Obama.

The prisoners are men like Mr. Webster, 46, a former cocaine dealer from the South Side of Chicago. And his old cellmate, Reynolds Wintersmith Jr., 39, a former teenage crack-cocaine dealer from Rockford, Ill., who has spent half his life in prison.

The two friends first met at the maximum-security prison in Leavenworth, Kan. That was almost 15 years ago.

"We were both younger then," Mr. Webster recalled.

Mr. Webster, bald, stocky and bespectacled, discussed his case several days ago in the spare visitors' room at Greenville. Signs everywhere said "no" this and "no" that. Nearby stood an artificial Christmas tree used by families as a prop to feign normality in holiday photos.

"I should have done time," Mr. Webster said. "But a living death sentence?"

Growing up, his family of seven barely survived on his stepfather's job as a parking-lot attendant. Dropping out of ninth grade to make money for the household, he wound up buffing at a carwash favored by a big-tipping drug dealer. Seeing hustle in 16-year-old Jesse's eyes, he offered the boy a job as his driver, $200 a week.

Mr. Webster never forgot what his friends had said and how they said it: "that I had moved up in low places."

He became a low-key freelancer in a hooked-up world, living in a doorman building, driving a Volvo and concealing a gun he never used. "I didn't do flash," he said.

In 1995, though, he learned that the law was looking for him, so he decided to turn himself in. One day a station wagon left the South Side for the North Side, jammed with his mother, brother and others who wanted to be there in support. "We all went as a family," his mother, Robin Noble, said.

Soon Mr. Webster was being cuffed from behind, an indelible moment. "The look on his face," Leon Noble, his younger brother, said. "Like he let us down."

Prosecutors offered leniency on the condition that Mr. Webster become a confidential informant against a powerful drug gang. He declined, which Matthew

Crowl, a prosecutor in his case, described many years later as a reasonable decision, given that the gang had already killed an informant.

Mr. Webster was convicted of participating in a drug conspiracy and filing false tax returns. His sentence of life without parole left his mother weeping and his brother's heart dropping to the floor. For a sentence like that, the inmate said, "I thought I'd have to hurt somebody, do bodily harm."

The federal judge, James B. Zagel, explained to the court that he was adhering to the mandatorily harsh sentencing guidelines of the day. "To put it in simple terms," the judge said before imposing sentence, "it's too high."

If it were 1986 or today, Mr. Webster would probably be sentenced to serve about 25 years. But he was sentenced in 1996, during a period when sentencing guidelines gave federal judges virtually no discretion in assessing punishment.

"That was at the peak of mandatory sentencing," said Vanita Gupta, the deputy legal director for the American Civil Liberties Union.

The A.C.L.U.—which highlighted the cases of Mr. Webster and Mr. Wintersmith, among dozens of others, in a recent report on lifers—estimates that more than 2,000 federal inmates are serving life without parole for nonviolent offenses.

What's more, in a sample study of 169 federal inmates incarcerated for nonviolent crimes, the organization found dozens who were first-time offenders, as well as many others who had only misdemeanors and juvenile infractions in their past.

And this was just in the federal prison system.

"We kind of lost our moral center and any sense of proportionality in our sentencing" during the so-called war on drugs, Ms. Gupta said. "The result was the throwing away of certain people's lives, predominantly black and brown people's lives."

Mr. Webster spent 16 years in federal maximum-security prisons, including Leavenworth, willing himself past the temptations, the lockdowns, the nearly hopeless reality. He received only three infractions—all minor, with the last one in 1997—and earned the trusted position of captain's orderly.

In July 2011, finally, he won a transfer to relative tranquility, here in Greenville. "Took me 17 years to get here," he said.

Up at 6:30. Bowl of oatmeal. Stretch. Clean cell. Work as a unit orderly. Run three miles. Push-ups and pull-ups. Shower. Lunch. Volunteer as a tutor to other inmates. Stand for count. Dinner. Work on job skills and résumé writing. Shower. Read the Bible. And call Mom, whose picture he keeps tucked into his bottom bunk's ceiling.

Family members say Mr. Webster lifts spirits on the outside when he calls from the inside, urging improvement, strength. Mr. Noble, for example, considers his older brother to be his role model.

All the while, Mr. Webster knows that the associates who testified against him have been free for years; that his mother is ill; that his daughter, Jasmine, who was 4 when he went away, has given him a grandson he has seen only once. That barring the secular equivalent of divine intervention, he will die in prison khaki.

A few months ago, Mr. Webster's lawyer, Jessica Ring Amunson, sent a thick packet of documents to the Office of the Pardon Attorney of the Justice Department. This office assists the president in exercising his power of executive clemency, including pardons and the commutations of sentences.

In these papers were Mr. Webster's life, the bad and the good. The particulars of his case, his achievements as an inmate, and many, many letters requesting a commutation of Mr. Webster's sentence, all effectively beginning with: *Dear Mr. President.*

They even included appeals for clemency from the prosecutors and the judge in his case.

"A commutation of sentence which would result in his service of 20 or so years in prison is enough punishment for his crimes," Judge Zagel wrote.

The packet also included Mr. Webster's letter, which had undergone several drafts as he sought concision in conveying to the president the essence of who Jesse Webster was, and is. "I didn't want a lot of mumbo jumbo," he says. "I know he's a busy man."

The odds never favored Mr. Webster, though, at least not this round. Nearly 2,800 other requests for commutation of sentence were pending—including one from his friend Mr. Wintersmith—and before last week, Mr. Obama had commuted the sentence of just one inmate.

Turkeys at Thanksgiving had a better chance at mercy.

"But you've got to keep up the hope," Mr. Webster said, shrugging, before leaving the visitors' room.

On Thursday, President Obama increased his number of commutations by eight (while also pardoning 13 others). He described his action as "an important step toward restoring fundamental ideals of justice and fairness," and called on Congress to come up with further sentencing reforms.

That morning, some inmates were gathered in the Greenville prison gymnasium, including Mr. Webster and Mr. Wintersmith. A voice came over the intercom, summoning Mr. Wintersmith to the associate warden's office.

Mr. Webster instantly knew what had happened, and what had not. He later said he was overjoyed for his friend, and hopeful that the president would remember the many, many others, and "spread his grace on us."

EPILOGUE

In March 2016, Jesse Webster heard his name announced over the prison intercom, ordering him to report immediately to the assistant warden's office. The last time he had been summoned was to inform him that he had been given the privilege of choosing the Christmas specialties to be sold in the commissary. He went with barbecue potato chips and some smoked cheeses.

This time, though, he was told that his lawyer, Jessica Ring Amunson, was holding the line on the office telephone. She had some news. Mr. Webster, it turned out, was one of 61 federal inmates, all serving time for drug-related crimes, whose sentences had just been commuted by President Obama.

All he could think to say was: "Wow."

Mr. Webster works now as a homeless prevention specialist for Catholic Charities in his hometown, Chicago. He is also taking classes in communication at the City Colleges of Chicago. And, he said, he travels in his free time to schools and churches to "tell my story about my choices and consequences."

That is the name of his company: Choices and Consequences.

On a Trip to Fenway,
Only the Game Was Meaningless

BOSTON, MASS. — OCTOBER 4, 2015

My good friend of 30 years has amyotrophic lateral sclerosis. Not much that he can do about this, beyond hoping for some major medical breakthrough, and nothing, really, that I can do. So let's go to a ballgame.

I meet my friend, Bill Malinowski, at his home in Rhode Island. He will drive his Acura wagon the hour to Fenway Park for a night game of no importance. I will drive back, because having A.L.S. is exhausting. These days, he's usually asleep by 9.

The diagnosis this spring only confirmed what he suspected. A superior athlete—marathoner, swimmer, biker—who chronicled his every mile in the chase after fitness, he knew his body. Now the body he so carefully nurtured had betrayed him in some cosmic bait-and-switch.

Cry. Curse the fates. Monitor the research. Keep working out as best he can for as long as he can. Keep his head clear as best he can for as long as he can. At least there's baseball tonight.

Bill walks to his car as if the pebbles and tree roots conspire to trip him. Gingerly he steps, wearing red linen shorts and a black brace on a weakening left leg that once helped to power him through 15 marathons, three triathlons and scores of road races.

Let's go.

"Amyotrophic lateral sclerosis" usually precedes "also known as Lou Gehrig's disease." It helps the less clinically minded to summon to memory Gehrig's iconic farewell speech in 1939, his head bowed, half-smiling to himself at the dark joke played on the durable Iron Horse. Dead within two years, at 37, the Yankees great had called himself the luckiest man in the world.

Bill loathes the Yankees.

The word "loathes" does not quite convey the depths of his tribal hatred. A Red Sox guy to the marrow, he roots against the Yankees with a negative-force vigor that has sustained him through this trying summer. His wife, Mary Murphy, says he sometimes wakes at night to check the Yankees score. A Yankees loss eases the approaching morning.

We head north on Interstate 95, two old friends, both 57 years old. With coffee hot in the cup holders, Springsteen low on satellite radio and not a cloud in the early-autumn, late-afternoon sky, we talk about everything and nothing, as we have so many times before. Only now even talk about nothing takes work, this disease named after a Yankee thinning his voice, requiring exertion for every word he utters.

"It's challenging to talk," he says, and I can hear it.

This is why we text now more than talk on the phone, our virtual conversations a mash-up of medical reports and baseball.

May 4: "Doc says I have ALS."

May 20: "Great joy! The Skanks have lost 8 of 11 & the Sox are pitching well."

June 2: "I despise A-Fraud. The ultimate jerk."

June 18: "I despise the Yankees, the most hated team in pro sports."

June 28: "Just got a leg brace on Thursday @ Mass General. It helps stabilize my walking."

July 27: "Just took the Detroit series!"

Sept. 8: "I can go with you to a night game . . . Just scheduled an appointment at Johns Hopkins . . ."

A veteran reporter at The Providence Journal, Bill has long been an authority on Rhode Island's expansive underbelly, with sources on both sides of the law and an expertise in gangs, guns, organized crime and municipal corruption. Last year, the New England Society of Newspaper Editors named him a "master reporter."

But the intense curiosity that drove his professional success has waned. He has little interest now in a state once described to me as a reporter's theme park. Of the few subjects he cares about, baseball sits at the very top.

"Why?" I ask as Bill drives below the speed limit in the interstate's middle lane, oblivious to the red-faced truck driver passing on the right, shouting epithets.

"It's just where I grew up," he answers.

He means, in part, that he grew up in southeastern Connecticut, at a time when everyone knew Walt Dropo, the Moose from Moosup, who once played for the beloved Red Sox, and big John Ellis, from New London, who once played for the dreaded Yankees. Bill was a batboy for Ellis's American Legion team; played winter basketball with Bill Dawley, a future All-Star pitcher; occasionally ran across Roger LaFrancois, whose major league career, one year as a backup Red Sox catcher, would end with a .400 batting average. (4 for 10!)

Bill's baseball devotion developed on the streets, not at home. His mother was always working the night shift as a hospital nurse, and his father was always reliving World War II.

Active in the Polish resistance, Mieczyslaw Malinowski spent more than four years in Nazi prisons and labor camps, had his teeth knocked out with a rifle butt and was once ordered to dig his own grave. Battling tuberculosis when he immigrated, he was sent to a sanitarium in Norwich, where he later found work as a porter.

No war movies allowed on the television, no "Hogan's Heroes" canned laughter. The inadvertent slam of a door echoed like gunfire in his father's ears, enraging him, leaving his wife and three children to tiptoe about their modest house in Norwich. The war-scarred immigrant never spoke of the past and rarely spoke in the present—but made it clear that he considered most American pastimes to be frivolous, including baseball. What is this baseball?

Bill wound up excelling at another frivolous endeavor—basketball—and was good enough to play at Connecticut College. But the Red Sox remained his true passion:

Tony Conigliaro and Rico Petrocelli and big George Scott; Fred Lynn and Dwight Evans and Jim Rice; and the constant, Yaz.

By the time I met Bill, in 1987, he had mostly recovered from the 1986 World Series, in which his Sox lost to the Mets for reasons that go well beyond a ball rolling through Bill Buckner's bandy legs. We were both reporters at The Providence Journal, and our friendship developed over shared interests in wiseguys, wisecracks and baseball.

Over the years, we shared many family vacations, including a few in the Adirondacks, where Bill continued to maintain and strengthen his body: 6 feet 3 and 225 lean pounds, with massive shoulders. Every morning he took a six- to 10-mile run, and every afternoon he swam a mile—often with me beside him, lazily kayaking, as he sliced the lake water with rhythmic precision.

Last fall, the runs became harder, the easy breathing a labored wheeze. He was covering the murder trial of a former New England Patriots football player, Aaron Hernandez, a fairly routine court assignment that by day's end left him spent.

"I reached a point where I couldn't run, I couldn't swim, I couldn't bike outside," he says, eyes trained on the road ahead. He became one of about 6,400 people in the United States who will be found this year to have A.L.S.

He says he cannot help wondering about the whys and hows of it all. Given the research into a possible link between A.L.S. and concussions, how could he not focus on that horrific collision on the basketball court at the Massachusetts Institute of Technology?

Playing for Connecticut College, Bill and an M.I.T. player collided head-on while chasing a loose ball and bam—lights out for several minutes. "A violent hit," he says, so bad that his dazed opponent air-balled the free throw. And Bill stayed in the game.

Was that it? A concussion nearly 40 years ago? All he knows is that some people at Massachusetts General told him they see A.L.S. among former soccer players. More soccer than football, in fact.

We keep driving, Bill, me and this, as K. T. Tunstall sings "Feel It All" on the radio. "It does make you wonder," he says after a while. "How does this happen?"

Bill is losing weight—13 pounds since June—because it is harder to swallow now, and A.L.S. tends to affect taste. He has also stopped taking the prescribed medication, Riluzole, because the constant nausea did not seem worth the minimal benefits. Sustenance comes instead in a book-and-movie project he's working on about the Rhode Island underworld, which has attracted the interest of some big names.

And, of course, there is still exercise: every morning to the local Y.M.C.A., riding a stationary bike and lifting weights, then recording the workout in his journal. This is his way of fighting back, mile by mile, pound by pound.

"Trying to push past it," he says.

We ease into downtown Boston. Bill notes how much gas prices have fallen. Says his leg brace is bugging him. Notes that the song on the radio, "Shut Up and Dance," is by Walk the Moon, a band that played during the All-Star festivities this year.

Baseball.

That beacon of Fenway, the Citgo sign, rises into view like a red-white-and-blue moon. We find a garage beside the park and pay the outrageous $40, figuring the closer the better. Still, Bill needs to balance himself against parked cars as he walks. Crowds of people, thin and overweight, young and old, rush past him to the Yawkey Way finish line.

Our excellent seats are beside the Red Sox dugout, compliments of a friend with an indirect connection to Pete Frates, a former Boston College baseball player with A.L.S. who began last year's charity rave, the ice bucket challenge. Johns Hopkins—where Bill has an appointment this month—has credited the charity with helping to underwrite a recent study that provides a deeper understanding of the protein clumps associated with A.L.S.

Tonight's game means nothing. Both the visitors, the Tampa Bay Rays, and the Red Sox are more than a dozen games out of first place. Still, Bill is looking forward to it, almost as much as he is to rooting hard against the Yankees in the playoffs.

He disappears for a few minutes, then comes back down the concrete steps, carefully, with a massive vanilla ice cream cone in his hands. Lots of calories and easy to swallow.

It will be a long night. We will not return to Bill's house until after midnight, and he will be wiped out. Then, in the early morning, he will rise before I do, drive to the Y and lift more weights to forestall what seems inevitable.

For now, though, there is baseball. Meaningless, late-season baseball, the innings blending one into the next in a game without a clock. The Red Sox are losing, and the scoreboard in left says the Yankees are winning.

That's all right. Bill finds hope in the young Red Sox ballplayers out there. Brock Holt, Mookie Betts, Blake Swihart. And this kid, Jackie Bradley Jr., who just hit a meaningless single in the bottom of the eighth.

The hell with the Yankees. Next year, he says. Next year.

A Force of Labor and
of Politics in Las Vegas Hotels

LAS VEGAS, NEV. — NOVEMBER 6, 2016

She begins her day in black, the natural black before dawn and the requisite black of her uniform: the T-shirt, the pants, the socks, the shoes with slip-resistant treads, all black. The outfit announces deference.

She crams fresh vegetables into a blender and holds a plate over its mouth as the machine whips up her green liquid breakfast. Its whine sounds the alarm for her four school-age grandchildren who, one by one, emerge sleepwalking from corners of their crammed rented house.

Time to go. Before shepherding the children into her silver Jeep Patriot, the woman straps on a fabric back brace and covers it with the last piece of her uniform, a gray and black tunic. Then, above her left breast, she pins two small union buttons beside her silver name tag. The combined effect says:

This is Celia. Underestimate her at your risk.

Celia Vargas, 57, with dark wavy hair restrained by a clasp, works at one of the hotels in perpetual gleam along and around the Strip. She is a "guest room attendant" and a member of the Culinary Union, one of more than 14,000 who clean hotel rooms while guests donate money to the casino of their choice.

Ms. Vargas, who is from El Salvador, and her Latina union colleagues are a growing force in the politics and culture of Nevada, vocal in their beliefs and expectations. Their 57,000-member Culinary Union, a powerful supporter of Nevada Democrats, is now 56 percent Latino—a jump from 35 percent just 20 years ago.

"The power and courage of guest room attendants are the foundation and a big source of strength of the Culinary Union," Bethany Khan, the union's communications director, says. These workers, she adds, "are the majority of the middle class in Nevada."

Most of the hotels on and around the Strip are union shops, but the one that employs Ms. Vargas has yet to sign a contract. Even though its workers voted to unionize last December, and even though it is violating the law by not coming to the bargaining table—a point reinforced in a decision and order issued on Thursday by the National Labor Relations Board.

So Ms. Vargas wears her back brace, hidden, but also her buttons, prominent.

A wooden rosary draped over the rearview mirror sways as her Jeep wends through a working-class stretch of Las Vegas; this is not where Donny and Marie live. She drops her grandchildren at their school, then goes to the house of a friend from the Dominican Republic. She is standing outside, dressed in the same black and gray.

The Jeep drives deeper into the Vegas peculiarity, past the 7-Elevens and massage parlors, the smoke shops and strip clubs. Soon the casino and hotel giants of the Strip are framing the view, including one that sticks out like a gold tooth in a wicked grin.

This is where Ms. Vargas will clock in at 8:30, and where she is expected to clean a checked-out room in less than 30 minutes and a stay-over in less than 15. Every room seems to reveal something about the human condition.

"Sometimes I open the door, and I say 'Oh my God,'" Ms. Vargas says. "And then I close the door."

Despite their name tags, guest room attendants are anonymous. They go unnoticed by many as they push their 300-pound carts to the next room, and the next.

A glimpse of what is expected of these attendants can be found at the Culinary Academy of Las Vegas, a joint venture between the culinary and bartenders unions and many properties along the Strip. Here, people are trained as cooks or baker's helpers, bus persons or bar apprentices—or guest room attendants.

A corner of the academy's building features a series of mock guest rooms, each one representing a specific hotel's style: a Bellagio suite, an MGM Grand, a Caesars Palace. Students learn how to lift mattresses without injuring their backs; how to wear gloves while reaching with care into wastebaskets; and how to maintain quality while moving quickly, because there's always another room.

"Get in and get out," says Shirley Smith, a former guest room attendant who now trains others.

Consider all the items on that cart. Linens, magazines, water bottles, coffee, toiletries, tissues, glass cleaners, disinfectants, bathrobes, dusters, a vacuum, and assorted brushes, including one for the toilet and one for the crevices around the tub and shower.

Now consider the job itself.

"We make the beds, dust, vacuum, mop, fill the coffee, the creamer, the sugar," Ms. Vargas says. "We wash the toilet, the bathtub, the shower, the Jacuzzi. Worst, sometimes, is the kitchen. We clean the kitchen."

All in a half-hour. Nine, 10, 11 times a day.

And when her shift ends in the early evening, Ms. Vargas has often sweated through her back brace and black T-shirt. Aching here there and everywhere, she drives home and tells her family that Grandma needs to lie down for a little bit.

Grandma's full name is Celia Menendez Vargas. She grew up in the city of Santa Ana, the daughter of a soldier and a nurse. As civil war engulfed El Salvador in the early 1980s, her husband was killed in a bus bombing, and various family members fled to asylum in Canada and Australia. She entrusted her two children to an aunt and sold her belongings to pay for illicit transport to the United States. She was smuggled in a wooden container on a truck bound for Los Angeles.

"Illegal," she says. "Like a lot of people."

She worked for four years as a live-in housekeeper, applied for residency and saved up the money to arrange for her two sons to join her legally. She remarried, gave birth to a girl in 1986, divorced and kept working. Newspaper deliverer. Garment factory worker.

Babysitter. School custodian. Food-truck cook, making pupusas, those Salvadoran corn tortillas filled with cheese or meat or beans.

In 1996, Ms. Vargas became an American citizen. Her reasoning is familiar, yet fresh: "For me this was very important. I always think this country was the best for the future of my kids."

Friends were urging her to come to the soccer fields some Sunday and meet a man who was also from Santa Ana, but her heavy work schedule precluded romance. "Always working," she says. "Working, work, work."

They met, finally, she and Jorge Alberto Vargas, and were married in 2003. A few years later they moved to Las Vegas, on word that jobs were plentiful in the neon oasis.

Mr. Vargas, who had a work permit based on political asylum, became a chef at a casino on the Strip, and things were fine until they weren't. Three years ago, he was

detained after being arrested a second time for driving under the influence, although the family maintains his second arrest was a medical episode related to diabetes. He spent more than two years being shipped to various federal detention centers—Nevada, California, Texas, Louisiana—before being deported back to El Salvador in July.

Ms. Vargas saw him last a year ago, for 30 minutes; she cries at the memory. She keeps his clothes boxed in the garage, and files document after document with the government, working toward that day when they might be reunited.

This and other travails consume Ms. Vargas. But she has returned to the work force, finding a job as a guest room attendant in this glittering gold nonunion hotel. It paid a little more than $14 an hour—about $3 less than what unionized housekeepers were making, and with nowhere near the complement of benefits.

Some of her colleagues began to agitate for a union vote. Union pamphlets and cards were surreptitiously exchanged in the parking lot, in the bathrooms, under tables in the employees' dining room. Ms. Vargas joined in, motivated in part by the $17,000 in debt she had accumulated by undergoing surgery for breast cancer; she wanted better health care benefits.

At one point she and a few other workers were suspended for wearing union buttons, but this concerted union activity is federally protected. After the Culinary Union filed unfair labor practice charges with the National Labor Relations Board, she was quickly reinstated with back pay, her buttons intact.

It has not been easy. Downsizing after her husband's deportation, selling her bedroom set, moving in with her daughter and her family. Publicly agitating for the union—and for the Democratic nominee for president—and then fretting that there might be retaliation at her nonunion, pro-Republican workplace. And working, constantly working.

"I tell my children, we have to work," Ms. Vargas says. "It's not for government to support me. We work work work."

She pulls into the employee parking lot of the gold hotel, set aglow now by the unsparing morning sun. Searching for a parking spot, she passes other women, many of them also in black and gray tunics, hurrying toward the service entrance.

Soon she is heading for the same door, one more guest room attendant who wears a back brace while cleaning rooms for a presidential candidate whose name is on the bathrobes she stocks, on the empty wine bottles she collects, on her name tag.

He will receive her labor, but not her vote.

A Refugee Home, Furnished in Joy

LANCASTER, PA. — DECEMBER 25, 2016

A dull gray house on a hillside has to become a home. Another Syrian family of refugees will be arriving soon, and this empty, echoing old place needs to be readied in welcome.

The word has trickled down from the State Department's refugee resettlement program. A mother, a father, his brother and four children, the youngest just 10. Muslims, traveling from Turkey. Flying into New York in the next few days.

Their imminent arrival explains all the commotion inside this slate-colored house in the small city of Lancaster, in south-central Pennsylvania. The state may have gone to Donald J. Trump, who likened the Syrian resettlement program to a "a great Trojan horse" for terrorists. But he isn't president yet.

That is why volunteers and staff members from the Church World Service, a nationwide nonprofit that helps the government take in refugees fleeing violence and persecution, are cleaning cabinets, carting furniture and doing their best to make things homey. Just not too homey.

"Doing too much can make a family feel like it's someone else's home," says Josh Digrugilliers, 26, the group's local housing specialist, whose crowded key chain jangles in reminder of all the refugees in need.

He scours a government checklist of housing requirements for a resettlement, mindful that whatever he spends is deducted from a refugee's one-time government grant of no more than $1,125. A family's combined grants must cover its rent and other expenses until the nonprofit has helped the adults acquire Social Security numbers and jobs.

The used furniture being trundled in reflects the emphasis on economy. Some comes from the donations hoarded in a cluttered garage, where a "Welcome Home" sign in Arabic is on display. Other items were acquired cheap—chairs for $5, tables for $20—at Root's Old Mill Flea Market.

New paint and flooring give the house the smell of a fresh start, thanks to the landlord, John Liang, who came to Lancaster as a child, one of the "boat people" who fled Vietnam on dangerously overcrowded vessels after the war. He spent a year in a notoriously hellish refugee camp before coming to Lancaster, where he and his family delivered newspapers, shoveled snow, did sewing and assembly-line work. Anything.

Now 45, Mr. Liang works overtime at a nearby Kellogg's cereal plant and manages several properties he owns, including this house, which he wants to be—just so.

"There are other people living a lot harder, tougher, than what I went through," he says.

A HISTORY OF ACCEPTANCE

Mr. Digrugilliers applies his checklist to the kitchen, where the counter is crowded with mismatched dinnerware, new appliances and clutches of flatware bound with rubber bands. Draped over the oven handle is a dish towel printed with a calendar for 1968, another tumultuous year.

Then to the bedrooms upstairs. The children's twin beds, bought at discount from the Lancaster Mattress Company, are covered with the black G of the Georgia Bulldogs, the winged wheel of the Detroit Red Wings and other invitations to sleep in cocoons of American culture.

Armed with a list of what he needs, he and a colleague, Orion Hernandez, climb into a beat-up van reeking of McDonald's. They head to Walmart, where Mr. Digrugilliers recognizes a thin man—a Nepalese refugee who resettled here two years ago—leaving as he is walking in.

"Hey, how are you?" Mr. Digrugilliers calls out. "Hello," the man calls back.

Such encounters happen often in Lancaster, whose rich history of acceptance is rooted, in part, in the influence of the Mennonites, Amish and other faiths. A glimpse of the local worldview came in January when a supportive rally of more than 200 people drowned out a much smaller anti-immigrant protest outside the Church World Service office here.

Sheila Mastropietro, the group's longtime supervisor in Lancaster, took heart in the moment. It reflected a communal understanding of both the global refugee crisis and the rigorous screening process that refugees undergo before coming to the United States.

Still, given a president-elect who seems averse to the country's modest commitment to refugee relocation, Ms. Mastropietro says, "We don't know what to expect."

Last fiscal year, the Lancaster office of the Church World Service helped to resettle 407 of the 85,000 refugees admitted to this country; this fiscal year, its target is 550 of a hoped-for 110,000.

"We are acting as if the numbers are going to be the same—until we hear something different," she says.

Decades of resettlement work have transformed the Lancaster area into a medley of cultures so rich that Amer Alfayadh, 34, a senior case manager, struggles to name them all: "Syrians, Iraqis, Somalis, Congolese, Ukrainians, Belorussians, people from Kazakhstan. Then, of course, Lebanese, Palestinians. Bhutanese, Nepalese, Burmese, Sri Lankans . . ."

Mr. Alfayadh himself arrived from Iraq in 2010. Though trained as an engineer, he worked at a Lowe's—customer service, paint, lawn and garden—and as a substitute teacher before being hired to help other refugees. He is accustomed now to urgent late-night calls from fresh arrivals unfamiliar with, say, locks on doors.

New clients are often at their breaking point, uncertain what to make of this exotic land called Pennsylvania. Knowing how difficult it can be for anyone in crisis to see ahead—to jobs, school, a future—Mr. Alfayadh says he tries to impart a simple message:

"O.K. Tomorrow will be better."

At Walmart, Mr. Digrugilliers and Mr. Hernandez commandeer two shopping carts each and begin racing through the cavernous store like contestants on the old "Supermarket Sweep" game show, grabbing specific items, down to umbrellas and sanitary pads.

His purchases complete, Mr. Digrugilliers mounts his cart and wheels it into the dusk like a skateboard, exuberant with hope that some refugee family's journey will be just as smooth.

It is not. The Church World Service soon receives word that this particular family's resettlement has been delayed—a not-uncommon development that could be caused by something as simple as a spike in an asylum-seeker's blood pressure at the airport.

But there is no shortage of tempest-tossed refugees. Mr. Alfayadh's supervisor, Valentina Ross, remembers that another Syrian family is arriving in a few days: a father, a mother, three daughters and a boy. They will need a home.

HOLIDAY SPIRIT ABOUNDS

Today is the day. A holiday spirit has taken hold in downtown Lancaster, with a colossal Christmas tree glittering in Penn Square and ancient brick houses swathed in festive lights.

A mile away, a Church World Service caseworker named Gaby Garver, a focused college graduate of 22, is collecting provisions for the new family at a food pantry. Signing some paperwork, she says, "And no meat products for the family, please."

As Ms. Garver prepares to leave with milk, vegetables and other items, a pantry volunteer asks: "Since you didn't take any meat, would you like some extra rice?"

Yes, please.

More food is needed. Ms. Garver guides her 1999 Pontiac through the cold rain to the Save-A-Lot supermarket, where many goods sit in cut-open cardboard cases. She leaves 10 minutes later with bread, fruit, beans, sugar, tea and a receipt for $26.58, to be deducted from the family's grant money.

Hunched against the weather, the slight young woman makes two trips carrying the food into the drab gray house. After stocking the refrigerator and cabinet, she conducts a last-minute inspection. The fridge is cold. The tap has hot water. The burners on the gas stove ignite.

Everything upstairs is fine as well, with even more homey touches added. New pajamas and towels. New clothes hangers. New picture frames, showing stock photos of cheerful families, on the shelves. And on one twin bed, a child's soccer ball, still in its box.

HUGS AND HANDSHAKES

The rain has stopped, a slice of moon risen. Ms. Garver is driving now to the home of a Syrian family that arrived seven months ago. The mother has cooked a hot meal for the refugee family that is about to land any minute in New York, a good three-hour drive away.

Inside, where five young children zip and waddle about, the prepared meal sits in expectation on the dining room table: a large aluminum tray bountiful with chicken and rice and a huge bowl of salad.

The oldest child, Mohamad, 14, helps Ms. Garver carry the food out to her vehicle, and she thanks him. He responds with the formality given to a new language being tried on for size.

"You're welcome," the boy says, and smiles.

Returning to the gray house, Ms. Garver fumbles in the dark to open the door while holding the tray of still-hot food. When she returns with the salad bowl, she stoops to collect a clump of junk mail, including a come-on addressed to "Our Neighbor."

Later tonight, Ms. Garver and Mr. Alfayadh will drive a Ford van to Lancaster Airport, where they will meet two representatives from the local Islamic Center. Soon after, another van will arrive from Kennedy International Airport.

Hugs and handshakes will be exchanged in the December air. Luggage will be collected. And six Syrian refugees will be driven the 20 minutes to a warm home perfumed by warm food, in a city made radiant by the multicolored lights of the season.

PART THREE

Misdeeds

Here you have your morning papers,
all about the crimes

A Rough Script of Life, if Ever There Was One

CHADRON, NEB. — SEPTEMBER 2, 2007

Item from the blotter of the Chadron Police Department: *Caller from the 900 block of Morehead Street reported that someone had taken three garden gnomes from her location sometime during the night. She described them as plastic, "with chubby cheeks and red hats."*

When you reach Chadron you're glad for it, because this Nebraska town is a long way from anywhere. Drive north on Main Street, past the Police Department, and you hit prairie; drive south, past the state college, and you hit prairie. In between, 5,600 people embrace, avoid and endure one another in a compact place that began more than a century ago as a remote railroad town.

Here, as anywhere, the specifics of most encounters between residents evaporate with the moment, leaving only those precious, fleeting bits, snatched from the ether and pinned by some dispatcher sitting at a desk behind the Police Department's service window. A call comes in, the dispatcher types and another brief paragraph is added to the continuing Chadron epic.

Caller from the 200 block of Morehead Street advised a man was in front of their shop yelling and yodeling. Subject was told to stop yodeling until Oktoberfest.

It is in this regard that Chadron is blessed. For here, life's gradual unfolding is measured and honored by Police Beat, a longstanding feature in The Chadron Record, the weekly newspaper. It records those small, true moments lost in the shadows of the large—moments that may not rise to the Olympian heights of newsworthiness, yet still say something about who we are and how we create this thing called community.

Caller from the 400 block of Third Street advised that a subject has been calling her and her employees, singing Elvis songs to them.

Police Beat repeats, almost verbatim, some of the calls that the town's police dispatchers receive and then dutifully log, often in a literary style that synthesizes the detached jargon of the police with the conversational language of the people.

Caller from the 200 block of Morehead Street advised that a known subject was raising Cain again.

Every day, except on those days when they don't feel like it, the dispatchers fax copies of their calls log to the ink-perfumed office of The Record, just around the corner. There, a young reporter named Heather Crofutt selects the most interesting

George Ledbetter

items, edits out the names and specific addresses and types them up for Police Beat. Although she is essentially transcribing the reports, she says, "People think I make it up."

Officer on the 1000 block of West Highway 20 found a known male subject in the creek between Taco John's and Bauerkemper's. Subject was covered in water stating he was protecting his family. Officers gave subject ride home.

George Ledbetter, the editor, says Police Beat rivals the obituaries in popularity, so much so that it has become an integral part of local culture. Not long ago, for example, the loud practice sessions of four Chadron State College musicians earned them a mention in the log. They instantly knew what to call their fledgling band: Police Beat.

Mr. Ledbetter struggles to name his favorite item; there are so many. But taken as a whole, he says, the feature is "such a reflection of human life."

Over the years, Chadron police officials have had a tolerate-hate relationship with Police Beat. One top-ranking officer complains that the feature seems to minimize the difficulty of police work. She says that while there are plenty of calls about animal encounters (*Caller on the 900 block of Parry Drive advised a squirrel has climbed down her chimney and is now in the fireplace looking at her through the glass door, chirping at her*), there are plenty of calls about far more serious matters: child abuse, domestic violence, you name it.

But Police Beat often reflects how heavily some of us rely on law enforcement for just about everything (*Caller from the 800 block of Pine Street advised that she had just left someone's home and she forgot her jacket, and requested an officer to get her coat),* and demonstrates how deft the police can be at defusing potentially volatile matters:

Caller from the 100 block of North Morehead Street requested to speak to animal control because caller felt that someone was coming into his yard and cutting the hair on his dogs. Dispatch advised caller to set up video surveillance on his house. Caller said he planned on it.

What emerges, then, is a kind of weekly prose poem to the human condition, where annoyance about barking dogs is validated, where nighttime fears born of isolation are reflected, where concern about others is memorialized.

Caller stated that there is a 9-year-old boy out mowing the yard and feels that it is endangering the child in doing so when the mother is perfectly capable of doing it herself.

In short, Police Beat is a rough script to the tragicomedy that is everyday life. And if the details preserved in the ever-expanding Chadron epic do not always find us at our best, there are moments, recorded for posterity, when we seek redemption, we make amends. We try.

Two weeks after the theft of those three chubby-cheeked, red-hatted garden ornaments, a brief item in Police Beat reported a break in the case. Two girls refusing to identify themselves had "brought in some gnomes."

Death in the Chair, Step by Remorseless Step

NASHVILLE, TENN. — SEPTEMBER 16, 2007

The window blinds to the execution chamber are raised shortly after 1 in the morning, in accordance with the Procedures for Electrocution in the State of Tennessee. And the condemned man is revealed.

He looks almost like a young child buckled into a car seat, with his closed eyes and freshly shaved head, with the way the black restraints of the electric chair crisscross at his torso. He yawns a wide-mouthed yawn, as though just stirring from an interrupted dream, and opens his eyes.

He is moments from dying.

The cause of death will be cardiac arrest. Every step toward that end will follow those written state procedures, which strive to lend a kind of clinical dignity to the electrocution of a human being, yet read like instructions for jump-starting a car engine. Remember: "A fire extinguisher is located in the building and is near the electric chair as a precaution."

Behold Daryl Holton. He is 45. Ten years ago he shot his four young children in his uncle's auto-repair garage, two at a time, through the heart. He used their very innocence to kill them, telling them not to peek, Daddy has a surprise. After he was done he turned himself in, saying he wanted to report a "homicide times four."

In seeking the execution of this Army veteran, now blinking in the cold, bright room, the state argued that Mr. Holton committed premeditated murder, times four, to punish his ex-wife for obtaining an order of protection and for moving away. He killed his children, so he must be killed.

In defending the life of this man—now pursing his lips, about all that he can move—his advocates argued that he believed his children were better off dead

117

than living in a profoundly troubled home; that he actually felt relief after pulling a tarpaulin over those four small bodies. He killed his children, so he must be mentally ill.

All the while, Mr. Holton adhered to a peculiar code of conduct that vexed all sides. Those fighting for his life often did so against his will. Those seeking his remorse were unrewarded.

Just days ago he said the crimes for which he was convicted warranted the death penalty, but he pointedly removed himself from that equation. Perhaps to suggest the killings were justified; perhaps to keep things theoretical. No matter. Now, at 1:09 a.m. on Wednesday, Sept. 12, 2007, at the Riverbend Maximum Security Institution, it is about to happen.

The warden, Ricky J. Bell, stands before him, supervising the first electrocution in Tennessee since 1960. Prison officials had hoped that Mr. Holton would choose to die by lethal injection, and had been gently reminding him of this option. But he maintained that since electrocution was the only form of capital punishment at the time of his crimes, then electrocution it should be.

Before the raising of those window blinds, Mr. Holton had started to hyperventilate, and Mr. Bell had sought to calm him by slightly loosening the straps. But now it is 1:10, the blinds are up, the clock is running. In accordance with procedures, the warden asks if the condemned has something to say.

The inmate's response is so slurred by his hyperventilating that he is asked to repeat what he has been planning to say for a long time. He says again, "Two words: I do."

This could be a joke of some kind, a cosmic conundrum, or maybe Mr. Holton's acceptance into whatever awaits him after life. It could be the use of his marital vow as a parting shot at his ex-wife, or perhaps a twisted re-affirmation of his belief in the sanctity of marriage and family.

The warden asks, "That it?" The inmate nods.

Two corrections officers step forward to place a sponge soaked in salted water on Mr. Holton's bald scalp to enhance conductivity. Next comes the headpiece, which the procedures describe as a "leather cranial cap lined with copper mesh inside." Finally, a power cable, not unlike the cable to your television, is attached to the headpiece.

The copper mesh pressing the wet sponge sends salty water streaming down the inmate's ashen face, soaking his white cotton shirt to the pale skin beneath.

When officers try to blot him dry with white towels, Mr. Holton says not to worry about it, "ain't gonna matter anyway."

After the white towels comes a black shroud to be attached to the headpiece. It is intended in part to protect the dignity of the inmate, now strapped, soaked and about to die before witnesses. His final expression, then, will be his own.

Time.

With the push of a button on a console labeled Electric Chair Control, 1,750 volts bolt through Mr. Holton's body, jerking it up and dropping it like a sack of earth. The black shroud offers the slightest flutter, and witnesses cannot tell whether they have just heard a machine's whoosh or a man's sigh.

Fifteen seconds later, another bolt, and Mr. Holton's body rises even higher, slumps even lower. His reddened hands remain gripped to the arms of the chair, whose oaken pieces are said to have once belonged to the old electric chair, and before that, to the gallows.

It is 1:17. Procedures require a five-minute pause at this point. A prison official off to the side watches a digital clock on the wall while chewing something, perhaps gum, perhaps to calm his nerves. Two minutes, three, four, the only things moving in the room are his eyes and his jaw, five. The window blinds drop, and a physician begins a private examination.

Later, in the foggy darkness outside the prison, someone will read a statement from the ex-wife, Crystal Holton, in which she says that all the anger and hatred can finally leave her, to be replaced by a child's innocent love—"love times four."

Later, well after sunrise, Kelly Gleason, one of the lawyers who fought to keep Mr. Holton alive, will set aside her mourning for a friend and give in to fitful sleep.

Later, in the hot afternoon some 50 miles to the south, four polished tombstones will again cast shadows toward a playground at the bottom of a cemetery's hill. Arranged in order of age, the stones bear the names of the four Holton children: Stephen, 12, Brent, 10, Eric, 6, and Kayla, 4.

But first confirmation, in accordance with procedures. And now the disembodied voice of Tennessee: "Ladies and gentlemen, this concludes the legal execution of Daryl Holton. The time of death, 1:25. Please exit."

A Violation of Both
the Law and the Spirit

RIPTON, VT. — JANUARY 28, 2008

Imagining that late December night of long darkness, you can almost hear these youths of Vermont tramping up to the isolated farmhouse to intrude upon the sanctuary stillness. The break of snow beneath their feet would be the least of it.

They had driven or walked a half-mile up a snow-covered lane called Frost Road, then trudged past a large blue sign that explained the historic significance of the farmhouse and the cabin beyond. And now they were entering the coldness of an uninhabited place, carrying with them cases of beer, bottles of rum and a store of ignorance about things that matter here.

Over the next several hours, more than 30 teenagers and young adults toasted their post-adolescence with liquor carrying the added kick of illicitness. By early morning they were gone, leaving a wounded house watched over by winter-stripped birches and sugar maples.

The damage left in their wake reflected some alcohol-induced mischief tinged with certain anger. Broken window, broken screen, broken dishes, broken antiques. Pieces of a broken chair used for wood in the fireplace. Gobs of phlegm spat upon hanging artwork. Vomit, urine, beer everywhere. And a blanket of yellow, pollen-like dust, discharged from fire extinguishers in parting punctuation.

Before long, distressing word spread from Ripton to Middlebury and beyond that the preserved farmhouse once owned by Robert Frost had been vandalized— desecrated, some said. If these children of the Green Mountains knew this house was once Frost's, then shame. If they did not know, then shame still; they should have. How many had been weaned on Frost? How many had tromped through here on class trips and family outings?

It seemed once that Robert Frost would be with us forever, like some lichen-laced stone in a field. But finally he did die, in 1963 at the age of 88, leaving biographers to quarrel about his merits as a man and readers to marvel over his body of work, which, among other achievements, twinned a mastery of language with wisdom about natural things.

Here, though, Frost lingers. Peering down from his portrait in the Middlebury Inn. Speaking through snippets of poetry displayed at the Robert Frost Interpretive Trail. Shuffling in spirit around the Homer Noble Farm, which he bought in 1939 and lived in during summer and fall: there in the rustic cabin above, writing, ruminating, while his close friend and protector, Kay Morrison, in the now-vandalized farmhouse just below, screened visitors eager for an audience with the great and garrulous bard—who might very well talk and talk until those visitors fairly begged to be dismissed.

Imagining still, as all poets invite us to, you can almost see Frost observing the vandalism and aftermath from that cabin above, wondering briefly whether these youths were, say, acolytes of Carl Sandburg, exacting revenge because Frost considered their hero poet second-rate. Sipping his tea, he rummages through his mind's deep storehouse for the metaphors that would provide context, that would find renewal in this destruction.

A day or so after the vandalism, a passing hiker alerted Middlebury College, which now owns the property, that the farmhouse door was open. Then a car wedged in snow off the main road led the authorities to a young man who said he had been at a party in the area. Oh really, said Sgt. Lee Hodsden of the state police.

With the help of Officer Scott Fisher of the Middlebury police, who is based mostly at Middlebury Union High School, Sergeant Hodsden gathered names, called in witnesses and heard accounts of that night, some delivered through tears, a couple with indifference. What emerged was a small-town epic about so much more than $10,000 in damages.

A 17-year-old boy who had once worked as a kitchen aide at Middlebury College's Bread Loaf campus recognized the remote farmhouse's potential for parties. He also knew a young adult willing to buy the central party ingredient, alcohol, at the Hannaford Supermarket. Word spread by mouth and text messages.

Mix 30 or more young people with 150 cans of beer, a few bottles of liquor and some drugs, put them in a museum-like, unheated house in the dead of winter, and the ensuing discussions will not center on the sublime construction of "Stopping by Woods on a Snowy Evening." Some played drinking games, some got sick, some did damage, and all followed that snowy path out, bound together by a secret that could not keep.

Even a frozen meadow sends ripples when disturbed.

Rippling through Middlebury College, which dispatched a cleaning crew to the farmhouse. Kelly Trayah was among those who cleaned up the vomit, repaired the furniture, wiped the yellow dust from the many books, and now he wonders whatever happened to respect for elders. He is 37.

Through the college's classrooms, where the English professor and nature writer John Elder, intimately familiar with the farmhouse and cabin, wonders what possibilities the destruction might provide. Could this violation of Frost lead to a celebration of Frost?

Through Middlebury Union High School, where administrators and teachers are talking about disconnection and, once again, substance abuse. For the rest of the year, the principal, William Lawson, predicted, "there will be a lot of Robert Frost quoted."

Finally, through the state police barracks, where Sergeant Hodsden had more than two dozen young people photographed, fingerprinted and cited for unlawful trespass, with a few also cited for unlawful mischief. He cannot shake the indifference of one youth in particular, who asked whether he could use his mug shot on his Facebook page.

In conveying his disgust over this communal breach, the police sergeant employed the Frostian technique of repetition.

"They should have known," he said. "They should have known."

A Name and Face No One Knew, but Never Forgot

FRANKFORT, KY. — APRIL 21, 2008

After the murder, the body was swaddled in bedsheets and a Mickey Mouse blanket. It was placed in a van, driven far from any road in rural Henry County and dumped in a narrow creek bed, just as another July day was dawning.

The summer of 1998 baked on. Autumn arrived to rain-swell the creek and send skull bits floating down the bed of silt and stone. Winter followed to skim the mesh of gray twigs and pale bones with a veil of ice. Then, one February morning, two hunters running their beagles were stopped cold in their tracks; the living, finally, took notice.

Soon came Dr. Emily Craig, Kentucky's well-respected forensic anthropologist, along with County Coroner Jimmy Pollard and a couple of state police detectives, all tutored in her lesson not to treat crime scenes as Easter egg hunts. She put on her latex gloves and thick boots, got down into the creek, and began handing up pieces of a broken human being, the evidence already shouting to her that this was a man shot dead in the head.

Investigators recovered most of a skeleton and some associated evidence, including a brown sandal, a gold bracelet and a mesh shirt bearing a Dallas Cowboys insignia. Now for the questions:

> Who were you?
> Who killed you?

Back in her autopsy room in Frankfort, Dr. Craig logged the case by pen in the official register: "John Doe," she wrote. Then she laid the bones in anatomical order on a stainless-steel gurney and developed a rough description. Male; possibly Hispanic; at least 30 years old; about six feet tall; extensive dental work, including a gold crown. Dead about six months.

The state police publicized a description of what the dead man might have looked like. Dozens answered, hoping and not hoping that their father, husband, brother, son, had been found. But nothing panned out. So Dr. Craig applied clay to skull to create a facial reconstruction for the public's consideration; again, nothing. She and the other investigators moved on to other cases just as sad.

They did not know that 1,250 miles away, in the South Texas town of Freer, a distraught mother had reported her 34-year-old son missing.

The bones were placed in a small plastic tub labeled "Henry Co. Doe" and tucked into an evidence room used to store books, Christmas decorations and the bones of Kentucky's unidentified dead going back 30 years. Here was a tub labeled "River Legs"; there, a bag labeled "Shelby County Babies."

More seasons passed. One day in October 2000, Detective Jim Griffin of the state police learned that a man just arrested for a minor crime wanted to talk about one of his old cases: the creek-bed body. The detective was skeptical, having wasted years of time listening to jailhouse lies. He arranged to meet the man; you never know.

The informant said he was awakened one night in July 1998 by two agitated acquaintances saying they needed his help. He so feared one of the men that he saw no way out. So he helped them lug a wrapped body out of a remote farmhouse and into a van, took a long ride, and then joined in dumping that body in a creek.

The skeptical detective asked the man for just one detail, just one, that no one else could know. The man paused, then said: The body was wrapped in a Mickey Mouse blanket.

"Gave me goose bumps," Detective Griffin recalls.

It eventually came out. Two men and a woman had met a man they knew as Jose, or Juan, or Miguel, or Mike, in the bars of Louisville. A plan was struck days in advance to lure him to a farmhouse and relieve him of this kilo of cocaine he kept talking about. His last words were for mercy. Please, please. Don't shoot.

In December 2002, the three defendants were convicted and given lengthy prison terms, even though no one in Kentucky, including those who killed him, knew who the victim was. He was known casually as Juan Doe; more formally as Unidentified Male, Case FA-99-09.

Out of diligence and with faint hope, Dr. Craig sent bone samples to an F.B.I. laboratory in Quantico, Va., to be processed for a DNA profile that could be uploaded into an unidentified-remains database. After that, the bones sat in the evidence room, among the unidentified, undisturbed, for five years.

But some never forget the unknown dead.

Volunteers for the Doe Network, an organization dedicated to examining cases of

A facial reconstruction

the missing and unidentified, were developing their own database. The Justice Department was starting an online repository, available to the public, called the National Missing and Unidentified Persons System, or NamUs. And a Texas Ranger, Sgt. Ray Ramon, was trying to find that mother's missing son.

Four months ago he received information that a body found not far from Dallas might be a match. It wasn't, but he decided to take a DNA swab from the mother, out of diligence and with faint hope.

Soon a description and photograph of the missing son was posted on the Texas Department of Public Safety's Missing Persons Clearinghouse Web page. About six feet tall; 34 years old; last seen in July 1998; and with these circumstances: "possibly en route to Kentucky."

In Mount Pleasant, S.C., a mother of two named Daphne Owings spends three hours a day searching websites to match the missing with the unidentified. "I really feel this is what I'm supposed to be doing," says Ms. Owings, a Doe Network volunteer.

She saw the Texas posting of the lost son "possibly en route to Kentucky" and compared it to a Kentucky posting of the unidentified dead man found in a creek. The man's photograph resembled Dr. Craig's facial reconstruction. This could be something.

Prompted by Ms. Owings's report and a similar one from another Doe Network volunteer, Dr. Craig and Sergeant Ramon worked to prove a match. They compared the missing son's dental records with the teeth recovered from the creek—including that gold crown—as well as the DNA culled from bone with the DNA taken from the mother.

Ten days ago, in the Texas town of Freer, a frail woman named Zeferina Garcia opened her door to an investigator from the local sheriff's department who represented, among others, Coroner Jimmy Pollard, Detective Jim Griffin, Doe Network volunteer Daphne Owings, Sgt. Ray Ramon and Dr. Emily Craig.

The investigator had bittersweet news: Ms. Garcia's playful, intelligent son, who had lived with her, served in the Army and kissed her goodbye 10 years ago, saying he had a job to do but would be back soon, was dead.

It was after hours last week when Dr. Craig closed out the case of Unidentified Male, Case FA-99-09. She removed a tub from the shelf, donned some latex gloves, and, with motherly care, collected the bones and placed them in a cardboard box bound for Texas. Then she opened the same register in which she had logged the case more than nine years ago.

She drew a pen line across John Doe, and, very carefully, printed the name: Miguel Garcia.

Facts Mix With Legend
on the Road to Redemption

He had said hey to the porter, he had made her cry, cry, cry, he had walked the line. Now, with another worshipful crowd sated and with the rest of the band already on the road back to Memphis, a troubled and restless Johnny Cash stayed to explore the magnolia-scented darkness of a place whose name he could not have made up: Starkville.

Searching for parties, he found them. Then, searching for cigarettes, he got arrested for public drunkenness—or, as he later put it, for "picking flowers." He kicked his jail cell so hard he broke a toe. Released after six hours, he collected his things in a motel, ate breakfast and left town.

What happened in Starkville stayed in Starkville. Few cared in May 1965 about the antics of a rowdy musician; fewer still connected those antics to a drug addiction. And while Cash later wrote a song about his experience called "Starkville City Jail," it never rose very high in the canon.

But since that night, and especially since his death in 2003, Johnny Cash has become for some the craggy patron saint of redemption, his rumbling voice imparting freight-train blessings for all of America. Fact swirls with legend, suffering with salvation, shots of cocaine with peace in the valley, defiance of The Man with obedience to The Lord.

Now, if you want to trace Cash's path to Damascus, you have to pass through Starkville, a town of 22,000 that last weekend celebrated its second annual Johnny Cash Flower Pickin' Festival. It promised the pardoning of sins and featured an amused Rosanne Cash, the gifted and firmly established singer and songwriter whose father happens to be an icon.

"I usually don't make a habit of making pilgrimages to a place where my father spent one night," said Ms. Cash, who rarely appears on the Johnny Cash circuit. Although she loved her father, she says, she has no interest in having people looking through her for him.

In 1965, when her father was deep in amphetamine addiction, rarely spending time with his family in California, Ms. Cash was a 10-year-old girl who knew only that something was wrong with Daddy. She did not speak of those days this weekend.

Instead, Ms. Cash said she came at the request of her dear friend Marshall Grant, 80, the last of the Johnny Cash and the Tennessee Two band and, for so many years, her father's keeper, the one who flushed pills down the toilet by the bushel. But she also admitted to being intrigued by the festival's swirl of fact, myth and redemption.

"There's something so American about it," she said.

The flower-picking festival was started by Robbie Ward, 30, a gangly Cash enthusiast who arrived as the Starkville correspondent for a regional Mississippi newspaper. He was struck by how few here appreciated their town's connection to Johnny Cash, or knew of the "At San Quentin" album that features "Starkville City Jail":

They're bound to get you.
'Cause they got a curfew.
And you go to the Starkville City Jail.

Mr. Ward soon wrote an almost mystical story about that long-ago May night. A man named Smokey Evans claimed that when he was 15 and drunk, he was thrown into the same cell as Cash. After Cash broke his toe but before he left, he recalled, the singer handed him his black shoes and said: "Here's a souvenir. I'm Johnny Cash."

The man called Smokey, who supposedly had worn the shoes maybe four times in 40 years, died in a fight in 2005. The shoes are now said to be in the possession of a nephew in Georgia who says the relics were left to him in a will. It is not known whether he wears them.

Mr. Ward left journalism for a public relations job here at Mississippi State University, but his research into Cash's night in Starkville remains a part-time job.

He eventually persuaded the town to begin holding a Cash festival, overcoming grumblings that it celebrates an addict's carousing by arguing that Starkville has the pedigree to become the host of the essential Cash festival.

"Johnny Cash was arrested in seven places," Mr. Ward said. "But he only wrote a song about one of those places."

He recounts Cash's Starkville wanderings with a zealot's fervor. How Cash wound up at a fraternity house after the concert in the Animal Husbandry building at Mississippi State. How he tossed his jacket to a student who had expressed admiration for it. How he made his way to a private party in the Longmeadow subdivision. How he got a ride to his room at the University Motel, where June Carter, a performer in his show and his future wife, was staying in another unit. How Cash was clearly not ready for sleep.

He was gaunt, suffering, not at peace. Mr. Grant, who with Cash and Luther Perkins created that signature boom-chicka-boom sound, recalls 1965 as "one of the worst years" of Cash's lifelong wrestling with addiction. "How dark those years were," he said.

So Johnny Cash went out for cigarettes. Did he wind up among the flowers on the Copeland property because he needed to urinate? Because he was picking flowers for June? His motive is lost to history; his arrest is not.

Room 22, University Motel

Come along, wild flower child. Don't you know that it's 2 a.m.

Cash left Starkville later that morning, addiction intact. He supposedly went clean to marry June Carter in 1968, definitely went clean when his son, John Carter Cash, was born in 1970, and alternated between addiction and sobriety the rest of his life.

But here now was Starkville, offering formal recognition of that painful struggle and providing a posthumous pardon—all with a street-festival silliness and quasi-religious vibe.

You could take a walking tour of Cash's journey, with stops at the Copeland property, the jail cell and Room 22 at the motel, where the door now bears a plaque that says:

JOHNNY CASH
MAY 11, 1965

You could eat fried pickles and listen to a band called Ring of Fire play "Ring of Fire." You could meet a deep-voiced man who says that after Cash's death, he asked for and received a sign from God that, yes, he should continue his impersonation of the Man in Black. You could draw pictures on the street with colored chalk.

You could listen to a lecture by Mr. Grant, who says he has never smoked a cigarette or tasted liquor; his voice sometimes breaking, he railed against the drugs that had laid low "the world's greatest human being."

(A note to those in search of a sign: Later, after being shown a photograph of Smokey Evans holding his jailhouse treasure, Mr. Grant said, "I must say that these look like his shoes.")

Late on Saturday night, Rosanne Cash took the outdoor stage to serenade hundreds. She opened with a sexy take of "I've Got Stripes," a prison song her father used to sing; she also sang his "Tennessee Flat Top Box" and, of course, his "Starkville City Jail."

Then, in the full spirit of redemptive rebellion, Ms. Cash took back the Starkville night by singing a few beautiful songs of her own.

An Old Mobster Lets Go
of a Long-Kept Secret

EAST PROVIDENCE, R.I. — DECEMBER 22, 2008

They came for the gravely ill racketeer last month, appearing at his North Providence home around dawn. His time was near, but not as near as the police officers at his door. He went peacefully.

Soon he was at state police headquarters, where veteran detectives knew him well: Nicholas Pari, once the smart-dressing mobster whose nickname, "Nicky," had clearly not taxed the Mafia muse. Now 71, with gauze wrapped around his cancer-ruined neck: Nicky Pari.

The arrest, for running a crime ring from a flea market, put him in a reflective mood, and he said some things he clearly needed to say, including that he was dying. Still, ever-faithful to that perverse code of the streets, he seemed insulted when asked about the deeds of others.

"He wouldn't cooperate beyond talking about himself and his past actions," says Col. Brendan Doherty, the state police superintendent, who knew Mr. Pari from long years spent investigating Rhode Island crime, back when it was more organized.

The gaunt man did not weep, though his voice softened as he spoke with regret about a life that had fallen far short of its promised glamour and riches, a life heavy with guilt over one particular act. And in confessing this one act, Nicky Pari gave up a ghost.

"He was making an attempt at an act of contrition," says Lt. Col. Steven O'Donnell, who also knew Mr. Pari from way back when and had listened to his old adversary's words of regret.

That same day, detectives took the mobster for a 19-mile ride, following his directions as he zeroed in on the past. To East Providence. To the Lisboa Apartments. To a grassy backyard bordered by a listing stockade fence.

What he indicated next, whether through words or gestures or even a nod, was this: Here. Deep beneath this blanket of dormant grass, you will find him—here. Soon the claws of backhoes were disturbing the earth.

Thirty years ago, organized crime in Rhode Island was still like a rogue public utility. Raymond L. S. Patriarca, the old man with bullet tips for eyes, still ran the New England rackets from a squat building on Federal Hill. And men, from the merely dishonest to the profoundly psychopathic, still followed his rules.

Among them was Nicky Pari, who supposedly declined the honor to join the Mafia because he preferred the freelance life. If not made, he was known, in part because he had done time for helping a Patriarca lieutenant hijack a truck with a $50,000 load of dresses.

In April 1978, he and another freelancer, Andrew Merola, decided to address the delicate matter of a police informant within their ranks, a droopy-eyed young man from Hartford named Joseph Scanlon. The theories behind his nickname, "Joe Onions," are that he made the girls cry or, more prosaically, that his surname sounded like scallion.

One morning Mr. Pari lured Mr. Scanlon and his girlfriend, who was holding their infant daughter, into Mr. Merola's social club, in a Federal Hill building now long gone. Mr. Pari struck Mr. Scanlon in the face. Then Mr. Merola fired a bullet that shot through the man's head and caught the tip of one of Mr. Pari's fingers.

The girlfriend was ordered to leave the room. When she came back, her child's father was wrapped in plastic near the door, his jewelry gone, his boots placed beside his body. A package, awaiting delivery.

The girlfriend, once described as a "stand-up girl" who wouldn't talk, did, and the two men were convicted of murder in a case lacking a central piece of evidence: the body. They successfully appealed their convictions, but in 1982 they pleaded no contest to reduced charges in a deal that required them to say where the body was.

Dumped in Narragansett Bay, they said.

Few believed this story, perhaps because it lacked the panache desired of a Rhode Island-style rubout. For years afterward, people would call the police and The Providence Journal with tips like: Joe Onions is in the trunk of a scrapped Cadillac. Check it out.

Perhaps, too, there was the inexplicable charm of Mafia sobriquets. In a state whose mobster roll call includes nicknames like "The Blind Pig" and "The Moron," one wonders whether Joe Onions would be remembered had he been known, simply, as Joe Scanlon.

The years passed. The paroled Mr. Merola opened a Federal Hill restaurant called Andino's, while the paroled Mr. Pari gravitated toward flea markets. They were often seen together, sitting in a lounge in Smithfield, or attending a testimonial for a mob associate in Providence, that damaged finger of Mr. Pari's, holding a glass or maybe a cigarette, always there.

Mr. Merola died of cancer last year, leaving Mr. Pari to bear their secret alone. He went on as a father, a grandfather and, apparently, the man to see in a grimy flea market in a stretch of Providence where auto-body shops reign.

Last month the police arrested Mr. Pari and a motley mix of others for crimes of the flea market that put the lie to The Life, including the supposed trading of guns and drugs for more fungible items like counterfeit handbags and sneakers. Still, he remained bound to Mr. Merola; in arranging to sell illegal prescription drugs for a measly $320, for example, he chose to meet an undercover officer at his departed friend's restaurant.

At state police headquarters, before that ride to East Providence, Mr. Pari expressed remorse for helping to kill Joe Onions, remorse that he admitted had deepened as he faced his own mortality. Seeing the anguish his own family was going through, he knew he could ease another family's 30-year pain by sharing one detail that only he knew.

Don't misunderstand, Lieutenant Colonel O'Donnell says. Mr. Pari could have shared this detail days before his arrest, months before, decades before—but he lied instead, for reasons known only to him. "It doesn't make him a good guy," the police official says. "But he's a human being."

Hours after leading the police to the place that had haunted him since 1978, Mr. Pari appeared in District Court in Providence, unshaven, diminished, in a wheelchair. Released on bail, he returned home to his hospice bed and oxygen tank.

Meanwhile, back in East Providence, backhoes mined the sandy past. They dug until dark that Monday afternoon, then returned to dig all day Tuesday, as detectives and spectators shivered and watched, as the November sun offered little warmth, as the smell of fried food wafted from a Chinese restaurant a few yards away.

Finally, late on that Wednesday, the scoop of a backhoe pulled up things of interest from more than a dozen feet below, including a boot that seemed to match a description. The mechanical dig stopped and a human dig began, with investigators using a sifting pan to separate bone from earth.

It isn't as though you can dig anywhere in Rhode Island and find a body. But Colonel Doherty, the state police superintendent, says he will not confirm this was Joseph Scanlon until a match is made with some DNA provided by one of Mr. Scanlon's siblings. He adds that even though 30 years have passed, among the Scanlons "there was always a hope that he was not dead."

On a cold night late last week, an old mobster died at his home in North Providence, freed of one secret he would not have to take to the grave.

A World Away from Wall Street, a Bank and a Robber

CARLETON, NEB. — JANUARY 26, 2009

The man entered the intimate Citizens State Bank with a balaclava covering his face and sunglasses shading his eyes. His attire did not seem too out of place, given that workers at the nearby grain elevator are known to wear similar protection against the punishing cold of Nebraska in winter.

Here in Carleton, the standard greeting—"Keeping out of trouble?"—gleans a "Yep" or a "Nope," both equally reassuring to its population of about 136. But this man stepped up to the counter, with its rack of candy canes and clear view of the silvery vault open in trust, and greeted the teller with: Give me your money.

The salutation received a classic Carleton response, something along the lines of: Are you serious?

The man answered by making sure she saw the pocket of his heavy Carhartt coat, bulging with his hand and maybe something else. Following bank protocol, which says no amount of money is worth a human life, she gave him the cash in her till, all the while taking quiet note of two physical traits. He had fat fingers and a fat nose.

He tucked the money into a zippered pouch and left without availing himself of either a candy cane or one of the complimentary yardsticks jutting from a bucket by the door. As soon as he left, the teller loudly called out words not common in Carleton: We've been robbed.

The bank's president, Michael Van Cleef, came running out of his office, where he had been discussing a farmer's financial situation with the bank's loan officer. He looked out the window just in time to see the grimy getaway, in a maroon, dust-caked Grand Am with a spoiler on the back.

The event took all of 55 seconds.

Proper protocol continued. The bank locked down, and someone called 911. Within nine minutes the sheriff's deputies arrived. Soon came the first of many calls of concern and support, a few of which, a smiling Mr. Van Cleef remembers, went like this: "Hear you've been robbed. Can I bring you over a pie?"

In this day of bank bailouts and subprime mortgage debacles, some of us might find Robin Hood charm in a Nebraska bank robbery. Some might whisper the lines to the old Woody Guthrie song romanticizing the violent bank robber Pretty Boy Floyd: "Some will rob you with a six-gun, and some with a fountain pen."

But the Citizens State Bank in Carleton has no connection to any of those banking conglomerates with names like AmeriCitiComGroup. It is the only branch of a small, family-owned business that has six employees, three of whom are family and none of whom are accustomed to junkets. It has a few hundred customers and about $11 million in loans out.

Its one-story brick building, built as a bank more than 100 years ago, has remained a local fixture while most buildings in downtown Carleton, such as it is, are bricked up or closed up: the old Weddel's grocery store; the old post office that partially caved in a few years ago; the old Little Café, where Thelma and Shirley sold fresh pies of apple and cherry.

Just outside the bank, a Cargill grain operation grinds away. Truckloads of soybeans and corn are weighed and dumped with a sound like a sigh into the mammoth grain elevators looming over the empty storefronts. Every few minutes, another long Union Pacific freight train loudly announces itself.

Inside the bank, Mr. Van Cleef, 46, is usually helping local farmers figure out how to finance the fertilizer, chemicals, machinery, fuel and irrigation needed to grow their crops, all while guessing what beans and corn will go for. There is no online banking here. It's all face-to-face, how are you, Mike, see you later down at TJ's for a burger.

The Van Cleef business has not exactly followed the Wharton School model. Mr. Van Cleef's father, Lloyd, 72, was a Navy veteran working as a meter reader for a gas company in Fairbury, about 40 miles away, when a local banker offered him a career change. He worked his way up the banking ranks and then, in 1975, decided to buy the Citizens State Bank in Carleton.

His teenage son, Michael, did not appreciate moving from a town with a Pizza Hut and a movie theater to a town where the passing trains served as entertainment. But he started working in the bank after high school, attended banking seminars instead of attending college, set aside aspirations of law school and eventually became a bank president without pinstripes.

"You do loans, you do deposits," he says. "You scrape the snow outside. You change the light bulbs."

Over the years, the bank, like Carleton, experienced some tough times. Lloyd briefly had to take a banking job in another state to help keep his own bank afloat. Michael's wife, Nancy, held three jobs for a while: mother of five, bank officer and waitress at an American Legion hall in Hebron.

The Van Cleefs recall a common-sense practice from those times, a practice that some larger institutions seem to have forgotten. "When things get tight," Michael Van Cleef says, "you don't get a bonus."

Maybe this explains why the bank and the Van Cleefs remain. Lloyd lives here with his wife, Marion, who comes once a week with mop and bucket to clean the bank. Nancy is an emergency medical technician. Michael is on the village board—overseeing a $100,000 budget and a single public employee—and was instrumental a few years ago in dissuading the Postal Service from shutting down the post office. ZIP code 68326 lives on.

This, then, is who a fat-fingered man robbed at 3:14 on the cold Thursday afternoon of Jan. 15. For the record, his was the fourth robbery at the bank since it opened in 1890, and the first in a half-century. Two were break-ins, and one, in

1950, involved a local man wearing a rubber mask and wielding a water pistol. He got away—briefly—with $12.50.

The robber and his dirty Grand Am probably turned right onto D Street, past the crumbling old post office, the new post office in the old library, and TJ's Café, where locals gather on Fridays for the Mexican night specials. A quick left, a quick right, across Route 4 and then onto a gravel road heading north, where the Van Cleefs say his dust trail was seen by more than a local herd of Holsteins before he vanished into the great American vastness.

Through that afternoon and into the night, people in cars rolled slowly past the bank to catch a glimpse of investigators working behind the yellow caution tape, while calls of concern continued: from TJ's, offering to send over some food; from banking competitors, offering to send over staff or money. Some said they had seen that Grand Am around.

Michael Van Cleef says he feels violated—as though someone had broken into his home—but is glad no one got hurt. And while he would not reveal how much had been stolen, he says the amount was not worth the robber's trouble.

He says he wonders what motivated the man with fat fingers. Did it have something to do with what investigators were saying? That with this economy, we're going to see more robberies in rural America?

No matter. On the morning after the robbery, at precisely 8:30, the Citizens State Bank once again opened its doors to the rumbles and sighs of Carleton.

EPILOGUE

Things are as they were at the Citizens State Bank in Carleton, Nebraska.

It remains a family-owned business, with Michael Van Cleef's father, wife, and son-in-law joining him in working there. And, as a result of some national banking scandals, business has been growing, he said. "People are calling up and saying, 'I'm looking for a small-town bank, where someone will listen to me and talk to me—and actually befriend me.'"

The robbery of the bank remains unsolved. "Sometimes I've seen a strange car in town, and I'll get in my truck and follow him around," Mr. Van Cleef said. "Just got to check him out."

Broken Trust Shakes Web from Farmer to Cow

FERNDALE, CALIF. — MARCH 23, 2009

In the verdant Eel River Valley of Northern California, where everyone is tied by blood or business, a dairy farmer named John Vevoda does his part. Though the roars of tractors have deafened an ear, and decades of nudging cows while milking have ruined a shoulder, he accepts his role and fulfills it.

He and his family keep a herd of 600. He employs Alan, Alberto, Dave, Edgar, Jesus, Jose and Umberto. He pays his bills. He recycles. And every two days, he forwards thousands of gallons of raw milk to the Humboldt Creamery, which rises five miles away beside the twisting, rushing Eel River.

The creamery looms as well over the area's economy, linking many through an understood compact: the 50 farmers who own it as part of a cooperative, including Mr. Vevoda; its 200 employees; on and on, down to those who count on its support of the annual Easter Seals telethon. Just recently the creamery began selling preferred stock so people here can own a piece of something local and organic that makes them proud.

But that delicate compact snapped last month when the creamery's longtime chief executive left one day and never came back, though he passed on word of possible irregularities in the books. Now the 80-year-old creamery is in jeopardy, as are the livelihoods of people like Mr. Vevoda. He joins the ranks of so many others who feel betrayed—by the Bernard Madoffs, the American International Groups and the predatory lenders who have come to define this distrusting time.

Mr. Vevoda's dairy-farm view of the world makes it hard for him to accept what has happened in Humboldt County. The way he sees it, you can't just skip a milking, or stay in bed when a cow is calving. These animals count on you, and you count on these animals. The same with people.

One Thursday about a month ago, while Mr. Vevoda worked his farm, his herding dogs galumphing about him, the creamery's chief executive, Rich Ghilarducci, left for some business in San Francisco. He and John grew up in nearby Rio Dell, and Rich was in the same class as one of John's sisters. Everyone here knows Rich.

Late the next day, a San Francisco law firm whose specialties include white-collar criminal defense called the creamery's lawyer with cryptic news. Expect to receive Mr. Ghilarducci's resignation letter any minute now. Also, you could have problems with the creamery's financial statement, so you might want to stop selling those preferred stocks.

The chief operating officer, Len Mayer, frantically kept calling Mr. Ghilarducci. Finally, he just left a message: "Rich. Give me a clue."

He has not received an answer. Mr. Ghilarducci and his wife, it seems, have left their Rio Dell home, a silver teapot on the stove, a classic car in the garage. A local newspaper, The Ferndale Enterprise, later found him at his second residence, in Arizona, and published a photograph of his right arm closing the door to questions.

The central question—what happened?—essentially remains unanswered. Mr. Mayer would not provide a figure for the creamery's financial hole, although he acknowledged that the $400,000 raised through the sale of the preferred stock could not yet be returned to investors; it's been spent. He also said the creamery had been in touch with three federal investigative agencies in San Francisco.

The damage, Mr. Mayer said, "is big enough to threaten the future of the creamery."

Mr. Ghilarducci's lawyer, Elliot R. Peters, declined to say why his client abruptly left his job, home, colleagues and friends. But he said that Mr. Ghilarducci had "never done anything he thought was contrary to the interests of the Humboldt Creamery."

In fact, he said, Mr. Ghilarducci had worked hard for the creamery, and had used $200,000 of his own money—taken from a home equity line of credit—to cover the creamery's payroll last year.

Mr. Mayer, though, said he was unaware of any financial rescue by Mr. Ghilarducci, beyond investments he had made along with other creamery executives. As for whether Mr. Ghilarducci has ever done anything contrary to the creamery's interests, Mr. Mayer answered in this way:

"He ups and resigns without any warning? And he's not reachable?"

On the Saturday after the resignation, while Mr. Vevoda tended to his Holsteins, unawares, creamery executives holed up at a bed-and-breakfast and pored over financial records. On the Sunday, while the Vevoda family attended church, the executives told the creamery's nine board members, all dairy farmers, what little they knew: holes in the financial records, an inability to re-create the balance sheet, and Rich in the wind.

Around 7 that Monday morning, a board member came to the Vevoda farm with a statement about to be issued by the creamery. It included phrases like independent inquiry and sudden resignation and inaccurate financial statements.

Mr. Vevoda exploded. He ordered the man to the family kitchen, because Kris, his wife, needed to be in on this. He then called his son and partner, Robert, and said, Get your butt up here. The three Vevodas stood around the dark granite counter while the board member, who was not offered coffee, stammered that he didn't know any more.

John yelled, Kris cried and Robert kept asking, "Are we getting paid?" But after a while, what can you say?

John Vevoda, 56, body aching, stared out the kitchen windows, past the hummingbird feeders, past the welcome flag waving over the herb garden, to the acres of Vevoda pasture. He thought of his 35 years as a dairyman and the many trials he had endured, none greater than this:

In 1987, his first wife, Margaret, and their 5-year-old son, John, drowned while swimming in the Eel River. Another son, the son now standing beside him in the kitchen, saw it happen; he was 9.

Things went haywire after that. But through all the drinking that never rinsed away the grief, Robert Vevoda, 31, recalls that his father made him breakfast every morning, packed his lunch for school and kept the dairy going.

Finally, John Vevoda's mother, Lotta, intervened by tracking down a high school girlfriend of John's from the Bay Area. Kris was the mother of three children, divorced and working as an assistant bank manager. When her secretary said someone was asking for her by her maiden name, she hesitated about taking a call from that deep in the past.

She took the call.

As he stared into the green beyond the kitchen, Mr. Vevoda did some math. The creamery owed them $120,000 for the milk they produced in January, money needed to pay bills. And they had another $380,000 invested in the dairy cooperative. All of it now at risk or gone.

That night, John Vevoda got out of bed and threw up.

For the next several days, forensic accountants hired by the creamery worked in Mr. Ghilarducci's office. There, under the gaze of dozens of his stuffed toy cows, they tried to make sense of the books.

The creamery's executives then met with the cooperative's 50 farmers in the turf building at the county fairgrounds. After a somber discussion, and with one executive near tears, the farmers voted unanimously to defer $2 million in payments for their January milk so the creamery could keep the doors open, pay employees, calm antsy vendors—and buy time while trying to figure out how to survive.

Matters had become that precarious. "If, say, the guy who sells us lids for our milk cartons wants to get paid immediately, everything grinds to a halt," Mr. Mayer said.

When the fragile compact is broken—when that responsibility to one another is betrayed—the repercussions are felt by people far removed from, say, an office filled with stuffed toy cows. There are the dairy farmers, some of whose families helped establish the Humboldt Creamery cooperative in 1929. The local Easter

Seals telethon, which no longer has the creamery's financial support. The creamery employees, truckers, suppliers of lids. Their families.

The Vevodas. John's mother, who lent them $10,000. Their employees. Their employees' families, including Edgar's two children, one 5 years old, the other 4 months old. The cows.

With their January payment short about $100,000, the Vevodas asked for time from their vendors and lenders. But the bank went ahead and processed a $20,000 mortgage payment. And one of their feed suppliers said that from now on, it's cash on delivery.

The Vevodas faced some hard choices; after all, Kris Vevoda said, "You can't just open the gates and tell the girls to have a nice life." So they held a staff meeting in the milk barn, while 24 Holsteins in the stalls waited to be milked.

We'll be using cheaper feed, John Vevoda explained. No layoffs, for now, but you'll be working five days a week, not six. No more overtime. Oh, and please don't cash your checks until after 3 on Monday.

The men listened. A silent exchange of glances told Robert the men wouldn't leave them in the lurch. Then the morning's five hours of milking began.

The other day, those employees were back in the barn, milking the cows, while John and Kris Vevoda worked in the office and tried to keep it together. At one point the phone rang, and they decided not to pick it up.

Soon there came the disembodied voice of a former employee, now retired, offering to help with the milking of the cows. "You don't have to pay me," he said. "We're praying for ya."

Click.

The words seemed to confirm what John Vevoda had been trying to say all along about our obligation to one another, and he almost smiled.

In Prison, Playing Just to Kill Time and Just Maybe to Help Solve a Murder

COLUMBIA, S.C. — NOVEMBER 16, 2009

In the down time before another head count, two prisoners play cards. One inmate shuffles and the other flicks his hand, a mystical cutting of the deck. The dealt cards land on the lid of a garbage can used as a table, falling on top of one another, face down.

A form of gin rummy breaks out in the courtyard of the Campbell Pre-Release Center as the inmates, Mark and Mario, toss their unwanted cards into

146

the discard pile. But from deuce to ace, nearly every card is a face card, looking up in silent appeal.

The cards ask: Do you know who killed me? And they ask: Do you know where I am? And they ask: Do you know something? Anything?

The South Carolina Department of Corrections started selling these decks in its prison canteens for $1.72 about a year ago; since then, inmates have bought more than 10,000 packs. Each card asks that you please call 888-CRIME-SC if you have any information about a case; each card also whispers, "Call *49," an anonymous prison hot line.

The seven of hearts spins to a stop, and gazing up is Victoria Duncan, last seen driving off with two men in 1998, later found beaten to death in York County. She disappears under the king of spades, Christi Hanks, a prostitute from the Anderson area, found dead in a field in 2006.

Here comes the 10 of spades, Tracy Ann Johnson, beaten to death in her home in Greer in 2000, only to be covered by the four of hearts, Richard Martin. He left Nancy's Lounge in Anderson one night in 1995 and was found an hour later, dying from blunt trauma to the head in the middle of Welcome Road.

Hands are won and lost as the inmates shuffle and toss the cards on top of one another. Their discards form kaleidoscopic arrangements in which the dead and the missing peer up together, as though from a deep, shared hole.

"You going down, mister," crows Mario to Mark, looking at the cards looking at him. The inmates sit six feet from a bank of public telephones.

Another discard spins into view: Brian Lucas, 29, forever smiling on the ace of spades. He was one of four people shot to death in an isolated motorsports shop outside Spartanburg on Nov. 6, 2003. My case is unsolved, his card says. Please call.

Brian Lucas's father, Tom Lucas, is the one who decided that his son would be the ace of spades, and that the three killed with him would also be aces. While he grieves for the other 48 murdered or missing people in the deck, he wanted to emphasize that this was our son, the son of Tom and Lorraine Lucas.

Aces, he says. "I had blood in it."

Their son, their motorbike-loving, fix-anything, father-of-two Brian, was killed at the Superbike Motorsports store where he worked as service manager. Also murdered were Scott Ponder, the owner and now the ace of diamonds; Beverly Guy, Mr. Ponder's mother and the ace of hearts; and Chris Sherbert, the shop mechanic and the ace of clubs.

After receiving the call, the Lucases drove six hours to South Carolina from their home in Kentucky, through fog and tears. "He cried all the way down," Ms. Lucas says.

While closure is a fiction, their wait for justice continues. The why of what happened that afternoon, amid the motorcycles and helmets and Suzuki paraphernalia, is still an open question: a quadruple homicide that, six years later, remains in a swirl of maybes: maybe drug-related, maybe business-related, maybe family-related.

The Lucases moved back to Spartanburg and began working to keep the spotlight on their son's case. They joined the Crime Stoppers Council, persisted with investigators and even talked to psychics. "We would have talked to Santa Claus if we could," Tom Lucas says.

In the midst of their frustration, Mr. Lucas learned of a company called Effective Playing Cards and Publications, which had produced "unsolved" playing cards that were being circulated in the state prisons of Florida, as well as in county jails in several other states. And he thought: Why not cards for unsolved South Carolina cases—like my son's?

Backed by the Crime Stoppers, Mr. Lucas met with Gov. Mark Sanford, collaborated with law enforcement officials, designed the cards and raised the money. He also worked closely with corrections officials to have the cards sold in the state's 28 prisons, as well as in many county jails. "There's a lot of information inside a prison," Mr. Lucas says.

He pressed police officials to choose the cases they wanted to include, and accommodated families whenever possible. For example, the family of Donnie Bell, killed in a hit-and-run in 2003, asked for the three of hearts because "that was his card," Mr. Lucas recalls. "I said, 'Certainly.'" But he always made clear that the four aces were taken.

The thought of a family member's image fluttering through prison card games is both jarring and reassuring, Mr. Lucas says. Many of the cases are cold, and families find hope in knowing that their loved ones have not slipped from memory—that they are, in a way, working their own cases.

Ann Hollingsworth, 54, of Anderson, agrees. Her sister is in the deck: Tina Milford, 23, kidnapped from a Li'l Cricket convenience store and shot to death in 1983. Ms. Hollingsworth says she endorses the program because a prisoner's memory, or conscience, or self-interest, might be jogged by a young woman's high school portrait on the 10 of hearts.

Twenty-six years have passed, Ms. Hollingsworth says. Her younger sister would be 50 in January—"if she'd lived."

Mr. Lucas acknowledges that the cards have yet to solve a murder in South Carolina, but he emphasizes that they have prompted dozens of tips, including one promising lead in a case more than a dozen years old. "It gives you something to look forward to," he says, studying the 52 cards arranged face-up on his kitchen table, including the ace of spades, his son.

Brian Lucas now appears and disappears in prisons throughout South Carolina. Here at the Campbell Pre-Release Center, he smiles from atop that garbage-can lid of a table, then vanishes until the next rat-a-tat-tat shuffle.

The cards are stored between the air fresheners and decks of Uno cards in the prison's canteen. When they first appeared a year ago to replace another brand of playing cards, they prompted several altercations. Inmates kept interrupting games by picking up a card in play to take a closer look.

The dead and the missing are known here. "I remember she was quiet," one inmate says of the three of diamonds. Says another of the five of diamonds: "People say he got what he had coming."

The "unsolved" decks, long since stripped of any reverence, are now part of the everyday prison culture here. Inmates say that the cards are too expensive, that the cards are not as sturdy as those they replaced, that sometimes a card is just a card.

"I'm tired of seeing James," says a man hunched around a hand he's just been dealt. James is James Oneal Boulware, shot to death in Rock Hill a couple of years ago. The two of spades.

James and 51 others are soon shuffled and spun across tables to form new combinations of faint possibility. Read 'em and weep.

The Holdup: A Mobster, a Family and the Crime That Won't Let Them Go

WORCESTER, MASS. — MAY 31, 2017

The aged gangster welcomed me at the door.

Hunched by hard time lived and served, his lean body scarred by several bullets and one ice-pick stabbing, he led a brief tour of the modest rental house he shared in a Massachusetts shore town. He paused to point out his three shelves in the communal refrigerator, a measure of his diminished domain.

This was Ralph DeMasi, once a feared member of the New England underworld whose long résumé included truck hijackings and home invasions, robberies and violence. Days shy of 80, he half-joked that at the moment he'd rather be holding up an armored truck.

He led the way to his small, well-ordered bedroom, where dozens of photographs formed a wall-to-wall collage of contradiction, a blur of toddlers and mobsters. Here, his ex-wife with their baby at an amusement park, and here, a friend at a picnic, shortly before his gangland murder.

"Rudy Sciarra," Mr. DeMasi said, motioning to a photo of a vicious Mafioso from Rhode Island, long dead. "And the one on the right, he's a wiseguy out of New York. . . ."

But he struggled to summon this mobster's name from his mind's darker recesses. "You forget people, like, as you go along," he said. "So the pictures kind of keep me up to—you know."

He kept more memories in boxes of correspondence arranged lengthwise on his bed, the dates of every receipt and reply recorded in his shaky scrawl. These letters, which he slept beside, were the coded missives of criminals, swapping family updates, sharing gun-rap loopholes. They often closed with "A friend always" and "With love," and were signed by public enemies named Bobo, and Gerard, and even Jim, as in James Bulger, the murderous former fugitive better known as Whitey.

Funny story: More than 40 years ago, Mr. Bulger and an accomplice shot Mr. DeMasi several times in the drive-by killing of another target.

Years later, after Mr. Bulger was captured, convicted and sentenced to prison forever, Mr. DeMasi sent him a letter—a message, really—that he summarized as: "Whatever transpired between us, it didn't kowtow me or make me any less of a man."

From this a pen-pal friendship grew. In one letter, written in slanted, nearly inscrutable script, Mr. Bulger suggested that Mr. DeMasi sell these notes; they might be worth something. In another, he evoked his time in Alcatraz:

"Thanks for writing and I really enjoyed your letter. Felt like I was hearing from friends way back in the Az years. Fellow Bank Robbers, not 'Organized Crime' guys. Life was simple back then."

The two men also exchanged yearly Christmas cards. But on this August afternoon last year, Mr. DeMasi sat on his bed, trying to remember something. Finally he said, "Whitey owes me a letter."

To his right, past the exercise ball he balanced on to do 1,000 situps every morning—he often invited people to test his taut stomach—was a closet crammed with still more memories: copies of indictments, appeals of convictions, transcripts of wiretapped conversations. ("I've got a crew of guys, I'll tell you, and we rob armoreds, we rob armored trucks. . . .") A half-century archive of persistent criminality.

Whenever the corpse of another wiseguy floated up to public consciousness, Mr. DeMasi was always in the mix of likely suspects. "Armed and dangerous" was stipulated.

"He didn't take any lip from anybody," recalled Tony Fiore, a mob associate and friend. "I mean, he was a tough guy."

"One of the most dangerous criminals in New England," said Brian Andrews, a former detective commander of the Rhode Island State Police. "A bad bastard."

No doubt, Mr. DeMasi would love to be back at it. Scoping out some strip mall for a week, a month, whatever it took. Getting the timing down for when the guard came out with that canvas bag of cash. Donning a nylon mask. Concealing a semiautomatic. Go!

"It's still in me," he said, with a desiccated laugh.

This was unlikely, though, given his age and his consideration for his ex-wife and three grown children, who had suffered enough. Besides, too many cameras out there now.

His quiet life in Salisbury seemed to suit him. He had family living nearby. He had those three refrigerator shelves. And to help him remember all that he had done and seen, he had a framed newspaper article on his nightstand: "Tips For Improving Your Memory."

"Make lists.... Put frequently used items in the same place each time.... Repeat information.... Make associations.... Exercise your mind...."

But some things cannot be forgotten.

A few months after my visit, on a December afternoon as clear and cold as a stare, other visitors came unannounced to Ralph DeMasi's door. And they were armed.

As a Providence Journal reporter covering organized crime a quarter-century ago, I was their deadline Boswell.

I eventually moved on, taking with me the noirish stories and vague threats. That time, for example, when the owner of a mob-connected strip club I was investigating mentioned during a tense interview the name of my wife and the address of the house we were about to buy.

Those days came flooding back two years ago when the documentary filmmakers Marc Smerling and Zac Stuart-Pontier contacted me about "Crimetown," a podcast focusing on the darker side of Providence. We began sharing our knowledge and research, which benefited me as I prepared a story about Maury Lerner, a minor-league baseball player who became a hit man for the Patriarca crime family.

The documentarians, it turned out, had gotten to know Mr. DeMasi, who had spent time in prison with Mr. Lerner. Mr. Smerling kindly arranged for the two of us to meet with the gangster and his ex-wife and close friend, Sue, at his home last summer, where our conversation wound up centering on Mr. DeMasi and his turbulent past.

"A journey and a half," Sue DeMasi called it.

In some ways, the man's journey seemed preordained. Born in 1936 to a teenager in a Connecticut home for unwed mothers, he was soon abandoned. So began his peripatetic life as a troubled foster child.

If his foster parents weren't happy with him, he once said, "they'll just call up the people that bounce you around and they just come and get you and take you somewhere else—take you to another foster home. But I don't hold that against anybody."

Many years later, Mr. DeMasi tracked down his birth mother, who by then had been long married to a man who knew nothing of her first child. She told her son never to call again. "I remember the tears coming out of his eyes," his ex-wife said. "He had spent all those years trying to find her."

In the distant blur of the 1940s and 1950s, who knows what truly happened to one forsaken boy? One version is that, at age 11, he finally found a foster mother whom he loved, a Mrs. Bowman, in Bridgeport. When her husband began hitting her, again, the boy grabbed the man's shotgun, threatened to shoot and ran away. He slept nuzzled beside the gun in a graveyard, then robbed a bookie's card game the next day by ordering everyone at gunpoint to strip naked.

That, at least, is the family story. But there is no question that the young Mr. DeMasi spent time in a reformatory, time in the Army and time doing time, his progress chronicled in newspaper police items:

> Ralph DeMasi was arrested after breaking into the Kingsway bowling alley in Fairfield and rifling a pinball machine . . . was remanded to the custody of the New York State Police after being charged with burglarizing a sporting-goods store in Brewster, N.Y. . . . was arrested at gunpoint behind a Boston furrier's, his car filled with $80,000 worth of furs, his pocket allegedly concealing a loaded gun.

In 1970, soon after being released from prison for the fur-theft conviction, Mr. DeMasi met his wife. He had stopped at her mother's house in South Boston with one of her brothers, who was working a con called the "short change"—in which the swindler uses confusing prattle to distract a clerk handling money. "You'd give them a 20 and say: 'Oh, wait a minute, I didn't mean to give that to you, take this dollar, oh, I need my change for the 20,'" Ms. DeMasi explained. "It's just fast-talking."

The ex-con and the flimflammer's redheaded younger sister were married within four months. Around the same time, Mr. DeMasi was suspected in the burglary of a suburban Boston home emptied of assorted valuables, including a mink coat, some jewelry and a saxophone. Searching the DeMasi apartment, the police found many of the goods, as well as a sweet but telltale note:

"Hi Honey! Went out with the cat & got nothing! Am going over to give Millie the money & then shall be taking a fast ride to Providence & try to get some money for the diamonds & the fur. Take care. Should be back by 3 p.m. Get ready & I will take you downtown. Took $19 out of your pocketbook? Love, Ralph."

When their first child was born on Christmas Day, Mr. DeMasi was in prison. During her pregnancy with their second child, he pulled up to their Rhode Island home in a rental truck one night and informed his wife that they were moving— right now—to California, where he was soon arrested. With the help of some Rhode Island connections, she was able to post his bail just before giving birth.

Ms. DeMasi spent most of her young married life waiting. Waiting and waiting for her husband to come home after a score, her heart pounding like cops at the door. "Like an eternity," she said.

Then there were waits that lasted for years, and his presence at home came in the form of his disembodied voice on cassette tapes mailed from prison. Amid the inmates' clatter, he would express his love and promise to change.

"I want to get out of here, and I want to be with you and the children," he said on one tape, from 1977. "Never again going through all them crazy runarounds. No way, boy. We just got to put it all behind us, baby, and get away from it."

He never did.

Back then, Mr. DeMasi was a valued associate of Mr. Patriarca, the Mafia boss who ran New England organized crime from his vending-machine business on Federal Hill in Providence. In the front of Mr. Patriarca's drab store sat broken cigarette machines and old arcade games, and in the back, the cluttered desk where he collected tributes, co-opted elected officials and ordered people dead.

Mr. DeMasi and Mr. Patriarca bonded while serving time in the Adult Correctional Institutions in Rhode Island, the two of them taking walks in the prison yard. The older Mr. Patriarca had also grown up without a father, and perhaps he saw himself in how his tough new friend avoided flash and kept his mouth shut. Even when Mr. DeMasi was wounded in that drive-by shooting, he refused to give names, including Whitey Bulger's.

The Patriarca connection paid off. During his frequent prison spells, Mr. DeMasi knew that his family would have food deliveries, the use of a car, a tree at Christmas. And every week, Ms. DeMasi said, she would go to Mr. Patriarca's storefront—"and there'd be an envelope with $200." All 20s.

In the brazen ranks of the Providence underworld, Mr. DeMasi distinguished himself as a dedicated family man who approached crime as a 9-to-5 job with the occasional late night. The police routinely watched him drive off in the morning to lay the groundwork for a planned robbery, then return home in the evening, leaving the carousing to others.

"And that was not like the other wiseguys I knew," said Mr. Andrews, the former Rhode Island law enforcement official. "Ralph was all about work."

Mr. DeMasi was so committed to his criminal profession that he might be in prison for one felony, on trial for another and under indictment for a third. He was almost as ubiquitous in the courts as the clerks and deputy sheriffs.

There was the time he wrote a Rhode Island judge an impassioned letter on nearly eight feet of prison-issue toilet paper. It laid out the injustice of being denied bail, but not before inviting the judge to use the paper for its intended purpose. His scatological cri de coeur lives on in court archives.

Then there was the time he represented himself against charges that he had conspired to murder a different judge by hiring assassins to blow up the man's home. For the two-week trial, Mr. DeMasi wore button-down shirts, slacks and brown Hush Puppies with white socks—never a jacket or a tie. According to The Providence Journal, he presented his case without opening a law book, relying instead on a mail-order paperback that explained how to win a criminal trial.

Mr. DeMasi, who has an eighth-grade education, wound up winning his own acquittal. He promptly accused the prosecutor of reneging on a $10 bet over the trial's outcome and invited all the jurors to join him for a drink. That evening, though, he drank his bourbon and Cokes alone.

New England back then had no shortage of mobsters like Mr. DeMasi, stealing, victimizing, doing harm. Colorful, but only from a safe distance. Then there was nearly everyone else, just trying to get by, like Ed Morlock.

Mr. Morlock was that guy behind you in line at Dunkin' Donuts, looking like he could use some caffeine. He was 6-foot-3 and a little heavy around the waist, with half-moon shadows under his eyes suggesting hardships endured.

He grew up in Winchendon, an old manufacturing town amid the hardwoods and pines of north-central Massachusetts. It once produced textiles, wood products and so many novelties that it was called Toy Town. But those factories had closed long ago, leaving the Winchendon of his childhood a self-contained place, detached from the Boston bustle.

By the age of 7, he was working on his family's dairy farm, tending the cows. By his teenage years, he was driving a milk route in a cream-colored truck. Stopping to make deliveries along Maple Street, he would often see a smallish teenage girl balancing herself like a tightrope walker on the guardrail cables along the road.

They never spoke. Sometimes, though, he waved.

Eager to see beyond the Winchendon horizon, the young man defied his father by joining the Marines, returned from service, found factory work, got married, had four children, all girls. One evening, at a wake, he was introduced to a cousin's wife, Jeannette, a petite woman with dirty blond hair. She had also grown up in Winchendon, one of 16 children of a French Canadian foundry worker and a homemaker.

You weren't that kid always walking on the wires?

Yes, and I used to see you go by. You never said hello.

Years later, Mr. Morlock was separated from his wife and living alone when he was invited to play cards at the house of that same cousin, whose relationship with Jeannette had soured. He had become abusive, she recalled.

One cold November night, she said, he locked her out of the house after she announced that she wanted a divorce. She had 95 cents and no coat.

"And who took me in? Ed did."

They married in 1968 and had one child, Ed Jr. Mr. Morlock returned to work at the dairy. Things, it seemed, would be all right.

Then one day, while he was clearing land for firewood, a malfunctioning chain saw bounced and cut his right leg to the bone. The injury left him with a permanent limp and profound circulatory problems that required him to wear pump-powered stockings to keep blood from pooling in his legs and feet. Discomfort defined his days.

The Morlocks moved around Winchendon, then down to Florida, then back to Massachusetts, where they eventually bought a small yellow Cape Cod house on a main road in the bypassed industrial town of Athol. One bathroom, and an endless whoosh of traffic just beyond the front door.

All the while, Mr. Morlock struggled to remain in the work force with his disability, laboring at the dairy, pumping gas, doing security, installing patios. He was also tending to his wife, who was having what she called emotional breakdowns that had them considering a move back to Florida.

In 1987, he found work as an armored-car security guard with Mass Transport Inc. Some days he was the driver and other days the courier, the one who got out to deliver or collect the cash.

He wore a two-tone brown uniform that his wife kept washed and ironed, along with a bulletproof vest that she and their son bought for him. The company feared that vests gave employees delusions of invincibility, but Mr. Morlock figured that, given all the blood-thinning medication he was taking, he would bleed out if he were ever shot. Best to wear the vest.

He also carried his own .357 Magnum, which he had yet to draw from its black holster in the line of duty.

His adult son eventually joined him at Mass Transport. The older Mr. Morlock had not been easy to get to know; for one thing, his disability had deprived the family of so much time and joy. But now, on those pre-dawn drives to the office in his blue Ford Taurus, the father opened up about his childhood, his years in the service, his injury.

"I didn't know my father very well until we started working together," Ed Morlock Jr. said.

It was a Saturday morning in May 1991. The Boston Celtics and the aging Larry Bird had just been eliminated from the playoffs. The Red Sox were in the midst of being swept down in Texas. And the older Mr. Morlock had agreed to fill in as a courier for a co-worker who wanted the day off to celebrate his birthday.

Before leaving, he told his wife that after work they would visit his mother at the nursing home and then have dinner at McDonald's. "And that was a treat for us," Ms. Morlock said. "Because we didn't go out much."

I've got a lot of things to tell you, he said.

Fine, she answered. We'll talk when you get home.

Armored trucks were money bags on wheels, often driven up to a bank or store at roughly the same time, day in, day out, depending on traffic. "There were always customers who wanted us to be there between this time and this time," the younger Mr. Morlock said. "Security-wise, it made no sense."

By the late 1980s, a finite number of New England gangsters, about two dozen, specialized in robbing these armored trucks. Prominent among them: Ralph DeMasi.

There were "two objectives," Mr. DeMasi told the "Crimetown" podcast. "Get the money and don't get caught getting the money."

A lot of preliminary work came first. You had to assemble your crew: gunman, wheelman, lookout. You had to spend weeks on surveillance: watching the police routines, the traffic flow, the arrivals and departures of the armored trucks, the habits of the armed guards. And of course, you had to plot your getaway.

"Everything had to be planned out," Mr. DeMasi said. "It couldn't be just spur of the moment."

Tony Fiore, a former comrade in crime, agreed. Mr. Fiore's reputation as a specialist in robbing armored trucks is memorialized by a tattoo adorning his chest. It depicts a thief wielding a gun, with a bag of cash at his feet and an armored truck in his sights.

"We used to go sit in parking lots from 7 in the morning until 5 at night before we would do a score," said Mr. Fiore, now 74. "We used to actually put more time into a score than people do if they were working a legitimate job."

The haul could be $100,000, $300,000, a half-million, with everything hinging on the element of surprise. By this point, law enforcement officials could narrow down the possible suspects to the same handful. "There weren't that many guys doing these jobs," Mr. Andrews said. "You always knew. That's Fiore. That's DeMasi."

In March 1991, the authorities arrested Mr. Fiore and his crew as they prepared to hold up an armored truck carrying $1 million at a mall in North Attleborough, Mass. The plan included having a grandfatherly thief in a wheelchair holding a semiautomatic under a blanket.

With Mr. Fiore and his accomplices in custody and about to spend the better part of two decades behind bars, the small number of criminals working armored trucks in New England shrank. Still, two months later, there came another holdup, this one in the second-largest city in Massachusetts: Worcester.

On that mild Saturday morning in May, an armored truck pulled up on schedule to a Shaw's supermarket at one end of an elbow-shaped strip mall on Lincoln Street in Worcester. Ed Morlock clambered out, his .357 Magnum snug in its black holster, and went inside to make his collection.

As he left with a bag of money and receipts, two men confronted him in the supermarket's foyer, and one tried to disarm him. A bagger inside the store saw Mr. Morlock standing against the wall, his hands raised. Then came loud popping sounds, with blood spattering the soda machines. He slumped to the floor, his gun beside him, out of its holster.

His assailants grabbed the bag, ran to an idling white Cadillac with stolen license plates and peeled out of the parking lot. The vehicle was found in an apartment complex a half-mile away, having been swapped for another getaway car. A chain blocking access to a back road out of town had been removed in advance.

The work of professionals, well planned, well executed. That is, if you looked past the blood.

On duty that morning was a young, clean-cut detective with street smarts and a military bearing named Steven Sargent, the son of a Worcester police lieutenant. Having grown up in a working-class neighborhood just down Lincoln Street, he knew this shopping center well. As a boy, he'd ride his bicycle to visit his grandmother, who lived in subsidized housing behind the plaza. As a uniformed patrolman, he'd take breaks at the Dunkin' Donuts.

Now it was his job to be with the wounded security guard, who had been rushed to the University of Massachusetts Hospital. His assignment: to collect evidence—the man's belt, his clothes, the bullets—and, if at all possible, to talk to him.

The detective watched the frantic struggle to save the guard's life under the surreal lights of the emergency room. He would never forget the bloodied uniform, the empty holster, the man's last breath. Ed Morlock was 52.

Soon after, a ringing telephone broke the quiet in a yellow Cape about 45 miles away in Athol. Jeannette Morlock was making the beds upstairs when she picked up. She did not quite believe what she was being told, even when two Athol police officers appeared at the front door, in confirmation.

Screaming, Ms. Morlock began pounding one of the officers on the chest. "He kept telling me he was dead, and I said, 'No, he's not.'"

Ed Morlock's wife and son never moved on; they just moved about. "When Ed got killed, my life—I just didn't care," Ms. Morlock recalled, crying.

She spent years helping to write and distribute a newsletter for families of homicide victims. She sang alto and soprano in the choir at St. Francis of Assisi Catholic Church and worked the post-Mass coffee break, where her confetti angel cake sold for a dollar a slice. She bought a .22-caliber Ruger and learned to shoot at the Woodsman Rifle and Pistol Club.

She also met a man named Bob Mathews at the McDonald's near her house. They're engaged now, but he knows she'll never marry again.

"You don't really forget things," she said. "It stays there. You push it aside—but it's always there."

As for her son, Ed Jr., he went on the road, working for a traveling zoo and an indoor circus, then for a series of retail outlets, then for a private school's horse stable. He married, had a daughter, divorced, remarried.

During his wandering, he collected more than a dozen tattoos that cover his arms and torso, including one of Anubis, the Egyptian god who watches over the dead.

By August of 1991—three months after the fatal Worcester holdup—Mr. DeMasi was many years divorced and living in the Pines campground, nestled among the woods and marshes of Salisbury. His furnished, tarp-covered campsite was conveniently close to his

Jeannette Morlock

children and ex-wife, who had briefly strayed from their marriage while he was in prison. He had forgiven her, she said, but she could not forgive herself.

Once again, the career criminal was being shadowed. Not long ago, he had boasted of his penchant for robbing armored trucks to a Massachusetts State Police officer working undercover on a drug investigation. "That's always been my thing, always been my thing," he was recorded saying. "Like I say, I love to go and get the cash."

He went on: "We put our thing together. We clock it, we clock it, we clock it, we clock it, we clock it, right? The guard's taking the money in the bank, or he's bringing it out or whatever. Then boom, we catch him. Boom, boom, quick—it's over."

Mr. DeMasi has many sides to his personality. He was so tough in prison that he pulled his own teeth, his ex-wife said, and spent years in solitary confinement rather than obey an order to sleep on his cell's mattress. He was also inordinately generous, known for giving away much of the money he stole.

"We did an armored car up in Taunton, and I don't know, he got maybe $50,000—and he's broke like two weeks later," recalled Mr. Fiore, his former partner. "I mean, gee, you just got $50,000. But he never forgot anybody, and he'd say like, you know, 'Ah, this guy's in jail, and his wife don't have this; his kids don't have that.'"

As his conversation with the undercover officer revealed, Mr. DeMasi also liked to brag, as if to prove that he was his own man, the head of his own crew—which by the summer of 1991 included a couple of degenerate gamblers, a hanger-on distrusted by other gangsters and an aimless young man from the campground.

Now, the Federal Bureau of Investigation was watching as the DeMasi crew monitored armored-truck deliveries to a strip-mall bank in Newburyport, not three miles from the campground. One afternoon, the men were photographed having a picnic in the parking lot, making and eating sandwiches around the trunk of their car while conducting surveillance.

We clock it, we clock it, we clock it . . .

Two undercover F.B.I. agents, both women, were also assigned to monitor Mr. DeMasi at the campground, but the case agent, John Egelhof, warned them to be extra careful. "This guy's extremely dangerous," he remembered telling them. "Any issue with him, blast him."

After several weeks of planning, Mr. DeMasi and his crew made their move on a warm September morning, guns at the ready. But as their stolen green van crawled toward the armored truck, F.B.I. vehicles raced up from every angle, disrupting the shopping center's ordinary rhythms.

Within minutes, five would-be thieves were under arrest—including a defeated but still defiant Ralph DeMasi, a bulletproof vest covering his chest and the nylon stocking on his head now looking silly. "He was cold," recalled James Mullen, a Rhode Island State Police detective who assisted the F.B.I. "No emotion. Nothing."

A few months later, Mr. DeMasi was sentenced in federal court to more than two decades in prison. When the judge asked if there were any other motions, the gangster said, "Kiss my ass."

"Motion denied," answered the judge.

Soon after, Worcester detectives visited the modest Morlock house. They explained that they knew who killed Ed Morlock, though they couldn't quite prove it. But at least there was this: Those responsible were now serving long prison terms.

The point, the younger Mr. Morlock recalled, was that his father's killers "were not out there whooping it up"—which gave him some peace.

"At least they got them on something," he remembered thinking. "And they were spending time in prison."

His mother took no such comfort.

"No," she said. "Not me."

So began another protracted prison stretch for Ralph DeMasi. The Clinton and Bush administrations came and went. Pay phones all but vanished. Email replaced handwritten letters. A black man became president.

Released finally in 2013, Mr. DeMasi said that he received some walking-around money—about $5,000 or so—from an emissary of Raymond Patriarca Jr., the son of the old mob boss, dead now 30 years and more. The gift would be in keeping with mob tradition, a recognition of a man's long and faithful service, but the younger Mr. Patriarca said through a spokesman that it never happened.

By now deep into his 70s, Mr. DeMasi melted back into a New England that had largely forgotten him. Continuing a kind of institutionalized existence in the squat house in Salisbury, he exercised, corresponded, followed a vegetarian diet, kept his cell of a bedroom neat. He also dreamed.

"I might rob an armored truck before I die," he told me on that summer day's visit.

Sitting beside his ex-wife, Sue DeMasi, at the kitchen table, Mr. DeMasi seemed not to remember many specifics of his wild criminal past. After she recounted her dramatic appeal for leniency at one of his many sentencings, he could not recall the case at all, even when she mentioned his accomplice, Tommy.

"Come on," Ms. DeMasi said. "You don't remember any of that? Wow."

"I remember Tommy," he answered. "Is he still alive?"

"No-o-o," she said. "Remember he got run over by Billy King and them guys? Ran him over so many times they had to shovel him up."

Ms. DeMasi got up to leave. Through the years she had held things together for the children while Mr. DeMasi was in and out of prison; she even did long-haul trucking. The two had had their ups and downs, and at times she had feared his facility for violence. But they continued to share an intense private bond impervious to outside judgment.

"If I had to do it all over again, I wouldn't change a thing," she said. "I still tell people today: Nobody on this earth—past, present or future—will ever love the way me and Ralph loved."

"Thanks for coming by, Sue," Mr. DeMasi said as she gave him a peck.

"O.K., Ralph, I love you," she said. "I'll talk to you soon."

"All right. You take care."

A quiet, domestic moment. Here, on this pleasant summer's day, was a mobster in twilight, about to go out for a vegetarian lunch that he would wash down with a bourbon and Coke.

Four months later, with the imminence of winter in the mid-December air, people with guns approached this same Salisbury house. Given the reputation of their target, these law enforcement officials, including two detectives from the Worcester Police Department's unresolved-homicide unit, were braced for anything.

But Mr. DeMasi went quietly.

That night I was Christmas-shopping at a mall in New Jersey. To be exact, I was in a Sephora cosmetics store, watching my 13-year-old daughter select stocking stuffers that were clearly not for me. Then Marc Smerling of the "Crimetown" podcast called, and my daughter would later imitate what I said:

"Ralph DeMasi? Arrested for murder?"

I had been planning to write a profile of Mr. DeMasi in the new year—something about the reduced circumstances of an aging, forgetful gangster reflecting the state of New England organized crime. But here was a murder charge.

I felt foolish.

The next day, Worcester County's district attorney, Joseph D. Early Jr., announced the arrest at a news conference. He then introduced the clean-cut Worcester police chief, who, 25 years earlier, had been the young detective dispatched to the hospital to be with the mortally wounded Ed Morlock.

As Chief Steven Sargent donned his glasses to read from a statement, he struggled to navigate his many emotions. The satisfaction and pride he felt were tempered by memories of having seen a man in a bloodied uniform die in the emergency room.

"This has always been a personal case for me," the chief said. "And today, it gives me a measure of satisfaction to say justice has been served for Edward Morlock and his family."

The two law enforcement officials declined to explain the break in the old case. Three men believed to have been involved in the fatal holdup had died, Mr. Early said, but he left open the possibility that others besides Mr. DeMasi were still alive.

"Maybe someone didn't want to talk before," he said. "Maybe they want to talk now."

Mr. DeMasi pleaded not guilty that morning, his cuffed hands holding a piece of paper, his expression somewhere between confusion and concern. Since then he has been in the Worcester County jail, awaiting a trial that may not begin until 2018.

"He strongly denies having any involvement in this armed robbery, which led to the death of Mr. Morlock," his lawyer, Michael Hussey, said.

As Mr. DeMasi was led out of the courtroom, someone in the gallery shouted "Dad!" It was his daughter, Sue DeMasi, who later told reporters that he was a loving grandfather who had been exhibiting signs of dementia—but who was still preparing Christmas cards to send to all his friends.

Also sitting in the gallery that morning was a small, bespectacled woman of 74 who had spent the past few years dealing with health challenges that included diabetes, lung disease, kidney cancer and heart problems so severe that her doctor had told her she might die at any time.

This was Jeannette Morlock, the murder victim's widow. And like the man charged with killing her husband, she too kept old photographs, among them a portrait of the family: a young boy of about 10, a short, smiling woman and a large man with half-moon shadows under his eyes.

Ms. Morlock had risen in the dark of early morning. She had bathed. She had chosen an outfit fitting for the occasion, a pale purple suit coat with slacks to match. Then she had taken the hour's drive down to Worcester from Athol, intent on being in court in time for the arraignment of Ralph DeMasi.

She wept at the sight of him.

PART FOUR

Intolerance

I'm always chasing rainbows

Yes, the Ill Will Can Be Subtle.
Then, One Day, It Isn't.

GREENWOOD, LA. — JANUARY 21, 2007

Midnight in a handsome one-story house on Waterwood Drive. Hours after Ernest and Shirley Lampkins say good night to their teenage daughter, Brett, and to the first Sunday of the new year, a Sunday of church-going and turkey and chili and some of those sweet frozen grapes that Ernest likes so much. Two bullets pay a call.

They explode through the living room window. They tear through the soft-yellow curtains that Shirley ordered from a catalog. They rocket past the Easter basket containing family snapshots, past Brett's bedroom door, past Ernest's antique upright piano, past the framed portrait of father, mother and daughter in serene pose.

One bullet strikes a golden candelabrum and splits: half whistles into a wall near the kitchen; half crashes through a French door—turning smooth glass into a spider's web of shards—and into the sunroom, four steps from the master bedroom.

The other bullet slams so hard into the living room wall that it has to be pried out. "It was a piece of lead about the size of my thumb," Mr. Lampkins recalls. "They use that for killing deer." There are no deer in the Lampkins home. Only Brett, 17, a high school junior, who has just learned to drive and wears slippers that look like kittens. And Shirley, 62, a retired high school English teacher and administrator, who enjoys gardening and makes a delectable fig cake. And Ernest, 78, a retired educator who has a doctorate in ethnomusicology and is known throughout Louisiana for reaching children through music.

Oh. One more thing about Ernest. He is also the mayor here in Greenwood, a quiet town of 2,600 a few miles west of Shreveport. Greenwood has a Dollar General store, a Mexican restaurant and some antebellum homes, including one once used as a Confederate hospital. It is predominantly white.

Oh. And one more thing about the Lampkinses. They are black.

On that night, Mr. and Mrs. Lampkins hear no gunshots, but their home alarm sounds, and they leave their bedroom to investigate. They stare at the shattered glass, and then at the holes in the front window. It does not register. Then it does.

As the police arrive to interview and to collect the shell casings from the street, it is hard to forget that several days earlier, the black mayor in Westlake, about 230 miles south of here, was found shot to death, and that some people there dispute findings that he killed himself.

The Lampkins family does not return to bed.

Ten days later, the mayor and his family sit in their sunroom, with its bullet-twisted Venetian blinds, and talk about music, food, Brett's love for dance. But the shooting has reduced these joyous subjects to fleeting diversions from two central questions: Who? Why?

"The town of Greenwood is not a racist town," Mr. Lampkins begins, noting that he was elected mayor with 56 percent of the vote. "There are racist people in Greenwood. That's different."

That said, he asserts, this was a racist act. A racist act perhaps stemming from the heated politics in town, but racist still. As racist as the For Sale sign he recently found planted in his lawn.

When asked how he can be so sure, Mr. Lampkins drops his voice, as if to emphasize that we are no longer discussing music and food. As if to underscore that this is a slave's grandson speaking, someone who heard his century-old grandfather talk of being the "house nigger" on a Kentucky plantation.

"I'm 78 years of age," the mayor says. "Don't you think I know what racism is in the South?"

Mr. Lampkins was elected to the Board of Aldermen in 2002, and he immediately sensed corruption. He was right: The town clerk was in the midst of stealing at least $130,000 from the municipal coffers. She is now doing eight years' hard labor.

He became the town's first black mayor in 2004, beating an incumbent who did not believe in graceful transitions of government. On the day Mr. Lampkins took office, he had to find a locksmith to gain access to Town Hall.

The steps he has taken to change the way of doing business, including firing several people from the old administration, have brought praise and vitriol. The monthly board meetings have at times devolved into shouting matches, with some spectators openly ridiculing the mayor.

Ellise Wissing, a board member, says the mayor often endures subtle racism. "These people can't stand the fact that there's a black man that's in control of this town," says Ms. Wissing, who is white. "That's so much smarter than they are."

Contributors to a website frequented by those from the anti-Lampkins faction—they like to mock the articulate mayor's pronunciation, for example—reject his assertion that racism is at play. A few even suggest that he orchestrated the shooting to shift attention from his administration.

The sadness of the suggestion is felt most acutely in the violated house on Waterwood Drive, where a decoy of a police car sits in the driveway, and a father confides that his daughter will suddenly just—cry.

Mrs. Lampkins tells her husband that he ought to return a call she just took from a political opponent of his. Maybe the man wants to express his concern, she says.

The mayor calls the man back. But the man never mentions the shooting. Instead he wants to know why a town building is closed.

Mold infestation, the mayor says. Mold.

The Names Were Separated, Though the Lives Collided

BUTLER, GA. — MARCH 18, 2007

The cool, busy lobby of the Taylor County courthouse features a bulletin board, a Dr Pepper vending machine and two framed rosters honoring local veterans of World War II. It is easy to spot the slight difference in wording that justifies displaying two plaques instead of one.

This list says "Whites," and that list says "Colored."

County officials explain that the segregated plaques continue to hang because state law says no publicly owned memorial dedicated to veterans of the United States—or of the Confederate States of America—shall be relocated, removed, concealed, et cetera, et cetera.

"Fifty-dash-three-dash-one, subparagraph B," recites Edward N. Davis, the county attorney. It is up to the state legislature to change the law, he says. Besides, he and other county officials say, some people like the plaques the way they are, and not all those people are white.

The names on these honor rolls—from Adams, Guy Smith, on one plaque, to Woods, Jesse, on the other—call upon you to imagine the lives lived. For example: Who was this man listed among the "colored," this Snipes, Maceo?

"Our favorite uncle," says Lula Montfort, her hair white, her memory sharp. He stands before her still: in his mid-30s, with brown eyes, a powerful build and a sixth-grade education supplemented by experience.

In early 1943, Maceo Snipes set aside his civilian ways—categorized by the government as "Farm Hand General"—and joined the Army. He served 30 months, including six in the Pacific theater, was honorably discharged, and received $100 in muster-out pay and $9.35 in travel pay. He returned to his mother in Butler, and

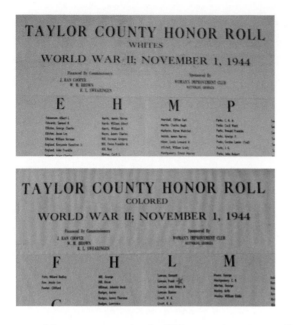

began summoning his dead father's farm back to life. Cotton, peanuts and corn became his life again.

Ms. Montfort, whose family were sharecroppers on a nearby farm, remembers Uncle Mace's challenge to embrace education: a trip to Macon, 40 miles to the northeast, if you got good grades. Soon, she says, she and her brother Ulysses were in the back of a bus bound for the big city.

Mr. Snipes reasoned that if he fought for this country, he should be able to vote in this country. On July 17, 1946, he was the only black person in his area to vote in the Democratic primary for governor—a bold move in a segregated state, where the candidate vowing to restore all-white primaries would eventually win.

The next day, white men in a pickup pulled up to the Snipes farmhouse, where even the floors, Ms. Montfort says, were kept "bright and shiny." They called for Maceo Snipes.

He came out. One of them, Edward Williamson, a fellow veteran who had stayed stateside, shot him. Then they drove off.

Ms. Montfort, then 13, remembers what she was told. Her favorite uncle stumbled back into the house. Bleeding from the abdomen, he walked miles to get help, alongside his mother—her grandmother, Lula, for whom she is named.

"Couple days later, they told us he was dead," Ms. Montfort says.

Mr. Williamson, who was related to a politically powerful family in the county, told a coroner's inquest that he had gone to collect a $10 debt. He said Mr. Snipes pulled a knife. He said he grabbed a gun from the glove compartment and shot twice.

The ruling: self-defense.

"Oh, please," Ms. Montfort says, 60 years later. "Really."

Fear, then, thrived like a healthy crop. A few days after the coroner's inquest, two married black couples were shot dead by a crowd of white men at the Moore's Ford Bridge, about 140 miles north of here. So no funeral for this veteran, no public mourning; he was buried in the woods.

That fall, with the crops harvested and fear alive, Lula Montfort's family said, Enough. They sneaked out of Butler, with Lula and other children hidden under canvas in the back of a truck, and went north, to Youngstown, Ohio.

The flow of time rubs against fact and memory. No one knows where Maceo Snipes is buried. Edward Williamson killed himself with a gunshot to the head in 1985, feeling bad about what he had done, or so some say.

And on Wednesday, an old farmer named Walter Snipes tried to share what he knew about his cousin's killing. But with heart failing and speech affected by two strokes, he could not. As his sister Nonie Gardner wiped his brow with a wet cloth, about all he could say was:

"Lord. Help. Poor. Me."

His prayers for relief were answered the next day. He was 84.

As communal memory fades, vilification of the dead becomes easier. A county official who does not want to be identified—and who recently and mistakenly maintained that Mr. Williamson had served time for the killing—suggests the deadly dispute concerned gambling and moonshine, not voting. When pressed, the official says, by email:

"Neither of them were exactly fine upstanding church-going citizens of the community."

"Oh, please," Ms. Montfort, a fine upstanding church-going citizen, says again. A citizen who took to heart an uncle's emphasis on education, and now has four college graduates for daughters.

She and other family members, along with several civil rights activists, especially John Cole Vodicka, director of the Prison and Jail Project, are pushing to have the Snipes case reopened and those segregated plaques in the courthouse taken down.

Ms. Montfort, who returned to Georgia a few years ago, says the plaques may have been well intentioned; after all, the county could have chosen not to recognize black veterans at all. "But this is 2007," she says. "If they're historical, then put them in a museum."

Last month, the three white and two black county commissioners came up with a compromise. They hung a third, integrated plaque beside the other two.

Now, among the hundreds listed together, are the names of Williamson and Snipes, two men who left one war to engage in another.

A Time of Hope, Marred by an Act of Horror

SPRINGFIELD, MASS. — NOVEMBER 17, 2008

As Election Night made way for a new day, a pastor named Bryant Robinson Jr. clicked off his television to accept a sleep of sweet promise. His mostly black congregation now had two blessings awaiting it in 2009: the inauguration of the first African-American president and the finished construction of a new church.

Give praise.

He could not have been asleep two hours before his telephone rang. It was his brother Andrew, whose home abuts the blessed construction site. "They're burning our church," shouted Andrew Robinson, who still doesn't know why he said "they."

Soon Bishop Bryant Robinson, pastor of the Macedonia Church of God in Christ, was standing at the grassy edge, as firefighters sprayed arcs of water meant not to save the building but to contain a fire clearly set. Black embers the size of fists shot skyward, only to float down like broken pieces of the cold New England night.

Someone eased him into a chair—he is 71, with bad knees and high blood pressure—and placed a blanket around his weary shoulders. He stayed there past dawn, when this new day's light revealed a smoldering test of faith: a skeleton of scorched steel and a cracked foundation upon which a church could no longer be built.

Sitting there, stunned, emotional, Bishop Robinson sought context for what had just occurred: A black president is elected, a black church is burned. He thought of dreams realized and dreams denied.

"It was so close I could taste it," he says. "I could just see it."

You could say that dream began more than 60 years ago, the moment his father, Bryant Robinson Sr., left Alabama for a place where his children could drink from

177

fountains of their choice. As soon as he arrived in Springfield he wanted to flee, so foreign was the place. But his train ticket, courtesy of a local pastor, was one way, so he settled in this community known as the City of Homes and sent for his family.

Though working as a parking attendant and then as an assembly-line worker, he found his true calling in the Church of God in Christ. Eventually the church's revered leader, C. H. Mason, resolved tension within the Springfield flock by directing the elder Robinson to start his own congregation, one that would be called the Macedonia Church of God.

For a while the congregation shared a storefront with another church, until it raised enough money to buy a former synagogue that featured rooms used for transitional housing. "Housing for people coming from the South," Bishop Robinson recalls. "Escaping segregation."

Finally, in 1961, the elder Robinson, now working as a stain spotter at a dry cleaners, persuaded his congregation to buy an old Episcopalian church that sat on a small corner lot on King Street.

For decades he juggled the dual tasks of cleaning clothes and saving souls. He immersed believers in the baptismal pool, presided over their weddings, talked Bible to them on Sundays, led others in prayer after they had gone. Years of footsteps formed grooves in the red stone steps leading to the church's wooden door.

The elder Robinson died in 2001 at age 86. Bryant Robinson Jr., his co-pastor and the oldest of his five children, took over the congregation, switching gears after more than 30 years as a civic leader and educator; at one time he had served as the city's interim superintendent of schools.

Bishop Robinson soon decided the church on King Street, now more than a century old, could no longer meet the congregation's needs. Parking was minimal, the maroon carpet old, the windows small and high; Oh Lord, could it get hot in those pews on a late-summer Sunday.

We deserve a church meant for us, built by us, he told his congregants, and they agreed. The weekly tithing and special offerings took on added urgency, as the bishop reminded people that when you invest in Kingdom's church, you cannot lose.

The church eventually bought four wooded acres on Tinkham Road, about five miles away, from Andrew Robinson, both a brother of the bishop and the congregation's music director. ("We got a favorable rate," the bishop says, smiling.)

Where others saw tall pine trees and sandy soil, he envisioned a soaring church with plenty of parking.

As time passed, enthusiasm flagged; the project sometimes seemed to be nothing more than an architectural sketch hanging in the back of the old church. As it changed in scope and required the purchase of more land, Bishop Robinson tried to re-ignite interest and to convey his commitment by announcing that he had long ago stopped drawing a salary.

Bishop Bryant Robinson Jr.

The response, he says, was "marginal."

Still, the project inched forward, thanks in part to the guidance of the church's lawyer, Bradford Martin Jr. He helped to secure a $1.9 million construction loan, and worked to allay the concerns of neighbors opposed to having a church in their backyard.

Finally, in April 2007, dignitaries and elders joined Bishop Robinson in breaking ground with shovels painted gold. "I was so elated that day," he says. "At one point I said we may be standing in the sanctuary. And you know where we were? In the parking lot."

After a while, though, parishioners who previously visited the site to mutter "This is too small" and "That's not right" would gaze upon the 18,000-square-foot structure and say only, "Wow."

"That became the descriptive word," the bishop says. "Wow."

Hardly a day would pass without a visit from the bishop. He would sit in his car, watch the workers—and visualize.

You would enter a foyer large enough for people to chat with one another after services. To the right, a men's room; to the left, a spacious ladies' lounge with large mirrors, because he remembered his father's fear of the sermon he would have to give if women stopped attending: "Finally, brothers, farewell."

A large meeting hall in the back, suitable for weddings and church gatherings. A row of prayer rooms to the right. A pastor's office in the left corner. A food prep room. A chandelier one day, but not now. And, of course, the 500-seat sanctuary, designed to be intimate, with video equipment to project the full-immersion baptisms on a screen for all to see.

Oh, and plenty of parking for a congregation sure to grow.

By Election Day, 75 percent of the construction was finished, with the entire exterior nearly done and construction workers planning to lay the water line in the morning. The bishop could taste it. He watched the election returns, felt pride in his country and turned out the light. And during his short sleep, someone set fire to his dream.

Investigators say the cause was arson, but so far they have no suspects or evidence that the crime was rooted in racism. Still, the bishop cannot shake the timing of it—timing that will now forever link two events, one of joy and pride, another of loss and horror.

As Election Night melted away, as memories of the past tempered thoughts of the future, the bishop sat in that chair, thinking, praying. Behind him were stacked five gold-painted shovels from the groundbreaking; in front of him, the fire; above him, the mysterious pitch of the night. And the thought came to him: Build again.

EPILOGUE

Two months after an Election Night act of arson demolished the new Macedonia Church of God in Christ, three white men in their 20s were charged with burning down the church to express their rage at the thought of a black president. Two pleaded guilty, and the third was convicted after trial, in a case that The Republican newspaper of Springfield, Massachusetts, described as a "blot on the whole city."

But Bishop Bryant Robinson Jr. and his congregation followed through on their vow to rebuild. In 2011, the smoke lifted to reveal a 20,000-square-foot church standing on top of an old crime scene, its sanctuary walls painted the color of a clear blue sky.

Bishop Robinson, now in his 80s, said that the church has nearly 400 congregants on its rolls. "Our challenge is to get them to all show up at the same time," he said, half-kidding.

Police, Protesters and Reporters Form Uneasy Cast for Nightly Show in Ferguson

FERGUSON, MO. — AUGUST 22, 2014

Late on Wednesday, a young man with a megaphone led a modest band of pro-testers in yet another loop around the traumatized commercial strip that is the stage for the nightly street theater of outrage here. But as the group passed an illuminated tent, the leader interrupted his chants for justice to say through his loudspeaker:

"Hey, Don!"

And Don Lemon, the CNN news anchor, preparing for yet another live shot, looked up and waved.

The fleeting moment, light and familiar, captured the Groundhog Day feel that now infuses these exhausted but edgy productions, known as the Ferguson Protests, that began after the shooting death on Aug. 9 of an unarmed 18-year-old black man by a white Ferguson police officer, a few hundred yards from this strip.

Exhausted, because the protests, deep into their second week, feature reporters and protesters with little new to ask, or say; everything seems stipulated. Yet edgy, because these nights also have included improvisational flashes—a protester's thrown water bottle, an officer's raised assault rifle—that can instantly transform an orderly protest into a jostling frenzy.

Then, whether conclusion is reached by consent or by force, the participants— protesters, reporters and officers—exit from West Florissant Avenue, prepared to see one another the next evening for a production with no clear closing night.

In the first days after the shooting of Michael Brown by Officer Darren Wilson, a murky event under federal and grand jury investigations, the violence and looting conveyed a sense of no one in charge. But now the nights follow a ragged, rule-bound routine that begins before dusk, when reporters check batteries, officers check weapons, and protesters prepare to repeat their calls for accountability.

At the nearby Northland Shopping Center, the packed parking lot would suggest robust sales at Target and the supermarket Schnucks, except that the vehicles are police cruisers, National Guard buses and news trucks, now that the space has been claimed for a command center.

Still, shoppers have adapted to seeing people carrying riot shields rather than grocery bags, and to navigating the many National Guard checkpoints—so much so that a maroon sedan rolled right past a checkpoint the other evening, causing an armed guardsman to shout: "Hey! Hey!" The stopped driver shrugged her shoulders, as if to say, "Oops."

As the sun descends, many reporters, some carrying gas masks, begin the long walk north along West Florissant, reserved now for armored vehicles, police cars and the occasional news truck. The people you pass say, "Y'all be safe," the preferred Ferguson greeting these days.

Soon there appears the asphalt stage: a quarter-mile cut of West Florissant, bordered by Ferguson Avenue to the south and, to the north, Canfield Drive, the road on which Michael Brown died. In between are many stores with boarded-up fronts bearing spray-painted messages that have been tweeted around the world.

"We're open," says Northland Chop Suey. "Our Prayers Go Out To the Michael Brown Family," says Sam's Meat Market. "Black Owned," says Yolo! Boutique.

By sunset, the production is well underway, as a procession of protesters—whose numbers can swell one minute and shrink the next—follows a loop, its members growing hoarse from their determined, ever-changing chants, including, "Hands Up, Don't Shoot."

The procession can never pause, per police orders. Officers who stand not quite at ease, sometimes holding rifles or long batons, frequently step out of their still poses to say keep moving, keep moving.

"Keep walking," an officer kept saying. "That's all I ask."

According to Ronald S. Johnson, the Missouri State Highway Patrol captain who was brought in by the governor to oversee security, the rule is intended to thwart stationary clusters that might give cover to agitators. "Because what happens is, the peaceful protesters gather, and the other element blends in," he said this week in response to a question from The Huffington Post. "Now they blend in, and that's what's been causing us some issues."

So the protesters, the reporters, the yellow-shirted observers from Amnesty International—everyone but the police—walk around and around. They might take a break in a designated area, or pause to study a glowing Anderson Cooper, his black shirt offsetting his shock-white hair, as he delivers his report. But then it's back to walking the oblong path, like exercisers on a high school track, or inside a mall.

There is a psychic loop as well, experienced by the many reporters, photographers and videographers populating the scene, looking for that moment, that shot, to justify their long night. But the weariness of the familiar has taken root; one reporter recently began interviewing a local man, only to realize in mid-interview that he had heard the story, almost verbatim, before.

Although the community's anger and sorrow are always present, informing the nightly theater, and although the setting evokes military siege, this week has also had moments, often unreported, that approach the festive. Here, one night, is an ice cream truck. Here, another night, are people sitting in folding chairs.

And here comes a Thomas the Tank Engine-like train, owned by a St. Louis amusement company, doing a loop to the strains of Marvin Gaye's "What's Going On."

"We do bouncy houses, kids' parties," said the train's minder, Jermaine Hayes. "And this is the 'peace train.'"

Even the police officers, standing in a row outside the closed but well-lit McDonald's, become background photo ops for selfies, now that the news media have had their fill of such images.

But then something happens—another tossed water bottle, say—prompting a finger-snap change in the dynamic, summoning recent memories of tear gas, and attracting the high beam of a helicopter's spotlight from somewhere above.

Late Tuesday, some clergy members held a prayer service to encourage a peaceful end to the day's protests, but you could detect a tense tug of war for control of the night. Something happened, and suddenly, clutches of armed officers were rushing into an area reserved for the news media.

Reporters scattered, tweeting and tripping.

This occurred more than once, the police thrusts nudging the crowd, alternately anxious and defiant, south, and out, to end the night and to highlight the news media's role in the story.

"Media, will you please get out of our way!" a police official demanded through a loudspeaker. "We're trying to do our job!"

Brian Schellman, a police officer and spokesman for the St. Louis County Police Department, said that a few agitators had been using the news media as shields. "You have a sea of media and a sea of protesters," he said. "When you're on street level—Who did that?—that's a real challenge to determine who."

But even jangled moments like this have become accepted into the rhythms of the night, as participants wait for a waning interest in protests; for the start of the delayed school year; for news on whether Officer Wilson is indicted.

As the days blur, the many participants continue to speculate about when the plywood might be removed from storefront windows to reveal a West Florissant not occupied by the police and the news media. But they know that periods of calm have come, and gone, before.

Wednesday night, at least, was less tense than Tuesday night. The ever-moving band of protesters was noticeably smaller, only a half-dozen people were arrested, and glorious lightning flashes caused most of the brightness from above.

Reporters walking back to their cars encountered several armed soldiers at checkpoints along the way. Good night, they said, and good night, we said, like people passing at the end of another long shift.

A Quiet Act of Decency Soars over Messages of Hate

COLUMBIA, S.C. — JULY 26, 2015

What the black state trooper saw was a civilian in distress. Yes, this was a white man, attending a white supremacist rally in front of the South Carolina State House. And yes, he was wearing a black T-shirt emblazoned with a swastika.

But the trooper concentrated only on this: an older civilian, spent on the granite steps. Overcome, it appeared, by an unforgiving July sun and the recent, permanent removal of a Confederate flag from state capitol display.

The trooper motioned for help from the Columbia fire chief, who is also black. Then, with a firm grip, he began walking the wilted white man up the steps toward the air-conditioned oasis of the State House. As they climbed, another state employee snapped a photograph to post on Twitter, where it continues to be shared around the world.

The meaning of this image—of a black officer helping a white supremacist, both in uniform—depends on the beholder. You might see a refreshing coda to the Confederate flag controversy; a typical day for a law enforcement professional; a simplification of racial tensions that continue. But what does the trooper see?

His name is Leroy Smith, and he happens to be the director of the South Carolina Department of Public Safety. He was at the rally, working crowd control, because he likes to signal to his 1,300 subordinates that he has their backs.

Mr. Smith said he was taken aback by the worldwide attention but hoped the image would help society move past the recent spasms of hate and violence, including last month's massacre of nine black people in a church in Charleston. Asked why he thinks the photo has had such resonance, he gave a simple answer: Love.

"I think that's the greatest thing in the world—love," said the burly, soft-spoken trooper, who is just shy of 50. "And that's why so many people were moved by it."

Earlier this month, Mr. Smith donned a dark business suit to join Gov. Nikki R. Haley and thousands of others in witnessing an honor guard of seven of his troopers march stone-faced toward a flagpole on the State House grounds. There, a few feet from a soaring Confederate monument, the white-gloved troopers lowered the Confederate flag in 30 seconds and presented it to an official from a state-supported museum.

Just like that, a red-blue-and-white battle flag—representing Southern white pride to some, Southern black oppression to others—was removed from the whims of the South Carolina breeze.

A different sort of photograph had helped to end the flag's official stature. After images surfaced of the suspect in the Charleston shootings, a white man named Dylann Roof, posing with the Confederate flag—and after families of the victims publicly forgave him—Governor Haley said: Enough. Legislation was swiftly drafted, a law was signed, and this flag of pride was demoted to relic.

As Mr. Smith watched the flag rolled up and history unfold, he felt chills running along his spine. "Very moving," he nearly whispered.

Now, on a hot Saturday afternoon eight days after that emotional ceremony, Mr. Smith was back at the capitol, only this time in his gray uniform and broad-brimmed campaign hat. A group called the Black Educators for Justice would be rallying in the early afternoon on the north side of the State House. And on the south side, a couple of hours later, the Loyal White Knights of the Ku Klux Klan would be demonstrating.

It promised to be a busy day.

Mr. Smith watched from the north side's top granite step as black demonstrators vented their frustrations. Then he walked through the blessed cool of the State House to the south side, which faces the back of a statue of Strom Thurmond, the longtime senator and segregationist.

Bike-rack barricades had been arrayed to separate the white-supremacist demonstrators from a swelling crowd of people, some fresh from the black-empowerment rally on the north side. "You could kind of feel the tension in the air," Mr. Smith recalled.

Soon the demonstrators, a few dozen, came marching from the west, flanked by Mr. Smith's "advance civil emergency response team." Many wore the black shirts of the National Socialist Movement, a neo-Nazi organization that, according to its website, believes: "Only those of pure White blood, whatever their creed, may be members of the nation. Noncitizens may live in America only as guests and must be subject to laws for aliens. Accordingly, no Jew or homosexual may be a member of the nation."

These people entered their State House pen and waved their Confederate flags. The public-address system they were said to have ordered never arrived, so all they could do was exchange taunts with hecklers and issue occasional bleats of "White power!" and "Wooo!"

The heat turned up a notch: a bottle thrown, some jostling at the barricades. Mr. Smith called his commanders down to a lower level because, he said, "we were getting ready to work a little."

Then a demonstrator directed his attention to an older man all but melting on a bottom step. "He looked fatigued, lethargic—weak," Mr. Smith said. "I knew there was something very wrong with him."

He called up the steps to the Columbia fire chief, Aubrey Jenkins, for assistance. Then, with his left arm around the man's back and his right hand on the man's right arm, he walked the swastika-adorned demonstrator up the steps, as many as 40. Slowly, steadily, all the while giving encouragement:

We're going to make it. Just keep on going.

A female demonstrator shadowed the climb. On the back of her black shirt appeared a familiar white-supremacist slogan ("Because the beauty of the White Aryan woman must not perish from the earth"). She kept asking Mr. Smith whether the man was going to be all right—as if his safety, as well as his health, might be in some jeopardy.

Up the steps the two men went. They didn't talk much, although the older demonstrator allowed that he wasn't from around here. A spokesman for the National Socialist Movement declined to identify him, other than to say he is a senior citizen who doesn't need people knocking at his door.

Mr. Smith isn't from around here, either. Born in Haines City, Fla., the fifth and last child of transplants from Alabama. Mom worked at home while Dad worked in the citrus groves. Went to an all-black elementary school and then to an integrated high school, where those with Confederate flags on their pickups never bothered him.

Four years in the Navy. Then, after a brief spell in retail—"I sold cars, and I was pretty good at it"—a long career with the Florida Highway Patrol, where he rose through the ranks. After that, his appointment in 2011 as the first African-American director of South Carolina's Department of Public Safety.

At this moment, though, Leroy Smith was a state trooper, helping a civilian suffering from the heat of the day.

As they approached the top step, someone nudged Rob Godfrey, 34, a deputy chief of staff to Governor Haley, who is known for his diligent chronicling of everyday history. He snapped a shot with his iPhone, sensing a distillation of the grace with which South Carolina has responded to these days of tragedy and strife.

"In that moment, Leroy Smith was the embodiment of all that," Mr. Godfrey said. He quickly shared the moment with the world—to the benefit, it must be said, of his boss, Governor Haley, as she tries to lead her state beyond its racially troubled past.

Mr. Smith did not know about the photograph. He knew only what was before him. He walked the man into the air-conditioned State House, led him to a green-upholstered couch, and left him there to cool down.

Realizing It's a Small,
Terrifying World After All

ORLANDO, FLA. — JUNE 20, 2016

The corner of Kaley Street and South Orange Avenue offers a tableau of American déjà vu, a sprawl of Subways and 7-Elevens so common in communities across the continent. This one just happens to include a gay nightclub popular with Latinos called Pulse, where gaping holes in the gray-painted exterior now reflect the infliction of a national traumatic injury.

It's easy to see Orlando as a place apart, our sanctuary of fantasy and escape, where fun trumps work and mouse ears are an accepted fashion accessory. But when a deeply aggrieved, heavily armed man burst into this unremarkable nightclub planted beside a carwash, the ensuing mayhem did not seem to occur in some distant, disconnected place. Instead, it became a sobering mash-up of so much that is contentious in American life.

Guns. Gay rights. Islamic extremism. Immigration. Latinos. Guns. Playing out just 20 miles from where George Zimmerman shot Trayvon Martin, in a state slowly receding into the rising seas, it felt like Disney Dystopia—just in time for Election 2016. Orlando is more than our preferred family vacation destination. Orlando is these fractured United States. Orlando is us.

Past tragedies tended to unify Americans, said Gary R. Mormino, a retired historian at the University of South Florida with a particular expertise in his state's experience. Here in Florida—"where roots are as shallow as Australian pines," he wrote in an email—some people will recall how, after Pearl Harbor, President Franklin D. Roosevelt's calm but assertive radio talks bonded the country, elevating hopes. Many more will remember the feeling of shared grief as the television broadcaster Walter Cronkite wiped a tear while reporting the assassination of President John F. Kennedy.

"But 2016 brings together the toxic elements of an election year, presidential candidates who polarize the electorate, voters who are afraid and angry, and a press eager to exploit the spectacle of division and disaster," Mr. Mormino wrote. "Alas," he added, "we live in a balkanized state and nation."

On some level, there's a chaotic, only-in-Florida quality to the calamity at Pulse. On the previous Friday night, a young singer named Christina Grimmie—famous for having appeared on "The Voice"—was shot dead by a stalker as she signed autographs. And on the following Tuesday, an alligator killed a toddler at a Disney resort.

But when Omar Seddique Mateen, 29, a security guard with thwarted law enforcement ambitions, entered the nightclub with a handgun and a military-style rifle—both legally and swiftly purchased—he was not coming from some foreign land. He was a first-generation American, born to Afghan Muslim parents in Queens and educated in the public schools of Florida.

And the community he was about to devastate was not some foreign place—not some stereotypical city of rednecks, snowbirds and Disney-besotted hordes. It was Tomorrowland today, a booming and diverse city of 250,000, in which the Hispanic share of the population has grown to 25 percent.

"I don't even know that I'd characterize it as a Southern city anymore," said State Senator Darren M. Soto, a Democrat who was born to Italian-American and Puerto Rican parents in New Jersey. "It's much more of a transplant, Hispanic kind of vibe in the city. We're an all-American town, but we're the new America," he said. "We have people from all backgrounds and walks of life."

That diversity includes gay men like Eric Rollings, 47, the chairman of the Orange County Soil and Water Conservation District. He recalled moving to Orlando from Michigan in 1989 and finding a small, sleepy-town L.G.B.T. community still reeling from the AIDS epidemic.

At the city's first gay pride parade, a quarter-century ago, he said, Ku Klux Klan members gathered at the corner of Magnolia and Pine to "greet" the marchers.

Now, he said, the gay pride festival is a popular signature event in the city. And on the January day that same-sex marriage became legal in Florida last year, he noted, Mayor Buddy Dyer of Orlando officiated the marriages of dozens of same-sex couples on the steps of City Hall.

Mr. Rollings recalled much of this while decompressing in a local restaurant called Santiago's Bodega. He wore a T-shirt adorned with slogans of determination—#OneOrlando, #OneHeart, #OnePulse—and an expression that changed by the minute. Now grief, now exhaustion, now disbelief, now hope, now grief again.

The nightmare unleashed by Mr. Mateen is a continuation of the shared nightmare we keep reliving—from Virginia Tech to Newtown to Aurora to Charleston. The names of the victims may change, but the Greek Chorus reaction is all too familiar. Shock and grief, candlelight vigils and calls for unity, vows for change and legislative paralysis, finger-pointing and vitriol, and, in the end, nothing much different—other than, say, South Carolina's vote to remove the Confederate flag from State House grounds after the Charleston shooting.

It took a 15-hour filibuster by Senator Chris Murphy, a Democrat from Connecticut with searing memories of the slaughter of 26 schoolchildren and educators in Newtown, to get modest gun-control measures to the Senate floor. Yet it had no more success Monday than similar proposals did after Newtown, with the Senate, largely along party lines, failing to advance measures that called for an expansion of background checks for all gun sales and a delay in selling guns to suspected terrorists (consider that phrase, by the way).

Add to that the profound displays of support for the grieving L.G.B.T. community here, offset by flashes of intolerance—a pastor in Sacramento lamenting that more hadn't died—and statements by more than a few politicians that somehow managed not to mention that many of the victims were gay, or Latino, or both.

Finally, the Pulse massacre provided more rhetorical fodder for Donald J. Trump. He suggested that President Obama was to blame. He trumpeted the positive aspects of racial profiling and reiterated his call for a temporary ban on Muslims entering the United States.

Mr. Trump also said the massacre highlighted the need for more guns, not fewer, and imagined a scene in which some in the nightclub had been armed. "And this son of a bitch comes out and starts shooting, and one of the people in that room happened to have it, and goes boom, boom—you know what, that would have been a beautiful, beautiful sight, folks," said Mr. Trump, the presumptive Republican candidate for the presidency.

It was too much, all this death and grief and discord, as if the horrors unleashed at the club were just another excuse to display our grievances and divisions. So respite was sought at one of the many Orlando-area theme parks: Epcot. The $121.41 cost of admission was paid, as well as the $20 for parking.

Then began a slog in 90-degree heat through this permanent world's fair. Past the margarita stands of fake Mexico, the pastries of fake Norway, the orange chicken with rice of fake China, the bratwurst of fake Germany, the tiramisù of fake Italy. On to the air-conditioned comfort of a colonial building featuring the "American Adventure" attraction.

An a cappella group called the Voices of Liberty serenaded visitors with a song that gave a shout-out to every American state. Then guests were directed to some closed white doors and instructed to remain on the blue carpeting and off the gold—at least until these doors opened to the auditorium.

Soon, an animatronic Benjamin Franklin and Mark Twain were leading a half-hour tour of American history, beginning with the Mayflower and ending with a montage of famous American faces and moments: Marilyn Monroe and Magic Johnson, Elvis Presley and Albert Einstein, Walt Disney and Sally Ride, the "I Have a Dream" speech of the Rev. Dr. Martin Luther King Jr., and the image of firefighters raising the American flag at ground zero.

The music swelled, a singer urged America to "spread your golden wings," and the lights came on. With the show over, the audience was directed to exit to the left, past white doors and into the hot glare of what seemed like another country entirely.

Ranchers Say Wall
Won't Help Chaos at Border

NACO, ARIZ. — JULY 24, 2016

John Ladd has two old pickups he uses to bang around his ranch, which rambles for 10 miles beside the Mexico line. One's a red Chevy that not long ago carried the body of yet another border crosser who had died on his property. The other is a blue Dodge with better shocks, and that's what he is driving now, along an unpaved road in an unincorporated place called Naco.

To his immediate right, cattle roam the mesquite and grass of his family's 16,000-acre ranch. To his left, a mix-and-match set of interlocking fences slices into the distance, this one 12 feet high, this one 18 feet high, this one a metal mesh, this one a vertical grille, section after section after section.

Mr. Ladd, 61, looks and acts the way a rancher is expected to, with brush mustache, hard squint and matter-of-fact affect, all kept tight under a sweat-stained cowboy hat. Bouncing westward, he points to spots where fencing had been peeled in the past like an upturned can of Spam. In the last four years, he says, more than 50 vehicles have rumbled through fence cuts and across his property.

What is the protocol when you encounter armed drug smugglers driving on your land? "You pull over and say, 'Adiós,'" Mr. Ladd says. "You don't get in their way, because they'll kill you."

Here is one aspect of everyday life along the southern border, where national demarcations are blurred by the supply and demand for what the United States continues to crave: drugs and cheap labor. The attendant casualties include human rights, property rights, civil discourse and the security of sovereignty.

But is the Great Wall of Trump, as proposed by the Republican candidate for president, the solution to the problems of ranchers like Mr. Ladd? If pixie dust sprinkled into the dry earth could make all the eye-crossing obstacles disappear, beginning with the multibillion-dollar cost, would a concrete divide constructed to Donald J. Trump's aesthetics ("beautiful," with "a big beautiful door") and ever-changing specifications (25 feet high! 35 feet high!! 55 feet high!!!) serve its intended purpose?

The answer heard time and again from Mr. Ladd and others along the border is a weary no.

"The wall?" says Larry Dietrich, a local rancher. "I mean, it's silly."

But what if this beautiful wall—and "wall" is the term used in the Republican Party platform—had a foundation deep enough to discourage tunneling? What if the beautiful concrete panels were designed to thwart climbing over or plowing through? And what if it stretched for hundreds of miles, its beauty interrupted only by rugged, virtually impassable terrain?

"It isn't going to work," Mr. Ladd says.

Ed Ashurst, 65, an outspoken rancher who manages land about 20 miles from the border, is more assertive, but he needs to address something else first. "I'll be straight up with you," he says with a scowl. "If Hillary Clinton gets elected, I'm moving to Australia."

Time will tell whether the Arizona rancher is forced to blend into the Outback, but his assessment of Mr. Trump's plan is just as succinct. "To say you're going to build a wall from Brownsville to San Diego?" he says. "That is the most idiotic thing I've ever heard. And it's not going to change anything."

The solution favored among ranchers is infused with a fatalism that nothing will change—government being government, and the cartels always one step ahead—so why bother. But here it goes:

Intensive, round-the-clock patrols along the border are required for a fence or wall to work; otherwise, those determined to cross will always find a way. But, they argue, if you have boots on the ground, you will have no need for anything so beautiful as the Great Wall of Trump.

It is easy, from a distance, to dismiss the ranchers along the border as right-wing Chicken Littles whose complaints hint of racism. Too easy, in fact.

Ranchers will say they saw people with backpacks trekking across their property last week, last night, early this morning. Some will say they have grudging agreements of access with drug cartels, as long as trespassers stay far from their homes. Dogs bark, motion lights flicker, things go missing.

The unnerving has become everyday life, Mr. Ashurst says, and then he asks my colleague and me where we live. Metropolitan New York, we answer.

Nice, Mr. Ashurst says, still scowling. "But how would you like it?" he asks, referring to the ebb-and-flow parade of strangers, some armed, past his door. "Do you think you're more important than the poor moron who has the misfortune to live along the border?"

True, the overall number of migrants has plummeted in the last 15 years or so. Here, in what the Border Patrol categorizes as the Tucson sector—about 90,000 square miles, with 262 miles of border—there were 63,397 arrests in the 2015 fiscal year, compared with 10 times that in the 2001 fiscal year.

Paul Becson, the patrol's chief agent for the Tucson sector, attributes the drop to an increase in officers and tactical equipment, an improvement in the Mexican economy, and the fencing erected along the border about a decade ago.

But Mr. Ladd and other ranchers say there has been an unsettling swap: fewer migrants, but many more drug traffickers.

Mr. Beeson acknowledges the change in demographics, and the challenge in facing an adversary with comparable intelligence and surveillance abilities. "They don't have to move their product today," he says of the cartels. "They can move it tomorrow. They can sit and watch, and they do that. Watching us. Watching us watching them."

But he says the Border Patrol continues to bolster its "tactical infrastructure"—higher resolution cameras, for example, and an increased use of drones. "It's unacceptable to us that folks along the border should be experiencing this type of activity," Mr. Beeson says. "We're doing all we can."

It is telling, though, that Mr. Ladd never used to carry a gun or a cellphone. That changed six years ago, when his friend Robert Krentz Jr., known to help people no matter their nationality, was shot to death on his family's ranch after radioing his brother that he had come upon another migrant in distress. His unsolved murder caused a national outcry, and it led to state legislation intended to crack down on illegal immigration. It also prompted Mr. Ladd's wife to demand that he carry a cellphone and a Glock.

But, really, what is a Glock going to do?

About 100 miles northeast of Naco, in a New Mexico dot called Animas, a few people gathered recently to sip iced tea and discuss where things stand. The Elbrocks—Tricia and Ed—set the tone by recalling how drug smugglers kidnapped one of their ranch hands a few months ago.

According to the Elbrocks, the smugglers threatened to kill his family, loaded his pickup with packs of marijuana and drove him and the drugs 75 miles to the Arizona town of Willcox. Then they tied him up and abandoned him and the truck the next morning.

A spokesman for the F.B.I. in Albuquerque said the kidnapping remained under investigation. As for the ranch hand, Ms. Elbrock said, "He's in counseling."

The fear, the frustration, the sense of being forsaken—it can be exhausting. "Nothing seems to work, because we keep buying what they bring to sell," said Crystal Foreman Brown, 62, an artist and the host of this iced-tea chat. "But Trump's fence issue at least brings up the issue that there is an issue. For officials in Washington to act like we're being silly and hysterical—it's kind of inconceivable."

Back in Naco, Mr. Ladd continues his dirt-swirling ride between Mexico and his ranch, along a 60-foot road called the Roosevelt Easement. His family has been in Naco for more than a century—before there was a Naco, in fact. Some say the name comes from combining the last two letters of Arizona and Mexico, but Mr. Ladd isn't so sure.

Naco is a drowsy dog of a place that seems not to have benefited much from being a sanctioned port of entry to Mexico. Adding to the stillness is a collection of abandoned barracks, built a century ago for American troops who chased after the Mexican revolutionary Pancho Villa after he attacked the New Mexico town of Columbus.

They never caught him.

Mr. Ladd says his family has sponsored three Mexicans for citizenship—but has seen more border sorrow than joy. Over the years, he says, the bodies of 14 people trying to get someplace else have been found on Ladd property. The last was in September. A party of six got caught in flooding; five were rescued, and the body of the sixth was found several days later.

Mr. Ladd waited for the authorities, but it was getting dark. So he moved the man's body in his red pickup to Route 92, where a funeral home took custody. He recalls the event in that same measured way that underscores how common the uncommon is along the border.

Rumbling west along the rutted road, Mr. Ladd points to his left and, referring to the cartels, says, "This is where they cut the wall down to drive trucks through."

He is like an art museum denizen who has memorized the history of the permanent exhibits, commenting on the changing fence designs as he drives, noting the insignia of the military units who installed some of them on behalf of the Department of Homeland Security.

The truck stops suddenly. "Well lookee there," Mr. Ladd says, pointing to his right. "I got a cut fence." Snipped again, and Lord knows how many times his cows have wandered off as a result.

The rancher slips white work gloves over his rough hands and reaches for a ball of blue hay-baling string. Soon he is stitching together what has been broken, as gunmetal rain clouds move east from the Huachuca Mountains and the wind whistles through the mesh divide.

PART FIVE

Hard Times

Hard times, hard times,
come again no more

Tending the Boulevards of Broken Dreams

FORT MYERS, FLA. — SEPTEMBER 22, 2008

The lawn mower's whine disrupts the morning peace of Coconut Drive like an alarm clock no one remembers setting. It rises and falls and rises again, as the angry machine cuts across the front-lawn jungle of an attractive house with great location and move-in potential.

Abandoned, in other words. Three years ago, sold for $660,000; today, a ghostly parcel of failure.

The lawn mower returns the grass to short uniformity, then growls toward the backyard, passing a two-car garage housing forsaken gardening tools, a basketball hoop no longer conjuring jump-shot dreams and a door leading to a kitchen with a granite-counter island. Now it begins to clear around an in-ground pool brimming with viscous water the color of cash.

The man operating the mower is not a landscaper making his weekly visit, but a city employee trying to stem the blight caused by a boom in property foreclosures. His name is Shayne Becher, and just two hours into his shift the 90-degree mugginess has saturated his city-issue cotton shirt. But that's how it is here in Fort Myers, in this season of rain and recession.

Mr. Becher works for the code enforcement division's rapid response team, which tries to keep up with an ever-growing list of abandoned properties needing to be mowed and boarded up. He is the team's foreman and its only member; his partner recently accepted the buyout the city was offering to reduce its budget.

So Mr. Becher mows and hammers and sweats from 7 in the morning until 3:30 in the afternoon, five days a week, sometimes with help, sometimes not. He may be unable to reverse the plummeting national economy, but at least when he's done, these deserted houses have a curbside appeal that neither offends neighbors nor attracts criminals.

With perspiration beading at the tip of his nose, Mr. Becher uses a blower to clean the sidewalk and driveway, then piles fallen coconuts and other debris at the curb for public works to collect. Before climbing into his truck, he pauses to assess his handiwork at what was once someone's dream house.

"Beautiful," he says. Then he drives a few blocks to another site of abandonment, on Sunset Place.

Come to Fort Myers, population 60,000, the seat of Lee County. Walk the Gulf Coast beaches. Cruise the Caloosahatchee River.

Witness what happens when banks dole out easy mortgages and homeowners forget that the money isn't free. Drive down McGregor Boulevard, or Cleveland Avenue, turn left or turn right, and see the empty houses, the overgrown lots, the signs saying AUCTION and FREE RENT.

Celebrate the fact that, according to RealtyTrac, a listing company, the Fort Myers–Cape Coral area no longer leads the country in foreclosure rates; that is so—July. In August the area ranked sixth, with one in every 66 housing units receiving notice of an auction, repossession or loan default.

One of the fallouts is wholesale abandonment. Michael Titmuss, a former Fort Myers police officer who became the city's manager of code enforcement seven years ago, is seeing new and disturbing trends in the city he loves. Failing condominium associations. Criminals renting deserted buildings they do not own to unsuspecting tenants. More and more no-shows at code enforcement hearings.

"They're desperate," Mr. Titmuss said. "They feel hopeless and they don't know where to turn. They're good people in a bad position. They perceive themselves as unable to comply, as being surrounded by a pack of wolves."

He didn't finish the thought because these days some things are understood: The homeowners walk away, leaving their properties to banks as unwanted parting gifts for having provided risky loans in the first place.

Here in Fort Myers, the code requires that grass be no higher than 12 inches. Otherwise, neighbors complain about property values, rats and snakes receive sanctuary and lurking criminals find easy cover.

If a lawn isn't mowed, a process kicks in. The city mails a courtesy postcard, saying: Time to mow your lawn, neighbor. After that it sends the rapid-response team—that is, Mr. Becher—to mow. Then it bills the homeowner for the service, though these bills often become liens on property that no one wants and banks are not eager to reclaim.

In July, the city mailed at least 600 courtesy cards—more than three times the number sent out the previous July. Still, codes must be enforced; lawns must be mowed. In hiring Mr. Becher several months ago, Mr. Titmuss passed on strange reassurance: "We will train you. And oh, by the way, we've never seen what you're about to deal with."

Mr. Becher, 39, is like a lot of people here: He's from someplace else. He moved a year ago from the small central Michigan city of Greenville, where he was a public works foreman. But his first marriage failed, his patience with small-town nosiness ran out and his side business as a builder came to what he calls "a screeching halt." Just like the Michigan economy.

Now here he is, driving a Ford pickup to Sunset Place, pulling a gasoline-perfumed trailer that contains two riding mowers, three chain saws, five weed whackers, two hedge clippers and a toolbox. He also has two jugs of water, a ham and cheese sandwich and a pages-long list of properties that need to be mowed or boarded up.

He pulls up beside a small, one-story house. City records include a photograph of this house taken in December 2005 that depicts a white convertible and a black dog in the driveway; today the house is a shell, with gaping holes where air conditioners have been yanked out, probably for scrap.

Mr. Becher sets down a foot-high traffic cone beside the knee-high grass, takes a "before" photograph to document the violation, and mounts his mower. He used to begin every job by tromping through the property, searching for debris or tree stumps that might damage the mower's blades. But he saw a snake not long ago, he says. "I'm not much of a snake man."

The mower begins its cringing whine, a kind of keening over these tough times. Mr. Becher expertly maneuvers around corners and bushes, the machine an extension of himself and of bureaucratic efficiency. Until, that is, it lurches to a halt, its gears entwined with a hose hidden in the brush.

"Holy smokes," he says. Using willpower and a knife, he extracts the snakelike hose and gets on with the job.

In the hours to come, Mr. Becher will mow two more lots. He will pass sign after sign saying FREE RENT. He will board up several buildings, including one house containing little more than auction brochures, and another, directly across from a public library, containing the detritus of a crack den. He will meet up with a code-enforcement officer, Ron Giddings, who will ask him: "Can you cut 4040 Rainbow tomorrow? It's next to a day care center, and she's complaining about rats and snakes."

But right now, he is immersed in tidying the messiness of failed plans. He finishes mowing, takes a photograph of a job well done, and closes the chain-link fence as though the property were his own.

"Another day in paradise," he says, standing on this street called Sunset.

Financial Foot Soldiers,
Feeling the Weight of the World

NEW YORK, N.Y. — NOVEMBER 3, 2008

"What's up, Lenny," a broker on the floor of the New York Stock Exchange says, just before the ringing of the Pavlovian bell that opens the financial market. Lenny answers this morning bid with the customary response: "What's up."

Posed less as a sincere inquiry into one's well-being than as a passing nod to another day in the financial scrum, the greeting can also be interpreted in these uncertain times as a question baldly seeking reassurance: What's up?

Stocks? Hopes? Layoffs? Blood pressure?

Leaving unexplored the phrase's deeper meaning, the two brokers melt into a blue-coated sea on the main floor of the exchange, where the Lennys have come to personify the amorphous, temperamental, life-altering thing called Wall Street—an all-encompassing name for the stock market, the economy, your 401(k).

From the balcony above this gladiator's pit, photographers crouch to capture expressions of joy, of anguish, of bewilderment, that are then presented as clues to how we should feel—even though that broker's frown may reflect nothing more than digestive disagreement with a wolfed-down fried egg sandwich.

Not long ago, a floor broker named Danny Trimble cocked a finger to his head and placed it against his temple, for reasons unrelated to the market; soon an image of Mr. Trimble "shooting" himself made the newspapers. No matter that he is not a hedge fund manager, bank C.E.O. or fat cat; no matter that he is just a financial foot soldier from Jersey, hoarse from shouting at his son's Pop Warner football games.

Mr. Trimble, 41, works at the edge of the exchange's main floor, shoulder to shoulder with six other men in a booth the size of an elevator car. Not everyone graduated from college, but all are resident scholars of the hurly-burly floor, educated in reading markets, hunting for matches and executing buy-and-sell orders. They are worth their commissions, they say, because they provide things a computer cannot, things like experience, intuition—a "feel."

Crammed into this booth with no place to sit are Mike Ackerman, Paul Davis, Billy Johnson and Nick Stratakis, of B and B Securities; Mr. Trimble and Chris Martin, of Greywolf Execution Partners; and Ralph Roiland, a clerk. Scrappy independents, all; no one works for Goldman Sachs.

Still, when they step onto Broad and Exchange Streets to breathe the autumn air, they sometimes get blamed for the world's economic crisis. "You walk out there and people think you're what's wrong with this country," says Mr. Martin, father of three, of Morristown, N.J.

With the opening of the market imminent, the men in the booth send instant messages to clients, asking, hoping, for interest in trading stock. But the volatile activity in recent weeks has unnerved many investors; some respond with noncommittal "Thanks" and "I'm away from my desk."

At 9:30 on the dime the opening bell rings, clanging off the century-old walls of white marble, the ornate ceiling of gold. Brokers rush to the center of the floor, where specialists in individual stocks track the last best data. Shouts of "Buy off 10,000, pair off 10,000," and "How's Marathon?" feed the low roar of business.

After a while, though, quiet returns. Brokers study computer screens in their booths, some to monitor stocks, some to play virtual games. In one corner, a man is deciphering a crossword puzzle, while three beside him play cards. The stock exchange has a different rhythm now, its denizens say, because of technological advances and the shrinking of the once-dominant house firms. It's not like before.

Many of the men, and it's still almost all men, remember the days when they stood several deep around the specialists, nudging, pushing, staying put for several straight hours, shouting "Squad!" for pages to hustle handwritten notes to clerks on the wings, jockeying at the banks of phones now hanging from hooks like relics.

Those were the days when black humor and practical jokes helped to blow off steam and show affection for comrades. The one-liners would fly minutes after, say, the space shuttle Challenger went down. A trader would return to work, disfigured, after a serious car accident to find at his station a toy car, burned and crushed. And he would laugh.

Billy Johnson, 48, a burly former firefighter from Oceanport, N.J., recalls how his floor colleagues helped him to toast his approaching marriage: by ripping his jacket and covering him with shaving cream, perfume and potato chips.

The jokes and put-downs still go on, and lately someone has been beeping a horn concealed in his jacket. But the humor is not quite as black.

"A lot of that stopped after 9/11," says Doreen Mogavero, 53, an experienced floor broker who points out that ground zero is a couple of blocks away. "It wasn't that funny anymore."

Gone too is the loud physicality. Headsets and hand-held computerized pads mean less running around, fewer clerks, softer voices, a smaller chance for error. Those technological advances have opened the market to just about anyone with a computer, making floor trading seem almost quaint. Many traders retired rather than change their ways; others were laid off, including one now walking through the exchange. Selling insurance, someone says.

Of the 1,366 broker's licenses available for an annual fee of $40,000, only 553 are being used. In 2006 there were 3,534 people working on the floor; today there are 1,273.

"The stress now is the lack of business," says Benedict Willis III, 48, a senior broker who started here in 1982. Moments later he is interrupted by applause. It is the sound of a lost job: A floor broker of 20 years has just been laid off from a major firm, and now his colleagues are showing their respect.

"They're clapping him off," Mr. Willis says. "It's the second one this week."

One of the brokers in that small booth, Mike Ackerman, leads a Scandinavian delegation on a brief tour of the exchange, past computer screens flashing red and green, past taped-up photographs of family members, closed baseball stadiums and the Lower Manhattan skyline when it was intact. As he takes them to the balcony, a delegate asks a question in halting English: Does Mr. Ackerman feel personally responsible for the collapsing economy?

Good question, answers Mr. Ackerman, 39, father of three, from Basking Ridge, N.J. Good question. But—no.

He and all the people down on that floor are executing trades on behalf of others, using a hybrid method that combines a computer's technology with a human's gut instinct. They do not deal in subprime mortgages; they do not get golden parachutes. But hey: Good question.

These brokers make money whether the market goes up or down; their earnings depend on the volume of trades, and the floor averages 117 million orders received a day. Still, they prefer north to south. "It's political economics," Mr. Willis explains. "We want to reassure investors that it's O.K. to come back."

Tomorrow the market will plummet in the very last minutes. Beaten brokers will repair to bars like Bobby Van's across the street, where the bartenders know their drinks before they've ordered.

But right now the market climbs with every tick toward the 4 p.m. closing, as though willed to rise by all the Lennys now eyeing the electronic board. Up, up, up.

"Two minutes to go," someone says at 3:58. "A lifetime."

At an Age for Music
and Imagination, Real Life
Is Intruding

NEWARK, OHIO — APRIL 15, 2009

Two days before their long-awaited trip to New York City, for many of them a foreign place, the members of the Newark High School Sinfonia noisily gather for rehearsal. The cacophony ends when the first of the first violinists, the best violinist, stands to lead others in tuning to an A.

Her name is Tiffany Clay and she is 18, with light brown hair tied in a ponytail and large eyes that always seem at the edge of tears. She has been on her own, more or less, since she was 16, and the violin in her delicate hands was bought for $175 on eBay by her music teacher.

She is a complicated young woman, says that teacher, and a gifted musician. Consistently at or near the very top of her class. Should be going to a top college, on scholarship. Should be, but won't be, because she feels a need to make money more than music.

Ms. Clay is a child of her age and place, worried about being laid off, uninterested in and maybe even afraid of imagining a life beyond central Ohio. Newark is what she knows: a pleasant, bifurcated city of 45,000, where concerns about unemployment temper the pride in local public art, and where affluence and poverty sit side-by-side in the classroom.

She once explored the idea of going away to college to become a music teacher. But it just didn't seem practical: spending four years studying the theory of music, which doesn't interest her, while here in Newark, the school system is constantly adapting to real and threatened cuts.

Music programs always seem among the first to go, she says. No job security in Tchaikovsky.

So she is maintaining high grades, playing in the orchestra, working 35 hours a week as a Sonic Drive-In carhop, paying $345 a month for the small apartment she shares with an unemployed boyfriend—and planning to study nursing for two years at a technical college in Newark.

"Everybody gets sick," she says, plotting her future.

Right now, though, she and the other students are rehearsing their string instruments for a high school orchestra competition that will take place in Lincoln Center. Soon the chatter of teenagers in a mostly empty school auditorium surrenders to the music of the masters.

"Listen," says their teacher, Susan Larson, her baton paused in mid-sway. "Listen."

Ms. Larson, 43, the Newark school system's music director for the past three years, faces challenges beyond those presented on sheets of music. The city's voters keep rejecting raises in the tax levy, forcing cuts in school programs, including music. Parents now pay $55 for a child to participate in activities like this orchestra, and $200 to play sports; if next month's proposed levy is defeated, Ms. Larson doubts that the orchestra, for one, will survive.

When she struggles to pay for repairs to instruments, many of which are long-ago hand-me-downs from another school district, she recalls her 15 years as the music director in Bexley, a more affluent city where her budget was nowhere

near as tight. She vividly remembers
the Bexley student who celebrated
graduation by smashing a $10,000
violin—his spare.

She cried then; it hurts more now.

Here in Newark, half the students
are poor enough to receive lunch free
or at a discount. The system also has
one of the highest dropout rates in
Ohio; nearly a third of the high school
students do not graduate. That elevated percentage seems out of place given the
Middle America setting, but officials have a theory:

Back in the day, you could drop out and still get a good job at one of the many
manufacturing plants in town. You could pay the mortgage, buy a car new, take
holiday trips—all without a high school diploma.

"Now those jobs have gone away," says Keith Richards, the city's schools
superintendent. "But the mind-set has not."

Mayor Bob Diebold, 48, who grew up here, agrees. "You could walk out of
school and get a job," he says. "You can't do that anymore."

Actually, you can—only those jobs are more likely to be at McDonald's and not,
say, at the Owens Corning fiberglass plant, for generations a vital part of the Newark
economy. Nine years ago the plant employed about 1,500; now, fewer than 700.

Rehearsal ends and the young musicians flee, a few in cars driven by parents.
Ms. Clay, though, drives her 1998 Chevy Malibu to wash clothes for her New
York trip at the Colonial Coin Laundry, then heads to her home in a weathered
apartment complex—the unit, she says, "right next to the Dumpster."

The apartment contains little more than a bed, television and couch, now
occupied by her boyfriend, Trevor Scanlon, who dropped out of high school but
says he's working on his graduate-equivalency diploma. Slinking about is their cat,
Easy Mac, named after a macaroni and cheese that you microwave.

The short life story Ms. Clay tells is of an adulthood come too soon, of parents
splitting up when she was young, of a mother gone to another city, of a father, an
electrician, dogged by employment uncertainties. She and her father clashed so
often, she says, that she moved out at 16, got a job and tried to figure out life—
rent, work, school, some health issues—on her own.

She returned after a year but left again several months later, for good, though she is in touch with her parents, and talks often of wanting to be around in case they ever need her.

While working full time at the Sonic, she has also maintained superior grades, taken several Advanced Placement courses and distanced herself from classmates. She bristles when some of them talk of what they have spent at the Easton Town Center mall—"That's a month's rent," she wants to say—but at the same time she admits to feeling jealous: "I want—that!"

Now wearing a yellow Sonic golf shirt and a Tiffany C. nameplate, Ms. Clay leaves to make $7.35 an hour, plus tips; it will be a long night. "Kids are in school during the week," she explains. "They leave at 9, and I stay until after 11."

Soon she is gliding on roller skates beneath neon reds and yellows that grow more garish as dusk descends. Spinning, speeding, stopping with effortless grace, she balances plastic trays of sweet and greasy food with those delicate hands. Her mastery of yet another world, this Sonic world, means she is again employee of the month, entitling her to a month of free meals.

And the lyrics of her night songs are:

"All right, I've got your three junior chili cheese wraps, a B.L.T., chicken strip sandwich, extra long Coney and a mozzarella stick. And a kid's hot dog meal and kid's hamburger meal, one with a grape slush, the other with a Powerade slush."

Two mornings later, buses whisk the Newark High School Sinfonia and its entourage to New York: Austin Modesitt, 16, violinist, who has never left Ohio, but whose mother, a factory worker, contributed her tax-refund check; Jessica Kunasek, 17, violinist, whose older siblings chipped in to pay her way; other students, who sold chocolate, washed cars, held a spaghetti dinner—anything to cover the cost of $850 a student.

Now it is Sunday. They have spent three days in a Manhattan wonderland, but the time has come to compete for something called the National Orchestra Cup. They file into the just renovated Alice Tully Hall at Lincoln Center and put on their school-owned tuxedos and gowns.

A few of the invited high schools had to decline; the recession, organizers explain. But others, from Ohio and California, New York and Indiana, have made it, and their instruments, at least in Ms. Larson's estimation, are of higher quality.

Newark is the last to perform, following a symphony orchestra—with strings, brass, winds, percussion and a harp—from Carmel, Ind., where the median household income is nearly three times that in Newark. The Carmel students seem at home in Lincoln Center; they play exquisitely.

The Newark students take the stage, led by concertmaster Tiffany Clay and trailed by director Susan Larson. First, a toccata by Frescobaldi. Then a cello duet by Vivaldi, sweetly rendered by juniors Bryn Wilkin and Alex Van Atta. Finally, the first movement of Tchaikovsky's Serenade for Strings.

Soon there come sounds just beyond articulation, of sorrow and joy and wonder, summoned from wood and string by the children of Newark, Ohio. And Ms. Clay, at the front of the stage, disappears into the music.

Enchanted by Pachelbel as a child, given free lessons by a teacher who recognized her talent, blessed with the gift of musical sight reading, Ms. Clay has not been as fortunate with other parts of her young life. Her worries are not about prom dresses but about family, and rent, and employment.

Soon, these students will be back in Newark, proud of tying for first runner-up, behind that orchestra from Carmel. And Ms. Clay will be back at the Sonic, spinning her wheels, singing her song of limeades and cheeseburgers, easy on the mayo. After that, nursing, probably.

What role music will play in her life, she doesn't know. But for now, at least, she is on a New York stage, wearing a borrowed black gown, playing a borrowed eBay violin, and Tchaikovsky holds her.

EPILOGUE

Tiffany Clay received a scholarship to Oklahoma City University. Her studies there and at Oklahoma State University centered mostly on nursing. She also became a mother.

In 2014, she and her son, Leif, moved back to Newark, Ohio. She reconnected with family members and eventually got a job as an employment specialist at Licking Memorial Hospital, where she works at what she says is the very rewarding task of helping at-risk high school students.

Music has taken a back seat in her life. Now she plays the violin—and, more and more, the piano—for enjoyment.

"Overall, life has improved," Ms. Clay said. "There are still moments, especially for people from lower-middle-class backgrounds. But that's okay: You just roll with it."

In a City Under Strain, Ladling Out Fortification

In the immaculate kitchen of an old social club now receiving the gray morning light, a deep silver pot has been filled with buckets and buckets of cold water. The cook measures not by the quart but by the heart, so if you ask exactly how much water, the answer is: exactly the right amount.

With her navy beans washed, her beef shanks unwrapped, her kale and cabbage ready to be chopped by hand, the time has come to make another batch of restorative soup for ailing Fall River. She lights the stove.

Her name is Ines De Costa, but the city calls her Vovó, familiar Portuguese for grandmother. She is 76, with salt-white hair and a small body transformed by spinal degeneration into the shape of a cupped hand. This means she must stand on tiptoe to stir.

Among the many soups in Ms. De Costa's oceanic repertoire are those with a specific purpose, including a chicken-and-potato concoction for pregnant women. But the soup she is making now, this Portuguese soup she learned from her mother, is for a working-class city with 16 percent unemployment, nearly double the average in Massachusetts and recently raised by the layoffs of dozens of police officers and firefighters.

For $3.50, you get a heaping bowl of nourishing soup, a fresh Portuguese roll and some butter. "It's a disaster in Fall River," she says, her accent still strong nearly 60 years after leaving the Azores. "No work, everybody loses their jobs."

So this is what Vovó says: You want another roll?

Ms. De Costa rises well before dawn from the hospital bed her children installed in her Somerset cottage several years ago. There, surrounded by portraits and statues of Jesus, the Blessed Virgin and a host of saints, including her beloved St. Teresa of Ávila, who suffered so, she begins her morning ritual of praying for you, me, everyone. Then a cup of coffee, decaf.

Every day except Monday, her daughter, Ines Bates, who tries in vain to get her fragile mother to cut down on these 70-hour weeks, drives her across the Taunton River to Fall River. Past the triple-decker houses and ghostly mills, the run-down housing project and the Portuguese bakery, to here: the St. John's Athletic Club, a social anchor of the Maplewood section since before the Depression, and the place where Vovó has run a restaurant for 30 years.

On one side of a wall: the bar, where Quaker Fabric factory workers once lined the counter two deep; no bar stools necessary. But the factory, which employed more than 2,000 people just a few years ago, closed in 2007, forcing the shot-and-beer bar to adjust. There is Friday night karaoke now, and if for some reason you suddenly crave an appletini, the St. John's can provide.

At 8:30 this morning, though, only a few men disturb the emptiness, a couple of them presiding over shot glasses with Dunkin' Donuts chasers.

On the other side of the wall: the kitchen-and-dining-room domain of Ms. De Costa, now chopping kale. She slices away the spines with surgical precision, rolls several leaves together, then chops, her gold wedding ring winking from the dark-green mound. Her cherished husband, Manuel, died 20 years ago; he too made a good soup.

She could buy the kale and cabbage already chopped, but she insists the strips sit better in the bowl when cut by hand. All leavings, by the way, from tired cabbage bits to day-old bread, are set aside for a man in Westport who keeps goats.

"Like St. Francis," she says.

The club is silent, save for knife-blade clicks in the kitchen and billiard-ball clacks in the bar. Ms. De Costa rarely goes into the bar, and only then to raise money for one of her many causes: an orphanage in Calcutta, a local nursing home, the occasional destitute dead in need of a coffin.

When asked if she takes a drink now and then, the saintly, knife-wielding Ms. De Costa snaps, "Hell, no."

The pot burbles. She reaches up with a spoon and stirs the brown broth.

Outside the club spreads a city of 95,000 that is all too familiar with hard times. Once a textile manufacturing capital, the city has spent most of the last

century trying to adapt, as the industry moved away, as fires burned the downtown, as revitalization plans remained only plans. Its motto, "We'll Try," sounds almost apologetic.

The mayor, Robert Correia, is the latest to try. This month he announced a many-faceted plan to turn Fall River into a center of renewable energy that would attract businesses, create jobs and make use of the city's many old mills. It includes the ambitious and expensive proposal to "daylight"—or unearth—the muscular Quequechan River, once the generator of power for all those mills, but diverted long ago into pipes beneath the city.

The city clearly needs daylight, hope—a plan. In the meantime, how about some soup? The mayor has known Vovó for nearly 40 years; he knows all about her charitable works, her influence on local-boy-made-good Emeril Lagasse, her portions so plentiful that customers usually leave with leftovers.

"She's one of these people you never hear from because they're too busy holding up the rest of us, and we don't realize it," he says. As for her Portuguese soup: "In Fall River you would say it's the kind your mother made."

At 11:10, Ms. De Costa removes the shanks to dice their meat. As she trims the fat, she remembers how her father used to love a piece of fat in his Portuguese soup, topped with a splash of red wine. When she arrived here in 1952 at 19, he told her: "Everybody in America drinks from the same glass"—meaning everyone's the same.

"As I find out, this is not the case," she says.

Soon Ms. De Costa has mixed all the ingredients together into the pot: kale and cabbage, beans and beef, some ground chorizo, and salt; just the right amount. She stirs again, then taps the spoon against the pot's lip, as if instructing the ingredients to cooperate with one another for the next two hours. She can be stern; just ask her waitresses.

The Tuesday lunch crowd arrives, if it can be called a crowd. Times are tough too at the club, where the motto on the lottery machine—"This is your lucky day!"—can seem like a taunt. A couple of years ago, though, Ms. De Costa bought a ticket, won $1,000 and immediately sent it all to those orphans in Calcutta.

Her daughter, Ms. Bates, has given up cautioning her mother about her endless giving of money and, especially, of food. Some days the business makes money, sometimes it does not. "She says God will provide," the daughter says, smiling a helpless smile.

Says the mother, "I like to see everybody leave full."

Sometime around 2, with drab skies threatening rain, Susan Bertrand, a nurse, and John Arruda, a cement truck driver, arrive for lunch. It's been a tough year, they say, as they count all the friends and relatives who have lost jobs. Mr. Arruda, in fact, just started working after a three-month layoff.

She orders the steak sandwich, he orders the chorizo sandwich, and they both order the Portuguese soup, now ready to be served. Out come two sustaining cups of Vovó.

Delicious, they say.

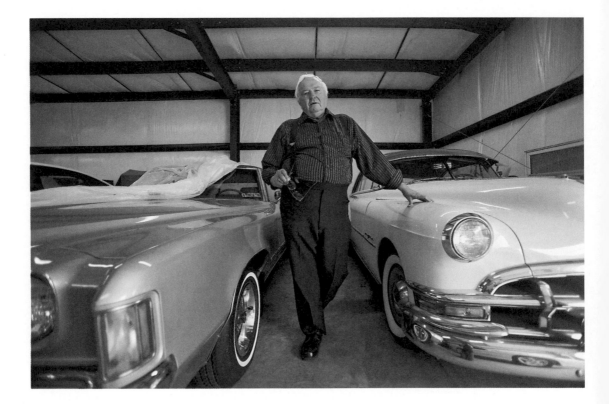

After Lifetimes Selling Pontiacs, Feeling Sold Out

HOUSTON, PA. — MAY 4, 2009

The Arnold Pontiac dealership is not one of those glass-encased bazaars winking from the main drag, with a showroom the size of a parking lot and a name that sounds like a law firm with too many partners: "Acme Chevrolet Buick Jeep Hyundai Volkswagen Kia Saab. How may I direct your call?"

No, Arnold Pontiac pretty much says it all.

The dealership sits exactly where the Arnold family began a car business back in 1916: on the corner of North Main and East Pike in the pit-stop western Pennsylvania town of Houston, right next to the First Presbyterian Church, where Arnolds are baptized. Small showroom downstairs, service and parts upstairs, free Pontiac calendars everywhere.

Until a few days ago, the Arnolds had a plan. In the tradition of his father and grandfather, Bob the white-haired elder, 74, would be turning the dealership over to his son, Bob the dark-haired younger, 44. The handoff would have happened sooner if not for the embezzlement of $400,000 a couple of years ago by a longtime employee who was like family and who, it turned out, liked to gamble.

But a far deeper betrayal came last week, the Arnolds say, when another family member and poor gambler, General Motors, announced that by 2010 it would close its Pontiac division and 2,600 of its 6,200 dealerships—all to convince a doubtful Obama administration that it had a business plan strong enough to beat a bankruptcy deadline of June 1 and to deserve more government loans.

Pontiac: The Official Car of the 2009 Economic Crisis.

Small, out-of-the-way Arnold Pontiac sells only Pontiacs, GMC trucks and used cars, so the Arnolds figure their G.M. warranty is about to expire. "It was just like getting kicked in the stomach," says the elder Mr. Arnold, who sold his first car in 1950, to a local man named Paxton. ("Pontiac Catalina. Two-door hardtop. It was cream and rust.")

His son, who started working at the dealership when he was 6, using a step stool to dust the tops of gleaming Bonnevilles and GTOs, is still trying to process the apparent evaporation of this chunk of his inheritance. "I'm not going to entertain that just yet," says the younger Mr. Arnold, who sold his first car in 1987. ("Green Sunbird.")

As Detroit and Washington work to save the car industry from going over a cliff like some roadster in a black-and-white melodrama, entire families have

been upended—families that long ago linked their surname to the name of Pontiac in commercial banns of marriage.

For example, the Arnolds are friends with the Mikans, a longtime Pontiac family in Butler, about 60 miles north of here. Robert Mikan, 76, and his son, David, 39, watched last Monday's devastating news conference on a computer screen in their dealership, in a back room where an old plaque from the Pennsylvania Automotive Association hangs tilted on the gray paneled wall.

After a while the son, whose first sale was a used white 1988 Pontiac Grand Prix, turned to his father, whose first sale was a gray 1946 Pontiac Torpedo, and said, "Dad, I think that's it."

They knew the end had come to a legacy dating to Robert's father, Ivan, who started a car business in the town of Trafford in 1924, sold Chryslers and Hudsons for a while, then settled on Pontiacs. That was 70 years ago.

Such excitement back then. Every year Ivan Mikan would paper over his showroom windows, building excitement, before unveiling the new Pontiac models at a reception where men wore suits and women wore dresses. Ladies and gentlemen, introducing:

Your 1951 Pontiac Chieftain! And yes, that hood ornament lights up! Your 1958 Pontiac Bonneville! America's No. 1 road car!

Your 1968 Pontiac GTO! We call it The Great One!

"That's a lot of years working for a brand and for a division that is now going to be defunct," says Robert Mikan, who keeps a 1975 Pontiac Grand Ville convertible, red with white interior, in a garage out back.

David Mikan, who runs the dealership now, says their sales of Pontiacs have steadily declined: 100 sold last year, compared with twice that in 2000. Although the emphasis has shifted to their Volkswagen line and their used cars, he says, the Mikans have always considered themselves a Pontiac family.

Still, a few days ago he removed all the preening Pontiacs from the front of the dealership and replaced them with shiny Volkswagens. Partly out of anger, he says, and partly because Volkswagen, not Pontiac, is central to the Mikan future.

Back in Houston, there is no Volkswagen fallback. The Arnolds have been hitched to Pontiacs since 1926, the year the car made its debut. Because of Pontiac, Bob Arnold the elder attended the General Motors Institute in Flint, Mich., more than a half-century ago. Because of Pontiac, then, he happened to meet his future wife, Angela, at an institute dance.

"Girls got in free," recalls Ms. Arnold, whose first car was a 1955 Pontiac Star Chief Catalina, turquoise and ivory. Now she drives a 2005 Pontiac Bonneville, candy-apple red.

It is quiet now in the dealership's office, save for the whoosh of passing cars outside, few of them Pontiacs.

A man pops his head in long enough to say: "Thanks, Bob. That was a good deal you gave my sister."

The visit underscores what Mr. Arnold has been saying about how small dealerships have cultivated relationships that span generations. Yes, Pontiac made mistakes, but Pontiac traditionally enticed younger people to join the G.M. family.

Mr. Arnold wonders about the future—what about their 20 employees?—and soon that wonder turns to complaint. G.M. should never have gotten rid of the Bonneville. G.M. sacrificed Pontiac to save Buick. It's all about the Buick market in China, which comes at the expense of American jobs. In the end, G.M. betrayed its family.

But Susan Garontakos, a G.M. spokeswoman, responds with a sobering perspective. The Pontiac line has been unprofitable for several years, she says. G.M. is trying to develop a survival plan under the government's deadline. Plants are closing and people are losing their jobs—including her son-in-law.

"It's hitting everyone," she says.

Mr. Arnold walks across the still showroom, shoes squeaking on the treated floor. He passes a display case of family memorabilia. Portraits of his parents and grandparents. A row of souvenir pens. A hood ornament whose amber glow once announced to the night: Here comes another Pontiac.

He starts talking about how discouraged he is, but interrupts himself long enough to hand a visitor a 2009 calendar, courtesy of Arnold Pontiac, Houston, Pennsylvania.

Under Gavel, Where Loss Transforms into Gain

SALT LAKE CITY, UTAH — JULY 6, 2009

Bid, Bid, BID, the auctioneer implores, serenading the curious and meek with the trills and yammers of his trade. Nearly 20 foreclosed properties are up for auction here in the great state of Utah, ladies and gentlemen, and now is your chance to turn an empty house back into a home.

Dozens of potential bidders sit before him in various states of intimidation, clutching bidding cards as thin as paper and heavy as brick. A few of them scribble out notes like racetrack rookies posturing as touts, calculating the odds of some dark-horse deal.

Whenever a bidder manages to lift a card, or nod, or wave, an auction assistant prowling the aisles gives praise—"Yes!" He wears a tuxedo, as if to bestow class upon an indelicate process in which one's gain comes from another's loss.

"Yes!" the assistant yelps again and again, making the Grand Ballroom of a Hilton hotel somehow less so. He challenges bidders in the throes of uncertainty with the cock of an eyebrow and the jut of a finger, as if to ask, Is there something wrong? Are you crazy? Don't you want to own your dream home?

"Yes! Yes! Yes!"

If it's Tuesday, then this must be Salt Lake City for a California company called the Real Estate Disposition Corporation; R.E.D.C., for short. Its employees barnstorm the country like a carnival troupe, staging auctions for banks and other lenders eager to reduce their groaning inventories of failure.

Since May 2007, the company has held more than 400 events, putting up for auction more than 50,000 houses and condominiums that fell into foreclosure during these singular times. But beware, you buyers with checkbooks in trembling hand. Each property has a minimum sales price unknown to bidders; if the auction doesn't hit that number, the lender can reject the sale.

Yesterday was Colorado, tomorrow will be Michigan, but tonight is Utah, where an R.E.D.C. representative begins the auction by commending those in the audience for being "part of the solution to the current economic crisis."

And now the auctioneer is singing his way down the brick-and-mortar list, sharing little more than the number of bedrooms and bathrooms in each structure.

So a modest $215,000 condo in Heber City (once owned by an electrician, said to have been a good father, dead of lung cancer at 38) is sold at $110,000. And a tired $139,100 condo in Orem (where a man sexually assaulted a woman one night, then lost his government job after being convicted) is sold at $95,000. And a hilltop mansion in Draper (where a man who calls himself a "preservation mechanic" mows the lawn and makes the creepy, cavernous place look both neat and lived in) is overvalued at $3 million and sold at $605,000.

Halfway through the night, the auctioneer comes to Item No. 1104: an eight-bedroom house in South Jordan. The bidding quickly hits 250, as in $250,000, then rises to 255, 260, 265, 270, while the auctioneer pleads and the assistant kneels before a potential bidder, as if proposing.

"I'm at 270!" the auctioneer calls. "Don't lose it! Don't lose it!"

But before another hand rises to bid, and before the auctioneer's gavel slams down in confirmation of deal closed, next deal, it might be instructive to visit this vacated house in South Jordan, on West Rambouillet Drive. A man named Paul Furse, who knows this house's every inch, stands at its locked door and begins to tell its story.

Years ago a developer bought an old sheep ranch and carved it into lots for sale. In the spring of 2002, Mr. Furse bought a third-acre parcel on a corner for $68,000. Then he set out to build a house by hand, although not alone; he had the assistance of his wife, Teri, and their four children, the oldest just 15.

Mr. Furse was 40, blond, sturdy, and nothing if not determined. He had never built a house before, but he had been in and around construction most of his life, remodeling rooms, jobs like that. "I got a bee in my bonnet and just wanted to build a house," he says.

The family, living then in a small house in a nearby town, assisted the architect by sketching out what they wanted: the bedrooms, the second-story catwalk, the office, the crafts room, the sprawling family area with a wood stove. A construction loan was secured, the foundation was laid—and just like that, the Furse Family Construction Company began to build.

The whole endeavor sounds improbable, but the family filmed the seven-month construction. Here is Kelsi, 15, using a pneumatic nail gun to assemble a wall; Kira, 13, holding steady a beam that will help to support the second story; Haylie, 10, nails in her mouth, applying shingles to the roof; Dean, 7, handing his father some wood, playing with a toy truck.

They listened to FM radio, broke for sandwiches at lunch, scraped knees, played on a makeshift swing, drenched themselves in water to keep cool, tried to keep up with schoolwork. Kelsi and Kira sometimes used carpenter's pencils to do their math-assignment calculations on the unfinished walls and floors.

Most of all, everyone just worked, sun-up, sun-down, six days a week. And when they were done, the Furses had built a home in time for Thanksgiving.

Peering now into the locked house, his head beside a "Warning—No Trespassing" sign, Mr. Furse recalls it all. The wedding portrait on display in the master bedroom. The color schemes chosen by each child for their bedrooms:

Dean, a bright green; Haylie, a sky blue; Kelsi, a tan with a rag-rolled look; and Kira, a crazy, Pollock-like spattering of blue, green and purple. The window view of a Mormon church's gleaming white steeple, set against the backdrop of the Wasatch Mountains.

It is difficult to say when the house that had become a home became just a house again. Mr. Furse used the property as security to finance a couple of business deals that foundered—mostly, he says, because of betrayals by partners. The money wasn't coming in, the tension built, and everyone sensed this wondrous family accomplishment turning into a burden.

"I could feel it slipping," Kelsi recalls.

Foreclosure proceedings came in 2006, followed by a bankruptcy filing to buy some time, and then, finally, a strangely welcoming release. Mr. Furse likens the experience to the last lingering days of a sick, older relative. "You hate to see them go," he says. "But what a relief."

Today the family is renting a much more modest house a few miles away—it has no view to speak of—while Kelsi, now a married mother of a toddler, lives nearby. Not long ago she drove past the house she helped to build, only to find it, she says, "remarkably alien." A home, she has decided, is where your family is.

Mr. Furse agrees. He says that even though he lost the house, the building of it bonded his family in ways beyond words. Still, he admits, "I'd have been happy if they'd have buried me in the backyard."

Bam! The auctioneer's gavel pounds home the deal for the winning bidders, who say they're looking to invest in real estate. Sold, subject to seller's approval, for $275,000: a house in which the calculations of children are in the woodwork.

Donna's Diner: At the Corner of Hope and Worry

ELYRIA, OHIO — OCTOBER 14, 2012

Another day begins with a sound softer than a finger-snap, in an Ohio place called Elyria. In the central square of this small city, the gushing water fountain applauds the early-morning chorus of sparrows. A car clears its throat. A door slams. And then: click.

The faint sound comes as 7:00 flashes on the clock of the Lorain National Bank building, looming over the square. The pull of a string—click—has sent life pulsing through a neon sign, announcing to all of Elyria that, once more, against the odds, Donna's Diner is open.

Its proprietor, Donna Dove, 57, ignites the grill that she seems to have just turned off, so seamlessly do her workdays blend into one endless shift. She wears her blond hair in a ponytail and frames her hazel eyes with black-rimmed glasses that tend to get smudged with grill grease. She sees the world through the blur of her work.

A dozen years ago, Donna found a scrap of serendipity on the sidewalk: a notice that a local mom-and-pop restaurant was for sale. After cooking for her broken family as a child, after cooking for county inmates at one of her many jobs, she had come to see food as life's binding agent, and a diner as her calling. She maxed out her credit cards, cashed in her 401(k) and opened a business to call her own.

Donna's Diner. Donna's.

You know this place: It is Elyria's equivalent to that diner, that coffee shop, that McDonald's. From the vantage point of these booths and Formica countertops, the past improves with distance, the present keeps piling on, and a promising future is practically willed by the resilient patrons.

It is where the recession and other issues of the day are lived as much as discussed. Where expectations for a certain lifestyle have been lowered and hopes for salvation through education and technology have been raised. Where the presidential nominees Barack Obama and Mitt Romney each hope that his plan for a way back will resonate with the Donna Doves, who try to get by in places like Elyria—where the American dream they talk about can sometimes seem like a tease.

But for now, at least, the door to Donna's is open. So take a seat. Have a cup of coffee. Maybe some eggs.

This morning, as usual, Pete Aldrich is helping Donna through the new-dawn isolation, turning on the coffee and being compensated by food and tips from the occasional delivery. In his early 50s, well-educated and from regional royalty, he has hit some hard times, and may or may not have slept in his car last night, cocooned by his bundled possessions.

Pete tries, though, he tries. He often leaves straight from Donna's for a job interview, hustling out with purpose, no matter that his thick-lensed eyeglasses are missing one arm. Something will turn up.

That is the communal hope. Donna, for example, is dogged by the day's anxieties. Why are her receipts going down? What lunch special can she offer to clean out the refrigerator? Should she buy less perch for her Friday fish fry?

Can she slide a month on her electric bill? Since she already doesn't have health insurance, what else can she cut?

"I'm just going in circles and circles and circles," Donna says one day, gazing through smudged glasses. "And not getting anyplace."

The fresh aroma of coffee face-slaps the air. Soon the Breakfast Club regulars, that gaggle of Elyrian past and present, will be here to renew their continuing discussion of what was, is and isn't in this city of 55,000. The presidential election sometimes serves as a conversation starter, like a curio placed between the salt and pepper shakers.

The talk will continue as yolk stains harden and refills turn tepid. Their Ohio is a swing state, after all, and their Elyria sits precariously on that swing. More Democratic than Republican, it has several global companies and the memory of many more; an embattled middle class and encroaching poverty; and the faint sense that the Next Big Thing better arrive before even its beloved park fountain, visible from the diner's front window, gets shut off.

Of course, the friendly political quarrel between the regulars Speedy Amos, 86, Republican, and Jim Dall, 89, Democrat, dates back to "I Like Ike" and "All The Way With Adlai." And John Haynes, lawyer, Democrat, and Jack Baird, councilman, Republican, will debate without ever changing minds. It will be others, the quiet, still-undecided ones, who will help to make the big decision, Obama or Romney.

The diner waits. Pete sips coffee and reads The Chronicle-Telegram through the damaged glasses he hopes to replace someday. Donna stands by the front door, near her Friday fish fry sign, peering through the plate-glass window with expectation. If it were only about location—well, she has it.

Her diner, in an 1880s brick building at the corner of Middle Avenue and Second Street, sits along the central park, Ely Square, where the fountain's mist blesses those who linger and a statue of a Union soldier rises from slab memorials for every American conflict from the War of Independence (1775-1783) to the War on Terrorism (2001-).

The diner is near the majestic old courthouse, circa 1881, now mostly empty, in some disrepair and too costly to renovate. It is a short walk from the sleek new courthouse, where the Judge, a regular customer (grilled chicken, cottage cheese, fruit), ruminates in his chambers with an unlit cigar in his mouth and a portrait of Che Guevara on his wall.

It is a few storefronts away from a temp agency, where a large man in an Ohio State cap (cheeseburger, fries) dispatches the work-hungry to fleeting jobs, and a short walk from Loomis Camera, 62 years on the square, where the nonagenarian owner displays a decades-old portrait of his wife, before her arthritis, back when she was a beautiful trapeze artist, an airborne ballerina.

Finally, the diner faces City Hall, where the new mayor (bacon-lettuce-tomato-and-fried-egg sandwich and a side salad) confronts the challenges of a postindustrial, recession-haunted American city. A fourth-generation Elyrian, Mayor Holly Brinda takes hope in the city's entrepreneurial hothouse of a community college and in northeastern Ohio's can-do DNA. But some nights she cannot sleep.

Donna also knows what it means to lose sleep in Elyria, as she stands beside her closed cash register, a diner's miscellany spread out before her: a jar of 25-cent mints that certain people think are free; a spill of business cards for Vinnie's Collision Center and LePue Drain Cleaning; a box of minted toothpicks favored by the Judge; a small Southern Comfort bottle half-filled with the maple syrup that sweetens Mr. Dall's pancakes.

When the diner's door is open, Donna can hear the aching thrum of another one of the Norfolk Southern freight trains that clatter day and night through the city. Bound for Cleveland or Chicago with endless containers of goods made across the country and overseas, they slice through Elyria, once more prominent as a maker of things.

The familiar freight-train siren can conjure memories of the writer Sherwood Anderson, who once ran a mail-order and paint business down by the railroad line. One Thanksgiving Day, he said goodbye to his secretary, walked out the door and followed the tracks east, out of Elyria. A breakdown, apparently, one that led to his fictional classic "Winesburg, Ohio," whose inhabitants, including some with distinctly Elyrian traits, ache for fulfillment.

Yes, Donna hears it. She also hears the Judge—James M. Burge, the meticulously dressed administrative judge of the Lorain County Court of Common Pleas—as he sits at the table reserved for him in the back and dines on that same health-conscious grilled-chicken lunch, day after day.

Donna, you're working yourself to death. Donna, you're not making any money. Donna, you have a heart—feeding people who don't have money, raising money for good causes—but there's no room for heart in capitalism.

Donna, how about this? Close up the diner, come across the street to the new courthouse and run the cafeteria: five days a week, a steady stream of customers and no worries about utilities. If you're interested, I can try to make this happen.

The Judge's words linger.

Imagine: no electric bill, no heating bill, no worries about security, air-conditioning. . . . Imagine, too: no Donna's Diner, open to all of Elyria. . . .

Donna has told the Judge that she'll think about it. Maybe one of these days she'll drive to Lake Erie. Sit on one of the benches. Gaze into the undulating blue. Clear her head. These are big decisions.

KITCHEN SALVATION

Cooking is vital to Donna. You can lose yourself in the stirring of sauce. You can nourish others and make things seem better, if only for a little while. This she discovered early on, as the turbulent marriage of her parents was upending her childhood.

Born on Flag Day 1955, Donna was the first child of a Navy man, Jerry Jacobson, and his Bay Village bride, Jean. But he refused to give up his beer and Black Velvet or his saloon romance with a woman named Sophie. Leaving a bar in Elyria one night, he drove into a telephone pole. When he awoke weeks later, he called out—for Sophie.

With her household's cash being slapped on bar counters instead of the kitchen counter, Jean raised extra money—between shifts at some factory or office—by making "sweetheart soap" arrangements for her children to sell door-to-door. Meanwhile, as the oldest, Donna tried to fill the parental void.

One day, holding her baby brother in her arms, Donna followed her mother into a Cleveland saloon to confront her father as he sat beside a new girlfriend, this one with a beehive hairdo. The mother said the family needed money for food. The oldest child seconded the plea. The father said get lost.

After the inevitable divorce, Jean moved her four children to a government-subsidized house in Elyria, where Donna found solace, or control, in the kitchen. She began having dinner ready by the time her mother came home from work.

"She'd always put a tablecloth out, and in the summer there'd always be fresh flowers on the table," recalls Jean, 78. "Dessert would be pudding, or fruit cocktail."

Donna clearly preferred the kitchen to Elyria High School, which she found to be too big—another way of saying integrated. She had spent most of her young life in the all-white bubble of Bay Village, 15 miles to the northeast, and now she was in a city high school with a healthy enrollment of black students.

She was intimidated by the unfamiliar, so she cut school. She became pregnant, so she got married, at 16. In the wedding photos, she and her husband look like children playing dress-up.

To say the pregnancy ended Donna's childhood is not quite accurate. In some ways, it had ended years before; in other ways, it continued. She tried to be a loving mother of two baby daughters, a doting housewife to a possessive husband, and a fun-loving young woman fond of the bar life—all at once. Not possible.

Divorce. Temporary loss of custody. A second marriage. Two more children. A third marriage.

But Donna caught her breath, summoning the resolve that had once empowered her to confront her negligent father. She earned her general equivalency diploma. She tended bar and cooked at Stan's Villa in Elyria, across the street from the General Motors plant. She fed inmates at the Lorain County jail. She worked in marketing for the county blood bank.

One day in 2000, when she was ready for a change, Donna picked up a newspaper notice on the sidewalk that said the Lunch Break Cafe on Broad Street was for sale. Destiny. She somehow scratched up the $35,000, and spent that Mother's Day stripping the restaurant clean, even throwing out its toaster.

Driving through Elyria to her own grand opening, she thought, "I'm going to make them remember me."

The diner did well at first, with its 1950s décor and sandwiches named after iconic cars. It became the headquarters for Donna's annual classic-car charity event, her community project to bake cookies for soldiers overseas, her Christmas toy drive for poor children.

"She walks the walk," the Judge says.

This does not include all the food that Donna gave away—to this event, to that person in need, to her father. Yes, Jerry Jacobson was back on the scene, a disabled alcoholic living above a bar in Elyria. But Donna took care of him; he was still her dad.

One day, he would be the charming Jerry, cadging beer money—Two bucks, darlin', c'mon, two bucks—or ordering hamburgers that he would sell for a shot and a beer down at Pudge's Place or Boomers. The next day, he would be awful Jerry, telling Donna's customers that they would be better off at McDonald's.

Father and daughter had a contentious relationship right to the end. When he died of a heart attack in 2004, what could Donna do but place $2 in his coffin, along with a cigarette and a beer?

As downtown Elyria declined, like so many other American downtowns, so did Donna's business. By late 2009, she was preparing to turn the diner's neon off for good, but then she sensed a second chance: An ancient storefront on Middle Avenue had opened up that was larger, closer to the courts and offered a view not of Bugsy's strip joint but of verdant Ely Square.

Over several generations, many had used the three-story brick building at 148 Middle Avenue, in a stretch once called Cheapside, as their claim stake—not to prosperity, but to the chance of it. The Candyland store, with sweets to cut the Depression's bitter taste. The H. W. Guthrie store, selling a dozen honey-dipped doughnuts for a quarter. The Roy E. Hultz store, for the supplies necessary to protect your barn.

The Jack and Jill children's store. Crandall's drugstore. Hess Pharmacy, for "sick room supplies, surgical belts and trusses." A real estate company, a title company, a law firm. The headquarters for local Democrats one year and for Republicans another year. Selenti's Pizza. Naples Pizza. Village Sub and Pizza.

In 1996, a proposal to demolish the building for a parking lot went nowhere. Two years later came Stackers Deli and Pizza. Then the Court Street Cafe. Then the Pulse Cafe. Now here was another aspirant, staking her claim in the Elyrian concrete.

DINER REGULARS

The unseen sparrows of Ely Square continue to dominate the morning conversation, save for the occasional beckoning of another passing train. A parks employee lost in his headset hunts for overnight litter. Coins tossed for luck tremble at the bottom of the fountain's animated waters.

Inside the diner, the sole customer eats scrambled eggs, while Donna and Pete have the kind of meandering conversation that effortlessly links a new casino in Cleveland to the diner's broken dishwasher.

"Some guy at the Polish Club supposedly hit for 130 grand," Pete says of the casino.

"It's never-ending," Donna says of her own gamble.

The dining room is as narrow as a railroad car, with the Breakfast Club's front table and the Judge's back table bracketing six booths and three small tables in the middle, all adorned with sprays of artificial flowers. Along the wall protrudes a coffee counter stocked with customer-donated mugs: "John Deere" beside "Cabo San Lucas" beside "Jesus Saves."

In the cramped other half of the bifurcated space, the kitchen competes for room with a freezer and two large refrigerators and cases of food and foam to-go containers and ripe bananas and a tub of Country Crock spread and the latest soda delivery and stacks of mismatched plates and a bucket filled with stale bread saved for a customer who feeds the crumbs to ducks.

At the center of it all sits the squat grill, the sizzling altar guarded by Donna with raised spatula. Orders scribbled out by her harried waitresses—her daughter Kristy, 38, and her granddaughter, Bridgette, just short of 21—are tucked into the grill's hood. But Donna knows her customers so well that sometimes a mere handwritten name will do. "Ken" means pork chops.

Donna knows their preferences, food allergies, moods, joys, sorrows. She knows to save some perch on Fridays for the Bullocks couple, Gloria and Forrest, who was born into a sharecropping family and is now a prominent civic leader. She knows to give turkey bacon to the retired judge who loves bacon but has heart problems, and to cut a distracting slice of lemon meringue pie for the cranky woman who bangs on the door with her walker and wants to know what's so good about the morning.

Even the people Donna doesn't know, she knows. Like that elfin man who comes in every Wednesday before going to the county sheriff's auction to bid for some law firm on the foreclosed properties that riddle Lorain County. He always orders coffee and plain wheat toast, always. Hence, his diner name: "Wheat Toast."

Donna knows how to handle the people who come in asking for a job. First thing, she escorts them to the grill to see if they can flip a frying egg. If not, the job interview ends.

She also knows how to handle Ike Maxwell when he wanders in, looking for money or food. Still built like a piston-powerful running back, he has not been the same since he was beaten on the head with a baseball bat 30 years ago. Once a high school football superstar who carried Elyria's Friday night hopes, he now loops its streets shouting "Golden Helmet," "They killed my brother" and other phrases that only a few Elyrians can decode.

But sometimes Ike's shouting becomes disruptive, even unnerving, and Donna has to order him to leave. He may protest by shouting a few names—President Obama! Mitt Romney! Les Miles!—but as he heads for the door, Ike often says something else, softly:

"O.K., Donna, O.K., Donna, O.K., Donna."

In this way, Donna's Diner has become a living thing, humming with the flow of the human condition, alternating between harried motion and fleeting rest. When lunchtime comes, an orderly chaos takes hold in the back, as the diner's telephone beckons with a "There's no place like home" ringtone and denizens communicate in a shorthand language rooted in the immediate.

"That's to go! That's to go! Put it in a box!"

"O.K., her Reuben went out. Are the tenders done? This is a crap microwave. This one's lettuce and mayo."

"I just spilled ranch all over the counter."

"I told Ryan I'd be there about 1:30."

"This have cheese-lettuce-tomato?"

"How much is French toast with scrambled eggs?"

"Four-seventy-nine. How come I only have two sausage links?"

"Hello, Donna's Diner?"

It can get to be too much, like the smell of toast burning. An unanticipated trigger—a forgotten order, a returned meal, a splatter of ranch dressing—can set Donna off, and her tirades will spill into the dining room like scalding coffee.

"Is she O.K.?" a customer asks one difficult day.

"My mom?" asks Kristy, the waitress.

"Yes," the customer replies.

"No."

Sometimes you can see why, as Donna hunches into the desk space she has carved from the back-room clutter and works through the mound of mail. "I'm looking for shut-off notices," she says, half-joking.

She also examines the income and expense figures she keeps in a brown spiral notebook. Last year, the daily receipts, in terms of hundreds of dollars, were in the threes, fours and fives; this year, they are in the twos, threes and occasional fours.

Meanwhile, the expenses keep coming. Rent, $650 a month. Electric, $1,416 a month.

"My bug guy, my pop guy, my towel guy, my window washer," she says. Cable. Orlando Bread. Port Clinton Fish.

She tries to lower expenses. When her vexing electric bill shot up a while back, she sold off several appliances and bought a cheaper, more energy-efficient freezer. She spent Mother's Day shopping for wholesale bargains on eggs and dish soap. She bounces from Rural King to Sam's Club to Giant Eagle, looking for the cheapest coffee.

She cannot afford health insurance, she says; it would be $1,500 a month for her and her out-of-work husband, Tim, who has congestive heart failure at 57. A while back, she tore something in her left shoulder while pulling a heavy box of bleach down from a shelf at Sam's Club. Never had it fixed.

Life has become cyclical. Every night, Donna returns to her modest two-story house in Elyria, with its untidy backyard that she never has the time or the energy to reclaim, and stares at the television until sleep comes. Every morning, she awakens to worries, beginning with what to offer for lunch.

Every day, after expenses, there is not much left—though, now and then, she peels off $20 to gamble at a video-lottery place she calls "the joint." And every week, after lunch, here comes Mark Ondrejech, the affable salesman for US Foods, a wholesale supplier, to provide counsel. He sits with her at a back table, opens his laptop and goes down his list.

"All your dressings are good this week? Meat broth, chicken broth, French fries? Onion rings, sauerkraut? Ketchup packets, crackers, chip bags? Foam containers are good? Dinnernapkins, straws—grape tomatoes. Steak fries, cinnamon rolls."

But Donna is ordering less and less from US Foods. She has raised her prices ever so slightly—two eggs and toast went from $1.99 to $2.39—in trying to strike the proper balance between fair profit and customer contentment. She is making her daughter and granddaughter occasionally pay for what they eat. She is holding on for better days, amid news that a new Taco Bell is replacing a downtown apartment building once occupied by Sherwood Anderson.

A Taco Bell.

All the while, the Judge's suggestion—that she consider moving to the courthouse cafeteria—preys on Donna's mind. "All you're doing is, you're working hard and you're entertaining your customers," she says he tells her.

But the diner's people matter to her: Pete, Speedy, the Judge, Gloria and Forrest, Ike, even that unpleasant woman who bangs her walker against the door. The diner matters. It all matters.

"I've got to figure out what I'm doing," she says. "When I get myself to this point, I can't see a way out."

HAUNTED BY FEARS

The Elyrian morning is now full-throated. Birds chirping, waters rushing, trains calling, music pounding from the cars stopped for the light just outside the diner. Sunlight paints the treetops of Ely Square.

Gazing at the park through her plate-glass window, Donna is reminded of a recurring image that she just can't shake: that of a short woman with unruly gray hair, hunting through the park's garbage for redeemable cans. Twenty years ago, Donna worked with this woman at a nursing home on East Avenue. She knew her to say hello.

The woman, Anna Hallman, redeems aluminum cans to pay a mortgage and make ends meet, getting about 50 cents for every 26 cans that she methodically crushes with her heel. She is 69, and other scavengers have kindly ceded to her the treasures to be found in the garbage bins downtown. And when she has had a good day, she sometimes treats herself to a meal at Donna's—something that sticks to the ribs, like meatloaf.

Anna's situation haunts Donna. Too close. Too possible.

How she needs to step away from the grill and take that drive to Lake Erie. No breakfast orders being shouted at her. No bills demanding her attention. Just Donna alone, sitting on a bench and staring into the infinite waters that calm her, help her think. Big decisions.

But now she has customers. The first two members of the Breakfast Club take their seats at the front table. Coffee for both. No breakfast for one, eggs over medium, wheat toast for the other. Orders taken, the owner of Donna's Diner disappears into the kitchen.

EPILOGUE

The diner's owner, Donna Dove, tried everything she could think of to keep the small restaurant open—from offering buffet-style service to applying for a liquor permit—but nothing seemed to work. Then her mother in Florida fell ill, which kept Ms. Dove away from the restaurant's day-to-day operations for prolonged periods of time.

Finally, in December 2016, after one last Christmas party, she hung a "See You Next Year" sign on the door—and that was that. She just didn't have the heart to tell her longtime customers personally, Ms. Dove said. "It hurt too bad."

So ended this big-hearted, hardworking woman's pursuit of success at a corner storefront in the small Ohio city of Elyria. At last report, another entrepreneur had moved into the space. The business plan: gourmet pizza.

PART SIX

Nature

The beautiful, the beautiful river

A Hand-to-Hand Struggle
with a Raging River

CANTON, MO. — JUNE 19, 2008

They sandbag by moonlight. The school superintendent and the judge, the police sergeant and the mechanic, the Amish man in a straw hat and the young man in a Budweiser T-shirt, they lay down sandbags as if making peace offerings to a vexed god called the Mississippi.

The only sounds on Tuesday night: the whine of all-terrain vehicles climbing up the levee to deliver more sandbags; the rustle of bags being lifted; the calling mmmf! of those tossing bags into the air and the answering ooof! of those catching them in the chest; the thump of bags dropped into strategic place; and, ever so faintly, a distant aaahhh of rushing, roiling water.

"You sit here and listen," Jim Crenshaw, a local emergency management official says with an awe just inches short of horror. "Normally you never hear it like that."

Behind him, the swollen moon sends a charged lightness skimming across the river's black surface and onto the white sandbags. Each bag tossed and each bag laid seems now to glow, as if containing something more than mere river sand. Mmmf! Ooof! Aaahhh . . .

And here, along the lip of the town's levee, remain the torn, whitish remnants of sandbags lifted, tossed and stacked before the disastrous flood of 1993, when the people of Canton somehow managed, almost against the odds, to hold back the river.

The men and boys catching the sandbags of 2008, then, are standing on the successful offerings of the past.

There is something almost too simple, even primitive, about sandbagging. In an age when anyone can receive a satellite photograph of where they're standing with the click of an iPhone, and when the river's southward swell can be tracked like a tagged animal lumbering along a worn path, we still heavily depend on a basic, communal practice: shovel sand in bag, place bag on ground, pray it works, as it often does.

The Army Corps of Engineers offers an appreciation for sandbags on its website; sandbags, it says, are "a steadfast tool for flood fighting." And by now, people along the Mississippi know the very specific instructions—fill bags to little more than halfway; start downstream and work up; layer bags just so—as well as the irony that their bags are often filled with sand dredged from the very river they are fending off.

But there is an ingredient just as necessary as sand: people. In the small towns along Highway 79, which meanders for dozens of miles alongside the river, people gather at firehouses, garages and street corners to participate in a ritual that combines hope and earth.

In Clarksville, for example, some inmates from the women's prison in Vandalia spend these days shoveling and packing while under the gaze of corrections officers in sunglasses. In white shirts stamped with "WR"—for work release—they form an assembly line that snakes away from a diminishing mound of sand toward the growing river, whose threat unites them with all those who will not be traveling 40 miles by van back to a prison.

Here are Sandra Miller, 48, and Thalisia Ervin, 40, basking in sweat and in the appreciation of Clarksville. Ms. Miller, who has already served 13 years for "being in the wrong place at the wrong time," as she puts it, says the weight of another bag caught sometimes knocks the wind out of her, but then she thinks to herself:

"This is for the good. This is for our good."

Still, Ms. Miller looks around, sees the water higher and closer than it was the day before, and she questions that good. "It makes me wonder," she says. "Does it help?"

"It does, it does," her sister inmate reassures her. "It's slowing it down."

The story is the same in other communities. Inmates and Mennonites, children who should be playing and retirees who should be resting, all answering the mayday calls, all racing against the lowering sun and the rising water. All sandbagging.

Tuesday had begun with the rise of another deceptive sun over Canton, a farming and college town of 2,500. The halcyon days of mere weeks ago, when the Mississippi River was content to be a vehicle of commerce and recreation, were gone; now its greedy waters had consumed the riverside park and a good chunk of the active rail line, and were still agitating for more, rapping against the town's three-mile-long levee.

The town's emergency management director, Jeff McReynolds, had issued a statement "highly, highly" recommending that residents east of Seventh Street sleep somewhere other than their homes until further notice. He had also called for all able-bodied men to report for sandbagging and levee duties.

This would explain, then, why a visitor driving through the high ground of Canton at evening time finds tidy homes, the tidy campus of Culver-Stockton College—and almost no people. That is because many of them are downtown, near the river, sandbagging: able-bodied and otherwise; men, women and children, including Dalton, an 11-year-old boy with a dirt-smeared face who keeps pestering local officials with, "What can I do now, huh? What can I do?"

They smile and point him back to the sandbags.

With the moon rising, getting brighter, Mr. Crenshaw, one of the local officials, patrols the levee, swatting away bugs, overseeing the sandbagging operation he helped put together. One night last week he and another man drove about six hours round-trip to Davenport, Iowa, to collect 250,000 empty bags from the Corps of Engineers. They arrived at 5:15 in the morning; by 7, sand-filled bags were being stacked.

First, he says, workers dug a shallow trench along the levee, hammered in stakes, put up a short wooden wall called a "batter board," laid some plastic sheeting—at this point Mr. Crenshaw is interrupted by the boy named Dalton, looking again for something to do.

"Hang tight, little buddy," the man says to the boy. Pointing to a cluster of young Mennonite women filling bags at a large sand pile, he says, "Can you help them load over there?"

The boy runs to the pile, and Mr. Crenshaw picks up where he left off, saying that Canton has gone through about 850,000 bags. And they need more in this battle of inches, of guessing how far above 27 feet or so the river will rise.

The absence of the sun lends menace to the river. The sandbagging normally stops at 9 at night, for safety reasons. But few sandbaggers stop; few think they have the time. They're still there—the civic leaders and local nobodies, those young Amish and Mennonite men tossing 50-pound bags around like pillows, that boy named Dalton.

In the hours to come, well into early morning, workers will race from wet spot to wet spot along the northern stretch of the levee, laying down sandbags to shore up what little separates a river from a people. The shoosh of shovel blade into sand, the rustle of bags, the exhalations of breath, under bright moonlight.

Another day will dawn with disaster averted, and by Wednesday afternoon there will be 50,000 sandbags. "Idle and waiting to be used," Mr. Crenshaw says, as if confirming that each bag contained more than river sand.

Learning to Love the Sea,
Then Torn from It

VENICE, LA. — MAY 3, 2010

Where the world runs out of road and into bayou, and all that is left beyond is the Gulf of Mexico, dozens of docked shrimp boats bob in place, restless. They should be out right now, green nets trawling for cash in crustaceans. But here they sit, their dry nets not even catching the air.

Among these many boats—actually, between the Capt. Andy and the Capt. James—there rocks the St. Martin. And on the St. Martin, there lives its owner, a small, muscular Vietnamese-born American named Thuong Nguyen, whose right forearm bears a tattoo that says, in his native language:

"Life is difficult."

Now his difficult, amazing life has been capsized by events not of his doing. Again.

Here is where Mr. Nguyen, 50, should be: on another 10-day trip out near Breton Sound, his two deckhands beside him, his lucky hurricane dog at his feet, trawling through the day and into the night, when all he can see is the celestial display he calls a "star soup."

But in another lesson of how all is connected, an offshore oil rig leased by a multibillion-dollar corporation exploded nearly two weeks ago. Which, in addition to killing 11 workers, ruptured a well. Which caused an ever-mushrooming oil slick. Which led to the closing of the country's most fecund fishing grounds, from the Mississippi River to Florida's Pensacola Bay, for at least 10 days.

Which has stalled, and possibly ruined, the livelihoods of thousands, including this diminutive man living on his boat at the very end of a place that calls itself the "end of the world." All he can do is paint, knock down some rust, and accept his boat's lullaby sway.

The pause fills Mr. Nguyen with anger, yes, but also guilt. In addition to providing for his family, he takes to heart the job of gathering some of the food you may eat tonight. "And now I cannot help out, so I feel like I'm—fail," he says. "I cannot bring in more seafood from here."

To find Mr. Nguyen in his fitful rest, take Louisiana Highway 23 south, the instructive road that bisects narrow Plaquemines Parish. The passing seafood shacks and oil tanks, the boat storage yards and the parked trucks of offshore riggers reflect the shared interests in the gulf's bounty.

Continue past the Riverside Restaurant, where Hurricane Katrina tried but failed to scrub away the marshland mural painted by an itinerant artist; past the damaged and ghostly shopping center; past the Katrina debris jutting from a landfill. The hurricane that defined 2005 nearly wiped this community away, but the people came back; adapted; are trying again.

The road unwinds and frays at the bottom, with one last strand ending at the Venice Marina. Many of the boats here are owned by Vietnamese men and women who, some 20 years ago, added a Southeast Asian flavor to the Cajun-Croatian stew of the parish. It took a while, but the stew has settled, mostly.

In 1991, Mr. Nguyen became another unfamiliar presence on the docks, altering the way things had always been. He would go out on his uncle's boat, chock-full of Dramamine, and hear the Asian slurs of other shrimpers coming across the ship-to-shore radio.

How do you respond? How do you quickly explain: I fled the Communists in a boat smaller than the one you are on now, crammed with three dozen others for 11 days. Little water. Vomiting. People praying to Jesus and Buddha. You cannot imagine.

How do you say: I am an American citizen now. I am married to an American. I have children. I was working at a battery factory in St. Joseph, Mo., when my uncle asked me to help him on his shrimp boat. So we live here now, in Plaquemines Parish.

Time washed away most of the tension. Mr. Nguyen, his wife, Dorothy, and their four children lived in a double-wide trailer in Buras, a few miles north of Venice. Eventually, he raised enough money to buy the St. Martin, a 65-foot used boat found in Houma; the purchase allowed him to promote himself to captain.

Once he was a man whose only maritime experience was a horrifying slog toward freedom; now Mr. Nguyen lived to be on the water. He would joyously tell his wife how, on the first day of shrimp season, the lights of the many boats gathered in the predawn looked like a city afloat.

Katrina hit while the family was out of town. Mr. Nguyen returned to a collapsed double-wide, two dead family dogs, and the absence of irreplaceable family photographs from Vietnam and Missouri. But he eventually found the St. Martin a mile from its slip, damaged yet upright. And he took in an abandoned puppy cowering near the dock; Lucky, he called it.

Mr. Nguyen insisted that his family start over in Missouri, while he repaired his boat. After several months, the rhythm returned. He would collect his two deckhands, buy ice, fill the fuel tank and the rice box, and head out.

The men would take turns steering, cooking and sleeping, as the boat moved, back and forth, back and forth, around the clock. The heavy chain dragged at the back would "scare" the shrimp into the nets, he says. And every four hours, the men would haul in, rinse clean the catch, and dump the take into the ice-laden hold, while Lucky chased away the hungry birds.

Sometimes, at sea, Mr. Nguyen would talk by cellphone—uninterrupted—to his wife and youngest son in Missouri, or to his daughter, married to a soldier, in Kansas, or to his oldest son, who works for an oil company, in New Orleans.

Sometimes, standing at the wheel, where bouquets of plastic flowers adorn the dashboard, he would talk to his second-oldest son, Bo—a soldier, he says, who has done two tours of war and is now preparing for a third.

Sometimes, under the starry soup that could make him feel as small as the creatures he pursued, Mr. Nguyen would forget about the threat of foreign imports, the fluctuating prices, the lingering tension along the docks. He would feel peace in his mission.

"I go out there, and I bring back seafood for this country," he says.

Several days ago, Mr. Nguyen learned of the large event disrupting his small world, an event that has denied him those offshore moments that fulfill him. He has no high school degree, no other training: Hauling shrimp is what he does.

He says he understands that oil is essential; it fuels his boat. What he doesn't understand is the delay and uncertainty, as shrimp boats remain tethered. "The company don't have a right answer," he says. "And the government don't have a right answer."

On Friday, Mr. Nguyen went to a meeting at a local school that focused on how to clean up hazardous materials.

On Saturday, he attended another meeting, this one held by the corporation whose accident has made his difficult life more difficult. He received a piece of paper saying that, according to the "BP Gulf of Mexico Operations," he had completed all requirements for "GoM Spill Response Efforts"—should his services be needed.

And on Sunday, as President Obama visited the Coast Guard station a half mile away, this tattooed man worked hard to suppress the call of the sea. He rinsed out some shirts, painted a boom and shared fresh catfish with his hurricane dog, Lucky.

As the Mountaintops Fall, a Coal Town Vanishes

LINDYTOWN, W.VA. — APRIL 13, 2011

To reach a lost American place, here just a moment ago, follow a thin country road as it unspools across an Appalachian valley's grimy floor, past a coal operation or two, a church or two, a village called Twilight. Beware of the truck traffic. Watch out for that car-chasing dog.

After passing an abandoned union hall with its front door agape, look to the right for a solitary house, tidy, yellow and tucked into the stillness. This is nearly all that remains of a West Virginia community called Lindytown.

In the small living room, five generations of family portraits gaze upon Quinnie Richmond, 85, who has trouble summoning the memories, and her son, Roger, 62, who cannot forget them: the many children all about, enough to fill Mr. Cook's school bus every morning; the Sunday services at the simple church; the white laundry strung on clotheslines; the echoing clatter of evening horseshoes; the sense of home.

But the coal that helped to create Lindytown also destroyed it. Here was the church; here was its steeple; now it's all gone, along with its people. Gone, too, are the surrounding mountaintops. To mine the soft rock that we burn to help power our light bulbs, our laptops, our way of life, heavy equipment has stripped away the trees, the soil, the rock—what coal companies call the "overburden."

Now, the faint, mechanical beeps and grinds from above are all that disturb the Lindytown quiet, save for the occasional, seam-splintering blast.

A couple of years ago, a subsidiary of Massey Energy, which owns a sprawling mine operation behind and above the Richmond home, bought up Lindytown.

Lights on at the Richmond home

Many of its residents signed Massey-proffered documents in which they also agreed not to sue, testify against, seek inspection of or "make adverse comment" about coal-mining operations in the vicinity.

You might say that both parties were motivated. Massey preferred not to have people living so close to its mountaintop mining operations. And the residents, some with area roots deep into the 19th century, preferred not to live amid a dusty industrial operation that was altering the natural world about them. So the Greens sold, as did the Cooks, and the Workmans, and the Webbs . . .

But Quinnie Richmond's husband, Lawrence—who died a few months ago, at 85—feared that leaving the home they built in 1947 might upset his wife, who has Alzheimer's. He and his son Roger, a retired coal miner who lives next door, chose instead to sign easements granting the coal company certain rights over their properties. In exchange for also agreeing not to make adverse comment, the two Richmond households received $25,000 each, Roger Richmond recalls.

"Hush money," he says, half-smiling.

As Mr. Richmond speaks, the mining on the mountain behind him continues to transform, if not erase, the woodsy stretches he explored in boyhood. It has also exposed a massive rock that almost seems to be teetering above the Richmond home. Some days, an anxious Mrs. Richmond will check on the rock from her small kitchen window, step away, then come back to check again.

And again.

A DICTATOR OF DESTINY

Here in Boone County, coal rules. The rich seams of bituminous black have dictated the region's destiny for many generations: through the advent of railroads; the company-controlled coal camps; the bloody mine wars; the increased use of mechanization and surface mining, including mountaintop removal; the related decrease in jobs.

The county has the largest surface-mining project (the Massey operation) in the state and the largest number of coal-company employees (more than 3,600). Every year it receives several million dollars in tax severance payments from the coal industry, and every June it plays host to the West Virginia Coal Festival, with fireworks, a beauty pageant, a memorial service for dead miners, and displays of the latest mining equipment. Without coal, says Larry V. Lodato, the director of the county's Community and Economic Development Corporation, "You might as well turn out the lights and leave."

In recent years, surface mining has eclipsed underground mining as the county's most productive method. This includes mountaintop removal—or, as the industry prefers to call it, mountaintop mining—a now-commonplace technique that remains startling in its capacity to change things.

Various government regulations require that coal companies return the stripped area to its "approximate original contour," or "reclaim" the land for development in a state whose undulating topography can thwart plans for even a simple parking lot. As a result, the companies often dump the removed earth into a nearby valley to create a plateau, and then spray this topsy-turvy land with seed, fertilizer and mulch.

The coal industry maintains that by removing some mountaintops from the "Mountain State," it is creating developable land that makes the state more economically viable. State and coal officials point to successful developments on land reclaimed by surface mining, developments that they say have led to the creation of some 13,000 jobs.

But Ken Ward Jr., a reporter for The Charleston Gazette, has pointed out that two-fifths of these jobs are seasonal or temporary; a third of the full-time jobs are at one project, in the northern part of the state; and the majority of the jobs are far from southern West Virginia, where most of the mountaintop removal is occurring, and where unemployment is most dire. In Boone County, development on reclaimed land has basically meant the building of the regional headquarters for the county's dominant employer—Massey Energy.

And with reclamation, there is also loss.

"I'm not familiar at all with Lindytown," says Mr. Lodato, the county's economic development director. "I know it used to be a community, and it's close to Twilight."

A FIGHTER

About 10 miles from Lindytown, outside a drab convenience store in the unincorporated town of Van, a rake-thin woman named Maria Gunnoe climbs into a maroon Ford pickup that is adorned with a bumper sticker reading: "Mountains Matter—Organize." The daughter, granddaughter and sister of union coal miners, Ms. Gunnoe is 42, with sorrowful dark eyes, long black hair and a desire to be on the road only between shift changes at the local mining operations—and only with her German shepherd and her gun.

Less than a decade ago, Ms. Gunnoe was working as a waitress, just trying to get along, when a mountaintop-removal operation in the small map dot of Bob White disrupted her "home place." It filled the valley behind her house, flooded her property, contaminated her well and transformed her into a fierce opponent of mountaintop removal. Through her work with the Ohio Valley Environmental Coalition, she has become such an effective environmental advocate that in 2009 she received the prestigious Goldman Environmental Prize. But no one threw a parade for her in Boone County, where some deride her as anti-coal; that is, anti-job.

Ms. Gunnoe turns onto the two-lane road, Route 26, and heads toward the remains of Lindytown. On her right stands Van High School, her alma mater, where D. Ray White, the gifted and doomed Appalachian dancer, used to kick up his heels at homecomings. On her left, the community center where dozens of coal-company workers disrupted a meeting of environmentalists back in 2007.

"There was a gentleman who pushed me backward, over my daughter, who was about 12 or 13, and crying," Ms. Gunnoe later recalls. "I pushed him back, and he filed charges against me for battery. He was 250 pounds, and I had a broken arm."

A jury acquitted her within minutes.

Ms. Gunnoe drives on. Past the long-closed Grill bar, its facade marred by graffiti. Past an out-of-context clot of land that rises hundreds of feet in the air—"a valley fill," she says, that has been "hydroseeded" with fast-growing, non-native plants to replace the area's lost natural growth: its ginseng root, its goldenseal, its hickory and oak, maple and poplar, black cherry and sassafras.

"And it will never be back," she says.

Ms. Gunnoe has a point. James Burger, a professor emeritus of forestry and soil science at Virginia Tech University, said the valley fill process often sends the original topsoil to the bottom and crushed rock from deeper in the ground to the top. With the topography and soil properties altered, Dr. Burger says, native plants and trees do not grow as well.

"You have hundreds of species of flora and fauna that have acclimated to the native, undisturbed conditions over the millennia," he says. "And now you're inverting the geologic profile."

Dr. Burger says that he and other scientists have developed a reclamation approach that uses native seeds, trees, topsoil and selected rock material to help restore an area's natural diversity, at no additional expense. Unfortunately, he says, these methods have not been adopted in most Appalachian states, including West Virginia.

Past a coal operation called a loadout, an oversize Tinkertoy structure where coal is crushed and loaded on trucks and rail cars. Past the house cluster called Bandytown, home of Leo Cook, 75, the former school bus driver who once collected Roger Richmond and the other kids from Lindytown, where he often spent evenings at a horseshoe pit, now overgrown.

"We got to have coal," says Mr. Cook, a retired miner. "What's going to keep the power on? But I believe with all my heart that there's a better way to get that coal."

Ms. Gunnoe continues deeper into the mud-brown landscape, where the fleeting appearance of trucks animates the flattened mountaintops. On her right, a dark, winding stream damaged by mining; on her left, several sediment-control ponds that filter out pollutants from the runoff of mining operations. Past the place called Twilight, a jumble of homes and trailers, where the faded sign of the old Twilight Super Market still promises Royal Crown Cola for sale.

Soon she passes the abandoned hall for Local 8377 of the United Mine Workers of America, empty since some underground mining operations shut down a couple of decades ago. Its open door beckons you to examine the papers piled on the floor: a Wages, Lost Time, and Expense Voucher booklet from 1987; the burial fund's bylaws; canceled checks bearing familiar surnames.

On, finally, to Lindytown.

THE COMPANY LINE

According to a statement from Shane Harvey, the general counsel for Massey, this is what happened: Many of Lindytown's residents were either retired miners or their widows and descendants who welcomed the opportunity to move to places more metropolitan or with easier access to medical facilities. Interested in selling their properties, they contacted Massey, which began making offers in December 2008—offers that for the most part were accepted.

"It is important to note that none of these properties had to be bought," Mr. Harvey said.

"The entire mine plan could have been legally mined without the purchase of these homes. We agreed to purchase the properties as an additional precaution."

When asked to elaborate, Mr. Harvey responded, in writing, that Massey voluntarily bought the properties "as an additional backup to the state and federal regulations" that protect people who live near mining operations.

James Smith, 68, a retired coal miner from Lindytown, says the company's statement is true, as far as it goes. Yes, Lindytown had become home mostly to retired union miners and their families; when the Robin Hood No. 8 mine shut down, for example, his three sons had to leave the state to work. And yes, some people approached Massey about selling their homes.

But, Mr. Smith says, many residents wanted to leave Lindytown only because the mountaintop operations above had ruined the quality of life below.

His family went back generations here. He married a local woman, raised kids, became widowed and married again. A brother lived in one house, a sister lived in another, and nieces, nephews and cousins were all around. And there was this God-given setting, where he could wander for days, hunting raccoon or searching for ginseng.

But when the explosions began, dust filled the air. "You could wash your car today, and tomorrow you could write your name on it in the dust," he says. "It was just unpleasant to live in that town. Period."

Massey was a motivated buyer, he argues, given that it was probably cheaper to buy out a small community than to deal with all the complaint-generated inspections, or the possible lawsuits over silica dust and "fly rock."

"Hell, what they paid for that wasn't a drop in the bucket," he says.

Massey did not elaborate on why it bought out Lindytown, though general concerns about public health have been mounting. In blocking another West Virginia mountaintop-removal project earlier this year, the Environmental Protection Agency cited research suggesting that health disparities in the Appalachian region are "concentrated where surface coal mining activity takes place."

In the end, Mr. Smith says, he would not be living 150 miles away, far from relations and old neighbors, if mountaintop removal hadn't ruined Lindytown. "You might as well take the money and get rid of your torment," he says, adding that he received more than $300,000 for his property. "After they destroyed our place, they done us a favor and bought it."

MEMORIES, WHAT'S LEFT

Ms. Gunnoe pulls up to one of the last houses in Lindytown, the tidy yellow one, and visits with Quinnie and Roger Richmond. He uses his words to re-animate the community he knew.

For many years, his grandfather was the preacher at the small church down the road, where the ringing of a bell gave fair warning that Sunday service was about to begin. And his grandmother lived in the house still standing next door; she toiled in her garden well past 100, growing the kale, spinach and mustard greens that she loved so much.

His father, Lawrence, joined the military in World War II after his older brother, Carson, was killed in Sicily. He returned, married Quinnie, and built this house. Before long, he became a section foreman in the mines, beloved by his men in part because of Quinnie's fried-apple pies.

After graduating from Van High School—that's his senior photograph, there on the wall—Roger Richmond followed his father into the mines. He married, had children, divorced, made do when the local mine shut down, eventually retired and, in 2001, set up his mobile home beside his parents' house.

By now, things had changed. With the local underground mine shut down, there were nowhere near as many jobs, or kids. And this powder from the mountaintops was settling on everything, turning to brown paste in the rain. People no longer hung their whites on the clotheslines.

Soon, rumors of buyouts from Massey became fact, as neighbors began selling and moving away. "Some of them were tired of fighting it," Mr. Richmond says. "Of having to put up with all the dust. Plus, you couldn't get out into the hills the way you used to."

One example. Mr. Richmond's Uncle Carson, killed in World War II, is buried in one of the small cemeteries scattered about the mountains. If he wanted to pay his respects, in accordance with government regulations for active surface-mining areas, he would have to make an appointment with a coal company, be certified in work site safety, don a construction helmet and be escorted by a coal-company representative.

In the end, the Richmonds decided to sell various land rights to Massey, but remain in Lindytown, as the homes of longtime neighbors were boarded up and knocked down late last year, and as looters arrived at all hours of the day to steal the windows, the wiring, the pillars from Elmer Smith's front porch—even the peaches, every one of them, growing from trees on the Richmond property.

"They was good peaches, too," says Mr. Richmond.

"I like peaches," says his mother.

Would Lindytown have died anyway? Would it have died even without the removal of its surrounding mountaintops? These are the questions that Bill Raney, the president of the West Virginia Coal Association, raises. Sometimes, he says, depopulation is part of the natural order of things. People move to be closer to hospitals, or restaurants, or the Walmart. There is also that West Virginia truism, he adds:

"When the coal's gone, you go to where the next coal seam is."

Of course, in the case of Lindytown, the coal is still here; it's the people who are mostly gone. Now, when darkness comes to this particular hollow, you can see a small light shining from the kitchen window of a solitary, yellow house—and, sometimes, a face, peering out.

EPILOGUE

The small West Virginia place called Lindytown is barely a memory.

The mining operation is idle, the surrounding roads are not maintained—making the family cemeteries nestled in the hills nearly impossible to reach—and the surrounding mountains "have been blown into dust," according to the environmental activist Maria Gunnoe.

Quinnie Richmond, one of Lindytown's last residents, died in 2017; she was 92. But her son Richard continues to live in the family home, in the shortened shadows of the diminished hills.

Losing Everything,
Except What Really Matters

COTTONDALE, ALA. — MAY 1, 2011

As the flight to Birmingham began its descent, the passenger in 8B, a barrel of a man wearing a camouflage baseball cap, peered out the window at the disfigured sprawl of Tuscaloosa below. There, he said, pointing: that light brown scar marks the tornado's path.

After studying it in silence, he snapped a few photographs with a cellphone that had in its memory another photograph, sent to him just hours earlier, of a one-story brick house that had been all but destroyed by that same tornado.

His house.

His name is Corey Soper, and he is 33. He lives just outside Tuscaloosa, but works as a welder on a pipeline in Nevada, because that is where the work is. Now, after a heart-pounding day of worrying from a distance for the safety of his wife and two young children, he was coming home to a broken house, clutching a blue luggage ticket that represented the only clothes he had left.

And yet he considered himself lucky, so very lucky. His family is safe, he said, his voice tight.

"And now we can build new memories."

For days now, those not in the path of the dozens of tornadoes that spun mayhem and death across several states on Wednesday have mostly experienced it through aerial photographs and film footage that tend to blend into one dispassionate tableau of destruction: stripped foundations, upside-down cars, bits of wood and brick that once were homes. Imagining the roar of freight trains and bee swarms, you can almost fool yourself into believing you were there. Almost.

But if you were able to zoom in, as though with a click of a newly updated version of Google Earth, you might come in closer, closer, closer, to one house on Rifle Range Road in Cottondale, where the roof has been swept away, bits of insulation cling to the grass like artificial snow and an eight-foot tree branch pierces the living room wall. This is the home of a very fortunate man.

He is fortunate because his wife, Alicia, 31, grew up with tornadoes and knows enough not to test them. When she was about 8, a tornado destroyed her home; when she was 12, another tornado destroyed her home. Now she is all weather all the time, listening to her hero, a local meteorologist named James Spann, and following reports from the National Oceanic and Atmospheric Administration.

So, when reports came on Wednesday of a "bruiser" of a storm, she chose not to use the storm cellar installed on their property, at her insistence, shortly after they bought their home in 2006. "Something told me, 'You have to leave here,'" she said.

Ms. Soper gathered the two children—Tommy, 10, and Gracelynn, 8—and drove her black S.U.V. to the DCH Regional Medical Center, a Tuscaloosa fortress, where her sister Michelle works as a scheduling clerk.

Meanwhile, her husband was in Nevada with his heart in Alabama. Mr. Soper watched the Weather Channel while talking to his wife, until their cellphone connection died. As he frantically tried to get back in touch, the tornado passed by the medical center, changing the air pressure so drastically that the ears of his family were popping.

Ms. Soper sent him a text message: "Its bad baby the tornadoe is headed straight for us dr. McKenzie brought us to the doctors lounge."

Then another text: "in the middle of the hospital." Mr. Soper texted back: "I lost you—call me."

An hour later, Mr. Soper managed to regain cellphone contact with his wife. They were fine. He was lucky.

Sometime after that, a neighbor sent Ms. Soper a text: "Your house took a hit."

All day Thursday, while her husband caught flights from Las Vegas to Houston to Birmingham, a numbed Ms. Soper sat on the smashed porch of her broken house and wept. Around her lay water-stained family photographs, and pieces of family bric-a-brac, and the three brick pillars that once supported the porch roof, still missing. She could find no strength.

"I lost it," she said. "My neighbor held me while I cried."

But once her Corey showed up Thursday evening, as the sun was setting and a coolness was coming to the pine-scented air, she found her strength again. He had driven through his devastated neighborhood, past the smashed cars and the downed power lines and the piece of metal wrapped in a bow in the trees, and he was home.

Mr. Soper looked around. It was not as it had appeared in that cellphone photograph. It was real.

The tornado had pried off the roof, collected some of the family mementos stored in the attic and distributed Soper photographs and Soper memories among the neighborhood's oak and sour-gum

Sunlight after the tornado

trees. It had exposed both the kitchen and the master bedroom to the sky. It had spackled the Whirlpool oven and the Kenmore dishwasher with green vegetation. It had possibly damaged the foundation, buckled what remained of the ceiling and blessed all Soper belongings with water.

At the same time, it had not disturbed the four Holiday Barbies from their perches of honor in Gracelynn's bedroom, nor rearranged any of the Alabama Crimson Tide posters in Tommy's bedroom. Even Ms. Soper's silver hoop earrings, weightless things, sat where she had last placed them on the counter in the ruined bathroom. A consolation prize, it seemed.

After spending Thursday night with Ms. Soper's grandmother in Brookwood, the Soper family returned to Rifle Range Road early Friday morning to face the inevitable question:

Could their home be salvaged? The home where every birthday was celebrated? Where Ms. Soper's extended family gathered every Christmas Day? Where you could sit on the porch and hear Roger across the street, a good neighbor, strumming his banjo to celebrate another Alabama night?

It remained to be seen. But the family had its strength back.

Ms. Soper drove to Home Depot, where the employees were so nice she almost cried, and to John Deere, to collect water and garbage bags and a new power saw.

As soon as she returned, she sat down again on the broken porch, only this time with resolve: to order a storage container in which to protect all the valuables—the baby clothes, the wedding album, the Soper things.

"O.K.," she said into her pink cellphone, responding to a sales representative's pitch. "O.K. O.K. O.K. O.K. . . ."

Mr. Soper, meanwhile, led a small army of power-saw-toting relatives and friends in clearing the jumble of fallen trees from his two-acre lot. If a tornado's call sounds like freight trains and bees, humankind's response sounds like growling, determined power saws.

He worked through the warm day, not a cloud in the sky, and into dusk, well aware that others in this state were mourning their dead. Sweat-stained and flecked with sawdust, he occasionally looked up to see his wife and his two children in their altered yard, working, making new memories.

His house nearly destroyed, he felt blessed.

Ready, Aim, Fireworks!

TERRE HAUTE, IND. — OCTOBER 27, 2011

Her Cadillac glides slowly through the rain-glossed streets of this traumatized city, her gat within reach. The ominous evening sky has yet to turn black, but it will. Oh, it will.

Her name is Joy Sacopulos. She is 72, bespectacled, and so small in her boat of a Deville that she seems at eye level with the wheel. But don't let her play you for a sap. By day she might be the civic do-gooder, planting dogwoods in the park; by night she is the dame packing pyrotechnic heat, intent on keeping the city's streets—and cars, and benches—clean.

Crows. That's right. Crows.

Ms. Sacopulos, of the Terre Haute Crow Patrol, eases over to 12th and Chestnut, a known hangout. Bingo. Hundreds of perps are getting all comfy in the treetops, cawing in mirthful defiance, unaware that they have just made her day.

She steps out. Loads her launch pistol as calmly as if she were adding milk to her tea. Leans Mannix-like on the hood. Fires, and fires again. The first shot sends a screaming firework over a housetop and into the trees. The second booms louder than the wail of the freight train passing by.

Black bits burst into the air, but soon return to where they were moments ago, like a jigsaw puzzle of a night sky reassembling itself. Then comes that taunt again: caw-caw, caw-caw.

Crows. So omnivorous, so opportunistic, so—like us.

Every fall, as many as 100,000 American crows choose to winter in this pleasant city of 60,000. It is believed that they are drawn to the closeness of the Wabash River, the bright warmth of the streetlamps, the variety of the cuisine. A hearty lunch in a rustic cornfield setting, followed, perhaps, by a light dinner at one of the city's finer Dumpsters.

But Terre Haute would rather shed its distinction as a winter resort for discerning crows—one shared by Auburn, N.Y., and Lancaster, Pa., among other cities. That is why it has created a Crow Patrol, with a mandate to enforce a kind of avian nimbyism.

Murders of crows, and that is the term for flocks of these birds, have mugged the quality of life here. If they roost in your trees, their mess will cover your property and their racket will disturb your evenings; you will run, not walk, from door to car.

And if they bless your restaurant, bank, or church with their presence and droppings, money is lost, faith tested.

Two winters ago, Union Hospital spent more than $100,000 to clean up after crows, an effort that included power-washing the parking lots. Last year, a crew shoveled 4,000 pounds of crow droppings from the roof of a building used by the Clabber Girl baking powder company. Trees have been chopped down. Recorded crow-distress calls have been played. Debates have raged between those who love all God's creatures and those who say the only good crow is a crow that has ceased to be.

Finally, everyone from The Tribune-Star newspaper to City Hall said enough, and a "crow committee" was formed last year to develop a comprehensive plan. As Mayor Duke Bennett explained in his 2010 State of the City address: "We can't shoot them. We can't poison them. We've got to figure out a way to transfer them someplace else."

A leading organizer was Ms. Sacopulos, retired schoolteacher, grandmother and bird lover known for Getting Things Done. She has championed urban forestry, worked to preserve a historic church, and led a drive to recycle electronics. Now she is focused on the crow, motivated in part by one image she can't shake: that of a car so thoroughly coated with droppings that its driver had to steer with door open and head peering out.

"O.K.," she recalls saying. "We have to do something."

But what? Humans have tried to keep crows away since forever. They have used scarecrows to feign human presence. They have hung sulfur-dipped rags to remind crows of gunpowder. They have mounted dead crows on sticks. They have sent out hawks, banged pots, laid out strychnine, shot off guns, paid bounties. Still the crows come, as if to peck away at our sense of superiority.

Crows are too intelligent to fall twice for most tricks. They care for their young and sick. They communicate through a vocabulary that goes well beyond "caw." They use tools. They take note of our behavioral patterns and, even, our faces.

"Who knows what they've got in terms of accumulated wisdom," said Peter Scott, a professor of biology at Indiana State University—which, by the way, has also had crow problems.

After several public discussions and many suggestions, including one to use the crows to feed the less fortunate, the Crow Patrol was established. Its costs would be covered by donations, collected mostly by Ms. Sacopulos, and its members would be trained in the shooting of fireworks. The intent was not to kill the birds but to launch a varied disruption so sustained that they would move to dedicated zones: an empty field, say, at city's edge.

All last winter, the boom of evening fireworks echoed through Terre Haute, with modest results. It turns out that crows don't believe in zoning.

"We were naïve, and so we've abandoned driving them to specified locales," said Jim Luzar, the chairman of the crow committee and an educator with the Purdue University Cooperative Extension Service. "This year our expectations are tempered. We're basically just trying to disrupt roosting behavior and dilute concentrations of roosting."

Last week, with gold flecking the trees and black flecking the skies, the Terre Haute Crow Patrol mustered once again. An hour before darkness, volunteers gathered around two "crow harassment" experts, Tim Christie and his son, Matt, as they distributed bright-orange Crow Patrol vests, launch pistols and bags of small fireworks.

Tim Christie, 62, a wildlife-management veteran who works for the patrol at a steep discount, has chased crows for many Terre Haute businesses, including the Honey Creek Mall. But in recent years there have been almost too many to handle, he said. "They keep moving back in, and moving back in."

The Christies tutored the volunteers once more on the proper way to load and discharge their pistols, while Ms. Sacopulos advised wearing earplugs before shooting. The leaders then divided the volunteers into teams and sent them out into the gathering darkness.

So here was Ms. Sacopulos, prowling Terre Haute streets in her unmarked Caddy. In the back seat, her latest issue of Birds & Blooms magazine ("Beauty in Your Own Backyard"); in the front, her pistol, her ammo, her resolve. All that was missing was a police radio's cackle.

As Ms. Sacopulos drove, she pointed out the places where crows loiter, including St. Benedict Roman Catholic Church—her church. She reflected on how crows always seem to be watching you. She whispered that they seem to be everywhere: "It gets so that you kind of feel they're there."

And they are: a murder of crows spotted in trees along Liberty Avenue. Ms. Sacopulos stepped out of her car in her vest of bright orange. She loaded her pistol, aimed and—boom! Startled crows darted into the air, while startled people darted from their homes.

"Crow Patrol," she explained, matter of fact.

EPILOGUE

The annual infestation of crows in Terre Haute continues to be, well, murder. As a result, the work of the crow patrol continues, although it is now handled by the city's code-enforcement unit.

Meanwhile, the indefatigable Joy Sacopulos reports that in the spring of 2012, she ended her crow patrol "tour of duty."

In Fuel Oil Country,
Cold That Cuts to the Heart

DIXFIELD, ME. — FEBRUARY 4, 2012

With the darkening approach of another ice-hard Saturday night in western Maine, the man on the telephone was pleading for help, again. His tank was nearly dry, and he and his disabled wife needed precious heating oil to keep warm. Could Ike help out? Again?

Ike Libby, the co-owner of a small oil company called Hometown Energy, ached for his customer, Robert Hartford. He knew what winter in Maine meant, especially for a retired couple living in a wood-frame house built in the 19th century.

But he also knew that the Hartfords already owed him more than $700 for two earlier deliveries.

The oil man said he was very sorry. The customer said he understood. And each was left to grapple with a matter so mundane in Maine, and so vital: the need for heat. For the rest of the weekend, Mr. Libby agonized over his decision, while Mr. Hartford warmed his house with the heat from his electric stove's four burners.

"You get off the phone thinking, 'Are these people going to be found frozen?'" Mr. Libby said. No wonder, he said, that he is prescribed medication for stress and "happy pills" for equilibrium.

Two days later, Mr. Libby told his two office workers about his decision. Diane Carlton works the front desk while her daughter-in-law, Janis, handles accounts. But they share the job of worrying about Ike, whose heart, they say, is too big for his bantam size and, maybe, this business.

The Hartford case "ate him," Janis Carlton recalled. "It just ate him."

Mr. Libby drove off to make deliveries in his oil truck, a rolling receptacle of crumpled coffee cups and cigarette packs. Diane Carlton, the office's mother hen, went home early. This meant that Janis Carlton was alone when their customer, Mr. Hartford, stepped in from the cold. He had something in his hand: the title to his 16-year-old Lincoln Town Car.

Would Hometown Energy take the title as collateral for some heating oil? Please?

Maine is in the midst of its Republican presidential caucus, the state's wintry moment in the battle for the country's future.

But at this time of year, almost nothing matters here as much as basic heat.

While federal officials try to wean the country from messy and expensive

Ike Libby, delivering oil

heating oil, Maine remains addicted. The housing stock is old, most communities are rural, and many residents cannot afford to switch to a cleaner heat source. So the tankers pull into, say, the Portland port, the trucks load up, and the likes of Ike Libby sidle up to house after house to fill oil tanks.

This winter has been especially austere. As part of the drive to cut spending, the Obama administration and Congress have trimmed the energy-assistance program that helps the poor—65,000 households in Maine alone—to pay their heating bills. Eligibility is harder now, and the average amount given here is $483, down from $804 last year, all at a time when the price of oil has risen more than 40 cents in a year, to $3.71 a gallon.

As a result, Community Concepts, a community-action program serving western Maine, receives dozens of calls a day from people seeking warmth. But Dana Stevens, its director of energy and housing, says that he has distributed so much of the money reserved for emergencies that he fears running out. This means that sometimes the agency's hot line purposely goes unanswered.

So Mainers try to make do. They warm up in idling cars, then dash inside and dive under the covers. They pour a few gallons of kerosene into their oil tank and hope it lasts. And they count on others. Maybe their pastor. Maybe the delivery man. Maybe, even, a total stranger.

Hometown Energy has five trucks and seven employees, and is run out of an old house next to the Ellis variety store and diner. Oil perfumes the place, thanks to the petroleum-stained truckers and mechanics clomping through. Janis Carlton, 35, tracks accounts in the back, while Diane Carlton, 64, works in the front, where, every now and then, she finds herself comforting walk-ins who fear the cold so much that they cry.

Their boss, Mr. Libby, 53, has rough hands and oil-stained dungarees. He has been delivering oil for most of his adult life—throwing the heavy hose over his shoulder, shoving the silver nozzle into the tank and listening for the whistle that blows when oil replaces air.

Eight years ago, he and another Dixfield local, Gene Ellis, who owns that variety store next door, created Hometown Energy, a company whose logo features a painting of a church-and-hillside scene from just down the road. They thought that with Ike's oil sense and Gene's business sense, they'd make money. But Mr. Libby says now that he'd sell the company in a heartbeat.

"You know what my dream is?" Mr. Libby asked. "To be a greeter at Walmart."

This is because he sells heat—not lumber, or paper, or pastries—and around here, more than a few come too close to not having enough. Sure, some abuse the heating-assistance program, he says, but many others live in dire need, including people he has known all his life.

So Mr. Libby does what he can. Unlike many oil companies, he makes small deliveries and waves off most service fees. He sets up elaborate payment plans, hoping that obligations don't melt away with the spring thaw. He accepts postdated checks. And he takes his medication.

When the customer named Robert Hartford called on the after-hours line that Saturday afternoon, asking for another delivery, Mr. Libby struggled to do what was right. He cannot bear the thought of people wanting for warmth, but his tendency to cut people a break is one reason Hometown Energy isn't making much money, as his understanding partner keeps gently pointing out.

"I do have a heart," Mr. Libby said. But he was already "on the hook" for the two earlier deliveries he had made to the couple's home. What's more, he didn't even know the Hartfords.

Robert and Wilma Hartford settled into the porous old house, just outside of Dixfield, a few months ago, in what was the latest of many moves in their 37-year marriage. Mr. Hartford was once a stonemason who traveled from the Pacific Northwest to New England, plying his trade.

Those wandering days are gone. Mr. Hartford, 68, has a bad shoulder, Mrs. Hartford, 71, needs a wheelchair, and the two survive on $1,200 a month ("Poverty," Mrs. Hartford says). So far this year they have received $360 in heating assistance, he said, about a quarter of last year's allocation.

Mr. Hartford said he used what extra money they had to repair broken pipes, install a cellar door, and seal various cracks with Styrofoam spray that he bought at Walmart. That wasn't enough to block the cold, of course, and the two oil deliveries carried them only into early January.

There was no oil to burn, so the cold took up residence, beside the dog and the four cats, under the velvet painting of Jesus. The couple had no choice but to run up their electric bill. They turned on the Whirlpool stove's burners and circulated the heat with a small fan.

They ran the dryer's hose back into the basement to keep pipes from freezing, even when there were no clothes to dry.

And, just about every day, Mr. Hartford drove to a gas station and filled up a five-gallon plastic container with $20 of kerosene. "It was the only way we had," he said. Finally, seeing no other option, Mr. Hartford made the hard telephone call to Hometown Energy.

Panic lurked behind his every word, and every word wounded the oil man on the other end.

"I had a hard time saying no," Mr. Libby said. "But I had to say no."

When Mr. Hartford heard that no, he also heard regret. "You could tell in his voice," he said. Two days later, Mr. Hartford drove up to Hometown Energy's small office in his weathered gray Lincoln, walked inside, and made his desperate offer: the title to his car for some oil.

His offer stunned Janis Carlton, the only employee present. But she remembered that someone had offered, quietly, to donate 50 gallons of heating oil if an emergency case walked through the door. She called that person and explained the situation.

Her mother-in-law and office mate, Diane Carlton, answered without hesitation. Deliver the oil and I'll pay for it, she said, which is one of the ways that Mainers make do in winter.

PART SEVEN

Grace

Ah! Sweet Mystery of Life

He Befriended a Serial Killer,
and Opened the Door to God

COTTAGE GROVE, WIS. — MARCH 11, 2007

The big wall clock tells the minister he has less than an hour before tonight's Bible class down at the church. No time for supper.

He finds his keys in the tight apartment that he and his wife, Susan, have rented for 16 years, shared now with an adult daughter, two cats and a dog. In this space the clock looms large, a treadmill dominates the living room, and bunny knickknacks everywhere signal the approaching season of rebirth.

A goodbye to Susan, a pocket pat to jingle those keys, and out he goes into the wintry Wisconsin sunset, Roy Ratcliff, minister of the Mandrake Road Church of Christ in Madison. No different from any other preacher, save for one baptism he performed long ago.

"My friend Jeff," Mr. Ratcliff often calls him. A child of God.

His friend Jeff was killed in prison in 1994, several months after his baptism and in a brutal fashion too quick and clean for some. To say that he confessed to killing 17 young men and boys only begins to hint at his grisly crimes. His full name was Jeffrey Dahmer, and his depraved actions once made the world recoil.

Mr. Dahmer left behind confused parents, dozens of distraught relatives of the victims, the traumatized city of Milwaukee—and this white-bearded minister, struggling still at 60 with the sense that he, too, had been condemned, for having the audacity to grant God's blessings upon the devil.

"I'm marked as the man who did that," Mr. Ratcliff says, his tone suggesting frustration, not regret.

Before this singular act came to define him, Mr. Ratcliff was just another modest minister of modest means, addressing the temporal and spiritual needs of a few dozen congregants. He tended to speak rapidly, with New Testament references seeming to tumble from his lips with each exhalation.

Then, one day in April 1994, Mr. Ratcliff found himself in a small room at the Columbia Correctional Institution in Portage, where an inmate had expressed a desire to be baptized. He had never met a serial killer; for that matter, he had never been inside a prison.

The young man entered smiling and unshackled. The minister calmed himself and got to the point: "I understand you want to be baptized."

In Mr. Ratcliff's mind, the shocking crimes of Mr. Dahmer were stipulated; the inmate had readily confessed to everything after his capture in 1991. What mattered now was whether this blond, pallid man before him understood that baptism cleansed his sins against God, not his crimes against the state.

Roy Ratcliff, minister

"He was seeking redemption," Mr. Ratcliff says, recalling how Mr. Dahmer often spoke of being the worst of sinners. "He was seeking forgiveness."

A few weeks later, Mr. Dahmer donned a white polyester robe and climbed into a steel-silver whirlpool normally used by inmates with physical injuries. The minister gently pushed him under the water until he was fully immersed, and baptized him with a short prayer.

When the convict emerged, the preacher said, "Welcome to the family of God."

Jeffrey Dahmer smiled.

Every Wednesday for months afterward, Mr. Ratcliff met with Mr. Dahmer to pray. The convict said he should have been put to death for his crimes, and his minister agreed. He talked about suicide, something the preacher had flirted with many years earlier, after being fired from another church. A shared faith drew the different men together.

A few days before he was killed in November 1994, Mr. Dahmer handed Mr. Ratcliff a Thanksgiving Day card that the minister keeps wrapped in plastic. "Dear Roy," the note begins, in loopy handwriting. "Thank you for your friendship, and for taking the time and effort to help me understand God's word."

After a discreet memorial service at the minister's church in Madison, after the notorious surname had slipped into the recesses of public consciousness, Mr. Ratcliff continued to be identified as the man who baptized the serial killer. Both in and out of the Church of Christ community, some embraced him for it, while others shunned him.

People would walk away when introduced to him or argue that they wanted no part of a heaven that included Jeffrey Dahmer. Some would praise him to his face, only to tell others that he had been duped. He was rarely invited to other churches to talk about the salvation of the least of us, because, he guesses, "there is a sense of shame."

At gatherings of preachers in the region, he says, one minister from Milwaukee constantly points him out to others and says: Do you know who that man is? Do you know what he did?

"I've become a little bit jaded by the hypocrisy," Mr. Ratcliff says.

Last year Mr. Ratcliff wrote a short book about what he calls Mr. Dahmer's "story of faith." The book, "Dark Journey, Deep Grace," has sold poorly—perhaps, he says, because people cannot see that a story about Mr. Dahmer is a story about all of us.

Mr. Ratcliff says he is a better man for having known Jeffrey Dahmer, but knows that some people will have trouble understanding this. He says he now visits several prisons a month. He says he has a keener understanding of faith, and of mercy.

It seems that Mr. Dahmer is rarely far from the preacher's mind. For example, that large clock looming in his family's apartment was bought at a kiosk in the mall, with the honorarium the Dahmer family gave him for arranging the memorial service. The Ratcliffs call it "Jeff's clock."

By the time that clock strikes seven, the minister is already at his church, turning on the lights, checking the heat, greeting congregants. Soon he joins them in song.

20,000 Days Down the Road, a Night on the Path

JAFFREY, N.H. — OCTOBER 14, 2007

Let us take a walk in the woods.

With no afternoon commitments, one of the great perks of retirement, this is what Jim and Eleanor McQueen decide to do: take a walk in the woods on a pleasant September afternoon. Nothing ambitious. Back in time for dinner.

Truth be told, Eleanor could do without the walk; she would be just as happy to work in her flower garden. But Jim has always loved to hike, and now with this new right knee of his, he is eager to make up for lost time. They are both 81; best they go together.

Twenty minutes later, their white sedan pulls up to a sign that welcomes them to the densely wooded Heald Tract. It refers to a "short, 1.5 mile hike that is part of a more extensive trail system." That's the one, says Jim, who researches these things—though Eleanor describes this research as getting mailings "from every cuckoo outfit out there."

Yes, the McQueens have quarreled now and then during their 55 years of wedded bliss. Or, as Eleanor puts it: "We're at swords' points all the time. All the time!"

The only trail opening they see is a few yards down the road; blue rectangles on trees seem to suggest the way for this short hike. If it's 3 o'clock now, they reason, we'll be out by 4. Short-sleeve shirts over T-shirts are fine. In they go.

They hike under maple and beech, past stone walls and small ponds, through an old orchard where they pluck some apples to eat. After a while, Eleanor says this is the longest damn mile-and-a-half she's ever walked.

Jim studies the pink map he picked up during his research, but it provides no comforting, geo-specific certainty. Overhead, a canopy of trees blots the sunlight. They keep walking, hoping to find that certainty around the next bend.

After another while, Eleanor asks, What time is it anyway? Jim reaches for his glow-in-the-dark Timex, the one with the broken wristband. Seven o'clock, he says, and they both know they have to get out of here now.

Their hopes dim with the fading light. They are not lost so much as trapped by the descending darkness. Jim suggests that they plop down for the night. Eleanor readily agrees, which pleasantly surprises Jim.

Are you having fun yet? Eleanor teases. Yeah, yeah, Jim says.

They do not worry about things that go bump in the night; they are 81. Their concern is the dropping temperature. They try to snuggle on the rocky, sloping ground, but their exposed arms are too cold. They slip their arms into their shirts, sit beside each other, and begin to talk.

If this were a movie, the McQueens would now reflect on their shared 55 years and profess their love for each other. But this is real life. Some things are just understood; stipulated, you might say.

Stipulated: That they were introduced at a Catholic social at Columbia University in 1950. Jim was a World War II Navy veteran of the Pacific theater and Eleanor was a nurse. They married and eventually settled in Somers, Conn., where they had three children.

Stipulated: That over the next half-century, they did the best they could. Jim, a chemical engineer, often suffered the vagaries of big business; the toughest came in 1970, when a new job meant uprooting the family and moving 100 miles north to Jaffrey. Eleanor kept the house together, then returned to nursing to help pay the tuition bills coming simultaneously from three colleges.

Stipulated: That in retirement, they may still butt heads, but they also still put heads together. On the dining room wall, for example, there hangs a framed saying: "May You Live All the Days of Your Life." She did the calligraphy; he made the frame.

Eleanor should be taking her blood pressure medication about now. Felix the cat is probably waiting to be let in. The cellphone is sitting on a windowsill. Jim wouldn't use it anyway, reasoning that the situation isn't dangerous enough; Eleanor would, though, just to alert people.

They amuse themselves by imagining their children's response to all this ("You did what!"), and shouting to a passing airplane ("We're here! We're here!"). They seek warmth by lying on top of each other, though this proves awkward, what with their arms inside their shirts.

We're babes in the woods, Eleanor thinks, and suddenly she is a child again, watching one of her older sisters—Grace, wasn't it?—in a junior high school production of the Humperdinck opera "Hänsel und Gretel." Grace would die in her mid-20s, but now here, in the wooded darkness, her baby sister is singing the evening prayer:

> *When at night I go to sleep*
> *Fourteen angels watch do keep*
> *Two my head are guarding*
> *Two my feet are guiding*
> *Two are on my right hand*
> *Two are on my left hand*
> *Two who warmly cover*
> *Two who o'er me hover*
> *Two to whom 'tis given*
> *To guide my steps to heaven.*

Hansel and Gretel veer between dozing and shivering. I wish two angels would bring us blankets. Having fun yet?

Dawn comes, and two people who have spent more than 20,000 days as husband and wife continue their walk through the woods—to the way out.

Soon the children will find out. Soon Eleanor will write down her account of the night, which will prompt Jim to write down his account. They don't exactly match.

But right now Jim and Eleanor are finding their way again, and she is carrying some of those plucked apples.

A Story of Exile and Union
Few Are Left to Tell

The peace of morning comes to the small village of famous isolation called Kalau-papa. Breezes rustle the berry bushes. Myna birds call from treetops to wild pigs below. Life stirs on this spit of land between the soaring Molokai cliffs and the stretching Pacific abyss.

The residents who call themselves patients move about in the hours before the day's few tourists arrive. Here is Danny, who first came here in 1942, lingering a moment in the peekaboo sun; Ivy, who arrived in 1956, standing outside the gas station she runs; Boogie, here since 1959, driving a clattering old van.

Boogie, whose given name is Clarence Kahilihiwa, gently explains why he considers himself a patient, not a resident. Some people, the state health employees and National Park Service workers, live here as part of their jobs. Others live here because this is where they were sent, against their will, long ago.

You see, he says, "We are—and you are not."

Those who are have Hansen's disease, also known as leprosy. Those who are represent the last few of some 8,000 people who, over a century's span, were banished to Kalaupapa because of an illness once called the "separating sickness." Many never again felt the embrace of loved ones living somewhere beyond the volcanic formations that rise like stone sentries just offshore.

Hawaii effectively liberated Kalaupapa by abolishing its isolation laws in 1969—more than 20 years after the development of medicine to control and cure the disease. Earlier this year, the state's Legislature formally apologized to the patients and their families for "any restrictions that caused them undue pain as the result of government policies surrounding leprosy."

Today, just 24 patients are left: 24 people who experienced the counterintuitive twinning of loneliness and community, of all that dying and all that living. Here, you may have grieved over the forced surrender of your newborn; you may also have rejoiced in finding a life partner who understood.

Ten live off-island, including eight in a hospital in Honolulu, 53 miles away. The rest live in Kalaupapa, now a national historical park with restrictions befitting its almost sacred nature. When asked why he stays, Boogie provides an answer so easy it's complicated:

"This is my home."

At 67, he is among the youngest patients, silver-haired and weather-beaten, quick to shake hands. When he was a young boy, a rosy spot appeared on his cheek, and his parents had no choice but to take him to a special hospital outside Honolulu. "When my parents left me," he says, "that is when I crossed the line."

Boogie moved nearly 50 years ago to Kalaupapa, where three siblings are now buried, including a sister who died at age 12. Although he has been off-island many times, visiting the mainland, shopping in Honolulu, his identity is here, where he has married twice and done everything from operate the theater's projector to preside over the Lions Club.

He is also on the board of Ka'Ohana O Kalaupapa, an organization that advocates for patients and the preservation of the settlement, which was established in 1866 amid growing panic about leprosy's spread. We must remember the story of this place, he says, a story that began with the sorrowful arrival of nine men and three women.

His dust-covered van pulls up to the gas station, where his wife, Ivy, 72, aims a hose's lazy spray on the windshield. As a Kalaupapa patient, she has known both liberation's joy, with trips to the mainland and Europe, and confinement's anguish: Her two children from a previous marriage were taken away immediately after birth because that was the law.

Husband and wife of more than 30 years gaze at each other through the distortion of running water on glass. Then he continues on, past the post office, past the wharf where, once every summer, a barge pulls up with building supplies, furniture and the occasional new car. "Christmas in July," they call it.

He turns onto a gravel stretch called Damien Road, past the overgrown spot where the famous patient Olivia Breitha—"Even if my skin is insensitive," she once wrote, "my heart and soul are not"—ran a chicken farm with her husband, John; past a tree-shrouded cemetery, where the rub of time has made tombstone almost indistinguishable from rock.

Farther on, Boogie points into a blur of dense green. "The picture of Damien, where he was kneeling down," he says, recalling a famous image. "It was here."

He reveres Father Damien, the strapping, strong-minded Roman Catholic missionary who came in 1873 to give hope and dignity to a place often called a "living tomb." With the help of patients, the priest improved St. Philomena Church, built houses, planted trees, created a water system, established a choir, nursed the living and gave proper burial to the dead.

After he contracted leprosy, Father Damien wrote that he was now "the happiest missionary in the world." He died in 1889 at age 49, and was buried a few yards from an open field that is believed to contain as many as 2,000 unmarked graves.

Father Damien's canonization is expected to take place late next year, and Boogie and Ivy plan to be there in Rome. For now, Boogie honors the man often called, simply, Damien, by pausing awhile at the priest's grave, hands clasped, head bowed.

The noon sun rises above Kalaupapa's lush solitude. Tourists, maybe two dozen in all, have traveled by mule down the cliff from "topside" Molokai, and are now lunching quietly in a grassy field. Boogie remembers the Boy Scout camp that was near here; gone now. He greets a couple of the tourists and moves on.

Toward day's end, a stop is made at the care facility where there reside some patients who remember when visitors were required to don gowns and have police escorts. When patients lived in a swirl of don't touch this, don't go there. When there were dances, and musical shows, and lei-making contests, and extremely competitive softball games with bats especially adapted for hands that could no longer grip.

Father Damien's grave

In one room, Makia Malo, a gifted storyteller of 74, sits in a wheelchair, sunglasses covering his compromised eyes. He so vividly recalls the morning he was sent as a boy to Kalaupapa that you share the child's excitement about boarding an airplane for the first time, even though you know the dreaded reason for the trip. In another room, Henry Nalaielua, 84, who wrote a memoir of his rich life in Kalaupapa, talks about the black-and-white photograph in his book, of a boy of 10, posed with hands across his chest to help document the state of his just-diagnosed disease. The boy glowers back at you from the harrowing past.

"I was scared and defiant," that boy as man says. "Or maybe I just didn't care to smile." Who will tell the story of Kalaupapa after Henry has gone, and Makia and Ivy and Danny and Boogie? Boogie says he thinks about this all the time: "Every time one person dies, we get less and less."

Still, he believes he has had a good life, with a loving wife and a remote paradise to call home. He prays daily to Father Damien. And when sea breezes stir the whispers in the trees, he listens.

Burlesque Days Again
for the Feather Boa Crowd

BARABOO, WIS. — OCTOBER 2, 2009

In a modest hotel suite at the Ho-Chunk Casino, a few women from out of town gather for a reunion. Homemade brownies sit on the counter, along with a peach pie, some cheese curds, several cans of soda and a long, sleek bottle of cherry vodka—a perfect name, they joke, for a burlesque queen.

There is no Cherry Vodka in the room. But Nocturne is here. And La Savona. And Ann Pett. And the Irish Mist. And Bambi Jones, also known as Bambi Brooks, Joi Naymith, the Black Panther Girl, the Mona Lisa Girl, the Garter Girl,

Evangeline the Oyster Girl—and, for a while there in New Orleans, "The Girl the Whole Town's Talking About."

And Pat Flannery, just Pat Flannery, may also show up. Nearly 60 years ago she did her "How Do You Do?" routine at the old Moulin Rouge in Oakland, wearing dark opera gloves, a polka dot gown and a look that said, You naughty boy. By act's end, only the look remained.

La Savona

But Ms. Flannery might have to cancel her Baraboo appearance. She is 83 now, using a wheelchair and living in a nursing home about two hours north of here—though there is hopeful talk of an overnight furlough for the woman who once saucily sang to would-be suitors:

"How do you do? But now, How do you do?"

Either way, Ms. Flannery is present in some of the photographs splayed on a table. Here she is in a skimpy sailor's outfit, saluting. And here is La Savona in midwrithe, during her signature Scheherazade routine. And here is Bambi in Miami, sharing drinks with Errol Flynn in the mid-1950s, and performing at a senior center in Connecticut just a few weeks ago, where she wowed them.

For that appearance she wore a pink Southern belle number that she proceeded to remove, slowly, before beginning a discourse on the history of burlesque. "I worked the walkers, and I worked the canes," says Bambi, a limber 79.

Outside this hotel door, civilians plod about, playing the penny slots, shuffling toward the bargain buffet. What do they know of the old bump and grind? Of enthralling men through skin and suggestion—and then puncturing the moment with a bawdy one-liner?

Bambi shares a few of those lines, but you'll have to catch her at the senior center to hear them; they cannot be repeated here. She also shares a basic burlesque technique. Imagine an apple to your left, an orange to your right, and a coffee bean in front of you. Now follow these pelvic thrusts:

"Hit the apple, hit the orange and g-r-r-ind the coffee.

"Hit the apple, hit the orange and g-r-r-ind the coffee . . ." Where were we?

Oh, yes, we are in Room 1223 at the Ho-Chunk Casino in lovely Baraboo, where the days blur and the chitchat says this is no quilting bee:

"I had been kicking chorus in Cleveland . . . I worked with Champagne glasses . . . It took 10 guys to get the snake off of her. And I said, 'So now I understand why you don't work Massachusetts.'"

"That cheese curd is delicious," Nocturne says. To which Bambi says, "Did you ever work Canada?"

Fifteen years ago, Tanayo, the Costa Rican Dream Girl, handed a worn address book filled with the stage names of lost friends to her civilian friend, Jane Briggeman. So began the Golden Days of Burlesque Historical Society, a nonprofit group dedicated to reuniting those who worked the circuit in the years before 1965: the strippers and dancers, the comics and straight men—the feather boa crowd.

The society had 235 members at its peak, many of whom helped Ms. Briggeman, 54, recover enough memories and photographs to write two books: "Burlesque: Legendary Stars of the Stage," published in 2004, a year after Tanayo died, and "Burlesque: A Living History," to be published this year. She continues the cause, in part by maintaining a newsletter with health updates, recent deaths and requests for help, as in:

"Lilli Marlene is looking for Luna, Goddess of the Spirit World."

But the hook of time has reduced membership to about 135. A list of attendees from a reunion in 2006 includes the names of Lee Stuart, a great straight man; Sunny Dare, the Girl With the Blue Hair; and Carmela, the Sophia Loren of Burlesque. Gone, gone and gone.

As Ms. Briggeman says their names, La Savona, petite, elegant, and wearing a blond wig, sits with a magnifying glass, reading her newspaper notices and advertisements from the days when she was the Czech bombshell who escaped the Communists. ("She's the Cinderella that upset European royalty! Now making her first Toledo appearance!")

At some point a knock at the door disrupts the memories. Pat Flannery?

No. A lanky, white-haired man, carrying in some chairs. Says his name is Bones. Outside, civilians and buffet lines. Inside, cherry vodka, rich desserts and stories about tassel applications and acts with animals. "I worked with this little girl, and she had parakeets," Nocturne remembers. "Parakeets in her purse."

Nocturne, 79, who drove up from Texas with her husband, is alone in saying her burlesque days were her darkest. She found stripping to be a lucrative humiliation, and she detested the pressure to mix with customers so they would buy a club's overpriced liquor.

But that is all behind her now, she says. Thirty years ago she found Jesus and has not had a drink since, "Praise God." She has come to Baraboo to see old friends and to remember the one aspect of burlesque she adored, those glorious costumes.

Bambi, also 79, is Nocturne's opposite: She left Holyoke, Mass., as a young woman and never looked back. Yes, some strippers would sabotage the outfits of their competitors, and yes, there was that abusive second husband, the one who forced her to flee. But one of burlesque's many charms is its service as a kind of witness-protection program; for a few years, then, Bambi became Holly Simms. Of burlesque over all, she says, "I loved it."

It is deep into the second day of the reunion now; time for a show. The coffee table has been moved aside, some chairs arranged. The Irish Mist will strut for a while, Bambi will grind that coffee bean, and a young burlesque star named Orchid Mei—who has been listening to the stories with undergraduate earnestness—will do an act that makes many in the room wish for 1955.

Another knock on the door. Is it Bones?

No: Pat Flannery. And what an entrance she makes: seated in a chariot of a wheelchair pushed by her elder daughter, Bekki Vallin, and wearing a pink sweatshirt, white socks that match her hair, and teal slip-on sneakers.

Her one-liners come out fast, most of them at her own expense. When she cannot remember the name of some Wisconsin town, she assumes a stage mentalist's pose, with a hand against forehead, and intones, "The mind has left the body."

Ms. Flannery watches the three women dance, one after another. She laughs at Bambi's wisecracks. She admires the fluid grace of Orchid Mei. And when the show is over, she is wheeled to a place where she enjoys a cigarette while looking out upon some grass.

How do you do.

Seeking God's Help
for a Wounded Gulf

In a small white building along the baptizing Bon Secour River, a building that once housed a shrimp-net business, the congregation of the Fishermen Baptist Church gathered for another Sunday service, with the preacher presiding from a pulpit designed to look like a ship captain's wheel.

After the singing of the opening hymn, "Ring the Bells of Heaven," and the announcement that an engaged couple was now registered at Walmart, the preacher read aloud a proclamation from Gov. Bob Riley that declared this to be a "day of prayer"—a day of entreaties to address the ominous threat to the way of life just outside the church's white doors.

Whereas, and whereas, and whereas, the proclamation read. People of Alabama, please pray for your fellow citizens, for other states hurt by this disaster, for all those who are responding. And pray "that a solution that stops the oil leak is completed soon."

In other words, dear God, thank you for your blessings and guidance. And one other thing, dear God:

Help.

The governor's words hung a moment in the fan-turned air. Then the preacher, Shawn Major, summoned the men of the church to the front to "ask God to do something special."

Two dozen men, many of them wearing short-sleeve shirts in summery colors, knelt and sat with heads bowed and eyes closed, while a half-mile down the street, other men—and women—underwent training in the use of a more secular form of hope, the laying of boom.

The wall between church and state came a-tumbling down on Sunday, as elected leaders from the five states on the Gulf of Mexico issued proclamations declaring it to be a day of prayer. Although days of prayer are not uncommon here—Governor Riley declared one asking for rain to relieve a drought a few years ago—these proclamations conveyed the sense that at this late date, salvation from the spill all but requires divine intervention.

In the two months since the deadly Deepwater Horizon explosion began a ceaseless leak of oil into the gulf, damaging the ecosystem and disrupting the economy, the efforts by mortals to stem the flow have failed. Robots and golf balls and even the massive capping dome all seem small in retrospect.

So, then, a supplementary method was attempted: coordinated prayer.

In Texas, Gov. Rick Perry encouraged Texans to ask God "for his merciful intervention and healing in this time of crisis." In Mississippi, Gov. Haley Barbour declared that prayer "allows us an opportunity to reflect and to seek guidance, strength, comfort and inspiration from Almighty God." In Louisiana, Gov. Bobby Jindal invoked the word "whereas" a dozen times—as well as the state bird, the brown pelican—but made no direct mention of God. In Florida, Lt. Gov. Jeff Kottkamp asked people to pray that God "would guide and direct our civil leaders and provide them with wisdom and divinely inspired solutions."

The suggestion by government to beseech God for help—to petition a power higher than any elected official—rang out in churches and halls from Pensacola, Fla., to Galveston, Tex., as well as here, in Bon Secour, where Brother Harry prayed with head bowed.

The Fishermen Baptist Church has been in this village, whose name means safe harbor, since 1989. An anchor is planted in its front lawn. Its walls are adorned with paintings of nautical scenes. Its collection boxes are a miniature lighthouse and a treasure chest. The dock across the street is used for baptisms and fishing.

These are all reflections of the church's founder and pastor, Wayne Mund, who grew up here. His father, grandfather and great-grandfather were fishermen, and so was he, until the age of 21, when he dropped his nets and went off to Bible school.

Pastor Mund, 66, lanky and proud to call himself a Bible Baptist, works hard to incorporate his seafaring past into his mission. He sees the Bible, from the Book of Genesis to the Book of Revelation, as a nautical book, and the sea as a mesmerizing draw. He will end conversation by warning that those who do not climb aboard God's boat of salvation "will drown in a sea of sin and despair."

And now the oily despair in the sea is affecting his small church, his community. Fewer envelopes are being slipped into the treasure chest and lighthouse at the back of the room because some of his 200 congregants can no longer afford to tithe. Fewer people are attending service because fishermen, who normally take Sundays off, are now working for BP to help clean up its goo, which is washing up in Gulf Shores and Mobile Bay.

"The sea, the sea, the sea," Pastor Mund says. "It has to do with the sea."

Pastor Mund expected to be out of town on Sunday, so he assigned an associate pastor, Mr. Major, to preside over the 10:30 service. Mr. Major is 46, stocky and more apt to smile than his boss when proselytizing. The spill affecting the river, the world, has been difficult for him to fathom, and he expects that the human toll will not be felt for another year.

Mr. Major spent Saturday with 70 men and women, all learning the proper way to lay boom. But now he was with 70 other men and women, all praying from nine wooden pews; all saying amen to his assertion that "We are still a Christian nation"; all nodding when he said that everyone knew "who ultimately will stop" the spill.

A missionary about to leave for Brazil was waiting to make a multimedia presentation, but first these kneeling men, led by Brother Harry—Harry Mund, a relative of the pastor's—needed to finish their prayer.

Please God, help us with "this awful oil spill," he said. In Jesus' name. Amen.

The men rose from their knees and returned to their pews, a couple of them rubbing the salty wet from their eyes.

Passion Play in Rural Florida Endures Time's Many Trials

WAUCHULA, FLA. — APRIL 21, 2011

With less than two hours until showtime, a man sits amid the backstage chaos and studies his image in a propped-up mirror. The eyes are grayish blue, the goatee trim, the long dark hair flecked with gray. Not there yet. He scoops another dab of makeup to continue the annual transformation of Mike Graham, now 58, into Jesus Christ, forever 33.

An assistant hustles over with a sky-blue robe that an anxious Mr. Graham wriggles over his bare torso and summer shorts. "Too little on me," he says apologetically, working his way out of it. Someone else asks him to assess a young girl's angel costume. "I'd like her to be glittered," he says, before asking whether the child has been warned how to behave around the camels.

Then the man who plays Jesus for a living turns back to his imperfect reflection.

For more than two decades, Mr. Graham, a preacher, has directed and assumed the lead role in a gritty Passion play, "The Story of Jesus," that unfolds 10 nights a year in the modest Cattleman's Arena, in rural Hardee County. Across its dirt-floor stage come chariots and sword fights, miracles and betrayals, exotic animals and a cast of hundreds.

Over time, Mr. Graham's play has survived many trials, some natural, some economic and some, he suspects, the work of the devil. In 2004, the production weathered both the competition of the Mel Gibson movie "The Passion of the Christ" and the wrath of a hurricane that nearly swept Wauchula away but spared the play's many costumes and long-suffering donkey.

Other challenges, he says, have included his divorce years ago, which alienated many followers; a decline in attendance, due in part to competition from the Holy

297

Land Experience theme park in Orlando; and other, curiously timed setbacks—a car accident, a sudden illness—that nearly prevented him from picking up his cross.

Finally, Mr. Graham knows the folly of trying to slow time, although he has tried. For one thing, he has enlisted a 27-year-old bridge inspector to play Jesus in certain taxing scenes.

"He handles the Trial, the Ascension, the Resurrection," Mr. Graham explains. "I do all the miracles, basically. The adult life of Jesus, the Last Supper, the garden of Gethsemane scene, and the Crucifixion."

Mr. Graham cuts his hair just once a year, and works out every morning in his home gym so that he is able to carry a heavy cross dozens of yards across the stage. Still, he has no desire to follow

The transformation

the great Josef Meier, who played Jesus in performances in South Dakota and in Lake Wales, just north of here, well into his 80s. A miracle in itself.

For now, Mr. Graham must set aside these concerns, and focus. The first Passion play of the season is just 90 minutes away.

PROPS, PAINT AND PETTING ZOO

Under the late-afternoon sun, white cast members take turns getting spray-painted a color called Sebring brown, a shade that Mr. Graham thinks approaches a Middle Eastern skin tone. A man in a "Sprayin' & Prayin'" T-shirt dilutes the chocolate muck in plastic buckets, while another man, with a praying-hands tattoo on his left leg, paints a succession of outstretched arms, splayed legs and wincing faces.

This ritual is one of many that have evolved over the last quarter-century, ever since Mr. Graham, as a guitar-wielding youth pastor from southern Illinois, staged a crucifixion scene at a church banquet with a few teenagers and a couple of props. Some of those here tonight have never been in a Passion play; others have never known a spring without one. They are united now by glistening coats of Sebring brown.

Alongside the arena, clusters of ticketholders gather for some nonalcoholic tailgating, while a Roman centurion trots past on a horse. In a tent nearby, volunteers set out various souvenirs for sale, including cardboard license plates that say: The Story of Jesus—I Was There!—Wauchula, Florida.

A kind of off-limits petting zoo has sprung up beyond the arena's back entrance, with pens containing ducks, sheep, horses, two oxen, a donkey and three camels, just arrived from Ocala. Their owner, Butch Rivers, 70, a former stunt rider who now uses a cane—"You pay for it," he says of certain passions—is excited to see the play again.

"The first time I saw this play it put chills on me," Mr. Rivers says.

An hour until showtime, and the Cattleman's Arena awaits its first-century bustle. The dirt has been raked and sprayed with water, to keep the dust down. All soda cans and other remnants of the future have been removed. The still-life setting is as serene as the blue-dyed river dug into the dirt, stage right.

But just a few yards away, in an exhibit hall serving as backstage, a large industrial fan stirs the nervous air. Actors hunt through a long rack of costumes that runs beneath a portrait gallery of beauty queens, the "Cattlemen's Sweethearts" of the near and distant past. Children wolf down treats and Gatorade before assuming the roles of angels and demons. Girding thespians reach for their fake spears and swords.

BEHIND THE SCENES

Here is Joann Grantham, 56, volunteer prop master, who has done everything from scour discount stores for plastic fruit to retouch the throne of the child king. She has also helped to decide whether you're a shop owner, an apostle or a member of the Sanhedrin. (Mr. Graham, by the way, is aware of the history of anti-Semitic Passion plays, and takes pains not to traffic in stereotypes.)

In the past, Ms. Grantham has often played a "false witness" who spits on Jesus. But she chose to remain behind the scenes this year, after undergoing chemotherapy and radiation for breast cancer. When she goes to Walmart, she says, she wears a hat to cover her bald head, but tonight she feels at home, hatless and happy.

Here, too, is Michelle Puma, 54, volunteer makeup artist, who has set up shop in the 4-H Club's concession booth. Everything is in its place: the long-haired wigs set on Styrofoam heads; the various jars of fake blood; the blue boxes of Jesus beards; the Ace Hardware bucket containing various props, including a crown of thorns.

One of Ms. Puma's challenges is to make young people look older, which is the opposite of Mr. Graham's task, as he peers critically into a mirror leaning against a menu board. "My hair's just crazy tonight," he says.

Mr. Graham's words seem rooted more in worry than vanity. Because he deeply believes that this play is how God wants him to spread the Word, his mind races with all the things that could distract from that message, and have: camels arriving a week late, a teenager texting on stage, a stray chicken flying out of Lazarus's tomb. How about the time a couple of camera-carrying tourists wandered into the John the Baptist crowd scene?

He is also thinking of a shortfall. The production costs about $250,000 a year, which includes the modest salaries for Mr. Graham and his wife, Diane, who will play Mary Magdalene tonight, and various rentals, from the arena to the camels ($1,000 a night).

And, of course, here he is again, trying to be 33. But Mr. Graham has a plan: to replace "The Story of Jesus," at least next year, with a new production, "The Story of Noah," featuring himself in the lead role of the biblical patriarch, who was said to have lived several hundred years. Maybe someday, if he raises enough money, he will be able to build an outdoor theater of his own.

Fifteen minutes to showtime. Mr. Graham, now in full Jesus attire, climbs on top of a table, near a sign promoting beef ("Real Food for Real People"), and uses a microphone to deliver some last-minute reminders.

No cellphones. No gum. No glasses. No watches. And if you're a teenage girl who is wondering, "Can I hang out with the Sanhedrin?"—the answer is no!

Mr. Graham leads everyone in a short prayer and a rallying hymn, then releases his energized flock with:

"Let's go! Do it!"

A HAPPY ENDING

Showtime, and on a dirt stage in a darkened arena, the Story unfolds again.

An innkeeper, played by a Sebring-brown student of Harley-Davidson mechanics, leads a couple to shelter. The baby Jesus, played by an infant named Angelina, is raised triumphantly into the air, while four white-robed angels, teenage girls strapped into harnesses, glide by pulley across the ceiling.

Hear the wails of mothers whose baby boys have been slaughtered by Herod's soldiers. See the colorful scrum of early commerce. Breathe the dust kicked up by the scurry of sheep and the plodding of oxen. Marvel as Jesus raises a child from the dead, halts the stoning of an adulteress and, thanks to a concealed harness and a fog machine, walks on water.

During the brief intermission, take in the orange-blossom air of the Florida night. Buy a "Story of Jesus" fan for $2. Enjoy some nachos, or a bowl of mini doughnuts slathered with whipped cream. Return, then, to brace for the bloody, violent passion. The scourging, the spitting, the echo of nails hammered into hands and feet. The death.

But everyone in the aluminum bleachers knows: This is not how the play ends.

Soon the resurrected Jesus returns to the stage in glory. His crown of gold glittering, his sword raised high, he races back and forth on a galloping steed, perfect in its whiteness. The applause and cheers of 1,400 ring through a rodeo arena in central Florida.

When it is over, Mr. Graham, exhausted, 58, ready to do it again tomorrow, takes the microphone to thank the audience and ask for parting donations. And if anyone wants to be baptized, there are robes, towels and a manmade river dyed a deep blue.

The Boy Who Became Judy Garland

NEW YORK, N.Y. — NOVEMBER 13, 2011

Down some dark stairs, past cases of empty beer bottles, in the brick warren beneath the Off Off Broadway cabaret called Don't Tell Mama, a middle-aged man helps his middle-aged brother adjust the blue sequined top that complements his black sequined skirt. Fifteen minutes to showtime.

"Grab it from here," says Tommy Femia, 52, who is also wearing pantyhose, three-inch heels and a dark-brown wig that belts out Carnegie Hall, 1961. "There's just the one button."

"No zipper?" asks his brother Bobby Femia, 58, who fumbles about Tommy's back like a safecracker searching in vain for the combination. He is wearing a black golf shirt, black pants, white sneakers and a porkpie hat that grunts Philadelphia, 1976.

No zipper, says Tommy, who returns to his metamorphosis. Something burning in the cabaret's kitchen is sending smoke through the muggy basement, but Tommy is focused only on the small round mirror in his closet of a dressing room, next to a humming Frigidaire. He checks his eyeliner. Sprays his hair. Applies his red lipstick.

Watching from the tight hallway, Bobby explains that his job is to make sure nothing goes wrong. His biggest responsibility, he says, is to open the door leading to the stage so that Tommy can make a grand and seamless entrance.

"He's a nice boy," Tommy says from his dressing room.

Ten minutes to showtime. These two brothers from Brooklyn—star and one-man entourage—walk up from the basement and slip into a dimly lighted room beside the packed nightclub. Tommy begins to pace, his high heels tapping out the Morse code for nervousness on the hardwood floor.

"Watch," Bobby whispers, as his brother begins to slip away. "There's a transformation." After some silence, Bobby calls out a heads-up—"It's 8:27"—and receives a soft O.K. in return.

Inside, dozens of people squeeze around the small tables gathered before the stage, many of them tourists and first-time visitors. But a pair of seats along the far wall are always reserved for two special guests, regulars.

The dimming of lights quiets the chatter. Showtime.

The side door swings open and is held in place by the unassuming man in a porkpie hat. His radiant brother sweeps past, giggling and waving to imaginary friends as the klieg lights turn plastic sequins into winking jewels. Tommy receives the applause and the microphone, and begins to sing.

> *Hey look me over, lend me an ear*
> *Fresh out of clover, mortgaged up to here*
> *But don't pass the plate, folks, don't pass the cup*
> *I figure whenever you're down and out*
> *The only way is up . . .*

Judy. It's Judy Garland. Judy.

The three Femia brothers grew up in the Dyker Heights neighborhood of Brooklyn, on the second floor of a corner building owned by a first cousin of their father's. They slept in a triple bunk bed: Bobby, the oldest, was the bottom; John, the youngest, was the middle; and Tommy was the top, always, as if determined to follow some Cole Porter credo.

Theirs was a typical Italian-American household, they say, with relatives wandering in and out, and people talking over one another during endless meals. They regaled and argued and laughed and cried and laughed again. Ann, the loving mother who could level you with a few choice words, worked as a supervising clerk for the state's Department of Insurance, while Cosmo, the dutiful father who could defuse any situation with a joke, ran his own bleach company. Together they raised these three boys.

Bobby on the bottom covered his share of the bedroom walls with posters of his favorite professional wrestlers, especially Bruno Sammartino, whose Italian heritage added to his appeal. He also displayed a photo of the Three Stooges; he was a Curly man.

After high school, Bobby ran messages on Wall Street, worked for a monument company in Queens ("You polish the tombstones, make sure everything is tidy for the funeral") and, for nine years, helped a cousin with a truck make deliveries of ricotta, mozzarella, and other Italian foods. He married, then divorced. Now he lives in Bensonhurst with Halina Flis, a Polish immigrant who works as a home attendant.

For the last 26 years, Bobby has been a security officer for the Waterfront Commission of New York Harbor. He works 56 hours a week, wearing a blue uniform and a shield that dangles from a chain around his neck. Truckers entering and leaving the container terminal in Red Hook have to check in first with Bobby.

"Nothing passes me," he says.

John in the middle, the baby, reserved his wall space for the Marx Brothers, although he also adored the Three Stooges; he was a Shemp man. He began developing an encyclopedic memory of comedy routines when he was very young, and before long he was performing dead-on imitations of Flip Wilson, Bill Cosby and Pat Cooper.

By the time he was 13, John was living in Los Angeles and appearing in "Hello, Larry," a short-lived television situation comedy with McLean Stevenson, and a few years later, he was being featured in "Square Pegs," a one-season high school sitcom that starred, among others, Sarah Jessica Parker. He was Marshall Blechtman, the class clown, who talked fast and often.

Cosmo Femia moved to California to be John's guardian, a job that Tommy took over a few months later. Ann Femia, meanwhile, guarded her youngest son's career with no-nonsense zeal, John says, making sure he would not be exploited by producers and higher-ups.

After "Square Pegs," John appeared once more on television, in a teen comedy that was broadcast as an "ABC Afterschool Special" in 1984. But as he grew older, he says, he came to be considered too ethnic—"too New York"—for most roles.

So, weary of a career that had come at certain cost to his childhood, he moved back to Brooklyn in 1989, when he was 23.

After a long layoff, though, John returned to show business a dozen years ago. Now 45, he lives in Manhattan with his girlfriend, Linda Maley, and works as an actor and a stand-up comedian. He also claims to be more amused than annoyed by a YouTube video that says the actor who played Marshall in "Square Pegs" died in 1989 of complications related to AIDS (the fate of another of the show's stars, Merritt Butrick).

"I never corrected it," John says.

And, finally, in that bunk bed: Tommy on top.

DECLARING DEVOTION, AND MORE

As a teenager in the Brooklyn of the mid-1970s, just before the age of "Saturday Night Fever," Tommy would lie in his bunk and listen to the albums he had culled from the collection at a record store in Bensonhurst. Not the Beatles, not the Rolling Stones, but Streisand, Streisand, Streisand and, a little later, Garland—especially the classic two-disc live recording from 1961, "Judy at Carnegie Hall."

"Zing! Went the Strings of My Heart." "Almost Like Being in Love." "Puttin' on the Ritz." "Swanee." "A Foggy Day." "Over the Rainbow," over and over and over, with Tommy singing along, belting it out. "I was 9, and I hated it," his younger brother, John, recalls. "I'd scream at him to stop, which, of course, made him do it more."

If Bobby had his wrestlers and John his comedians, Tommy had his women: Glossy photographs of Monroe, Harlow and Crawford adorned his share of the bedroom's wall space. He hated the posters of those hairy beasts of wrestling; give him—Garbo.

In a way, Tommy was not only declaring his devotion to Barbra and Judy and the rest. He was also announcing his homosexuality to his old-school Italian family at a time, John says, "when homosexuality was not an option in an Italian home."

The oldest brother, Bobby, knew, because he occasionally gave Tommy a ride to one of the gay bars in Greenwich Village. But the others never knew—until they did. According to Tommy, his father had no problem with his sexuality, but his mother's scorn was so unrelenting that he left home at 18 and moved in with a boyfriend in Hoboken.

Before he left, though, his father asked to speak with him. "He told me that he loved me, and he gave me some money," Tommy says. "He had never given me money before."

The hurt went both ways. "It was difficult; it was difficult," Mrs. Femia recalls. "But I did some reading. I spoke to some professional people. And I came to understand it was God's will. He was born that way."

Three months after Tommy left the family apartment in Dyker Heights, three months in which mother and middle son never spoke to each other, Mrs. Femia broke her silence.

"She invited me over for dinner," Tommy says. "And it was like it never happened."

No discussion. No analysis. Just—eat.

Helping his brother

A graduate of the High School of Performing Arts, the setting for the musical "Fame," Tommy worked for a while Off Off Broadway, taking any role that he could, no matter how wacky. He supported himself with a day job as a radio monitor for the American Society of Composers, Authors and Publishers, listening to recordings of programs to make sure that members got paid for their work.

Then, in the early '90s, he teamed up with Hal Simons, a high school friend who did a mean Ann Miller, for a revue called "The MGM Society"—for "Miller Garland Maniacs."

It became a hit, first at Don't Tell Mama and then at Rose's Turn, in the West Village. Within a year, being Judy had become Tommy's full-time job; soon, and with the support of his longtime partner, David Stevens, he was appearing regularly at Don't Tell Mama and juggling gigs around the country.

At first, Tommy says, "My mother was panicked: 'You're gonna typecast yourself as a drag queen!'" Now, he says, she has come to be his greatest fan and most pointed critic, never holding back in assessing his performance or his wardrobe.

"You have great legs," she tells him. "Do it up to the knees."

Every Friday, Bobby guards the Red Hook piers from 8 in the morning until 4 in the afternoon. He drives home to Bensonhurst, naps, eats a little something, then returns to begin a double shift—midnight to 4 p.m.—in his glass-encased security booth, where a television distracts from the long hours of nothing.

But every other week, the knowledge that his brother Tommy is performing that Saturday night fills him with joyful anticipation and a certain air of responsibility. In his mind, he is part of the show.

On these days, after working 24 of the previous 32 hours, Bobby drives home in his 1998 tan Toyota Camry—bought used—gets cleaned up, and then collects his parents in Dyker Heights. Cosmo is 83, Ann is 80, and both have some trouble moving around. But they never miss a show.

They follow the same routine every time: over the Brooklyn Bridge, north on the West Side Highway, park in a lot on West 46th Street and get something to eat, either at Don't Tell Mama or at a favored Japanese restaurant nearby. John sometimes joins them.

The parents find those seats reserved especially for them along the cabaret's wall, while Bobby heads downstairs, past the cases of empty beer bottles, to his brother's dressing room. This is where he becomes hairdresser, confidant, all-around everything. Or, as Tommy says in thanks at the close of every performance: "Mr. Robert from Bensonhurst."

"I help him zip up," Bobby says. "In case he needs anything, I'm there."

The metamorphosis begins again, as Tommy tries to strike a 50-50 balance between Garland and Femia. "I want to make her relevant, but I don't want to do a Xerox," he says.

"It's not a look-who's-back-from-the-grave show. She never left."

Beyond the sequined outfits and pantyhose, the makeup and wig, this requires a kind of psychic immersion into the wounded artist who was Judy Garland: the vaudevillian childhood and early fame; the frailties and addictions; the exhaustion and self-doubt; that singular voice. And the almost supernatural ability to transform applause into the revitalizing oxygen needed to take a performance to its greatest heights.

The boy from Brooklyn, then, becomes the little girl from Grand Rapids, Minn. He becomes the overworked and tortured star who died of an accidental drug overdose in 1969, at the age of 47. He is not campy so much as he is seen-it-all weary, though ready at a finger's snap to sing the encouragement for everyone—his mother, his father, everyone—to come on, get happy.

Before that takes place, though, two brothers, one in sequins, the other in a porkpie hat, stand near that door leading to the stage. Bobby conducts one last examination of Tommy as Judy before opening the door.

"I grab his hand and he grabs my hand," Bobby says. "And I say, 'Go get 'em, kid.'"

Not Official, but Still
a Wisconsin Pardon

BOSCOBEL, WIS. — JUNE 4, 2014

Aware of the awkwardness, the two men arranged to meet in the evening quiet of the local community center. Their only previous encounter, a decade ago, had ended with a thrown punch and a broken nose.

Both dressed as if for a Sunday service, in button-down shirts. The larger man, a piano mover by trade, sat on the floral-patterned couch, his tight haircut correctly suggesting ex military. The thinner man, owner of a floor-covering business, sat in an easy chair, his nose slightly bent to the right.

The punch they shared had come out of who knows where, maybe Iraq, to still a long-ago liquid night. But its impact was still being felt by the former Marine, who threw the right jab just days after returning from a second deployment; the victim, who has not breathed the same since; and the governor, who chooses never to exercise an executive power of ancient provenance.

To show mercy.

The former Marine, Eric Pizer, seeks a pardon because he aches with remorse, and because his one-punch felony conviction means that he cannot possess or own a gun, disqualifying him from his desired career in law enforcement. He has only one smudge on his record. "This one night," he said. "This one time."

On this one night, back in 2004, Mr. Pizer and two buddies headed in his mother's Chevy for the small city of Boscobel, birthplace of the Gideon Bible. Their sole intention: to change the subject from war to fun.

Opposite: Steven Frazier

311

Mr. Pizer was two days back from Iraq. A straight-up Marine, he had committed to the corps even before his high school graduation in 2000, and was at Camp Lejeune in North Carolina a year later when an officer interrupted a class on sexually transmitted diseases to share the latest from Lower Manhattan.

We got bombed, boys, the officer announced. We're going to war.

Mr. Pizer spent half of 2003 in Kuwait and Iraq, fueling tanks and trucks in a tense environment. He returned for seven more months in 2004, this time as a corporal who felt so responsible for the "newbies" on his team that he extended his tour by two months.

Eric Pizer

Now he was cutting the September cool of a southwestern Wisconsin night, bound for Boscobel to hang out with a buddy's cousin and two other women he had never met before.

The men and women drank and played cards in the cousin's garage, then headed to Snick's Fin 'N Feather to shoot some pool and drink some more. When they returned to the garage, two local men, one of them named Steven Frazier, stepped in to disrupt the free-and-easy night.

Mr. Frazier believed that an out-of-towner—not Mr. Pizer—had gotten a little too familiar with one of the women: his wife. There soon followed beer-fueled shoves and shouts about straying hands and absent wedding rings.

Mr. Pizer, 6-foot-2 and 210 pounds, and Mr. Frazier, 5-foot-10 and 140 pounds, both claim to have been trying to keep the peace. But Mr. Pizer says that he heard Mr. Frazier threaten to kill one of his buddies, saw movement and reacted with his right hand.

"I just popped him once," he said.

That pop pushed Mr. Frazier's nose nearly two inches to the right. He went to the hospital, while Mr. Pizer went to a bar nearly 30 miles away, where, he says, he all but held out his hands to be cuffed when the police found him.

Mr. Pizer finished the last three months of his Marine hitch in North Carolina, then returned to learn the sobering news that his status as a first-time offender, just back from war, was not enough to convince the prosecutor, Anthony J. Pozorski Sr., to reduce the felony battery charge to a misdemeanor.

Back then, Mr. Pizer did not fully understand the consequences of having a felony on his record. "I had never been in trouble before," he said. "I wasn't quite prepared."

The former Marine worked as a construction laborer before getting hired to lug Steinways and Schimmels up stairs and around corners. He completed probation and paid off the $7,165.59 in restitution. He met a woman with a child, married, fathered a son, and received joint custody in the divorce.

All the while, he remained a felon.

Several years ago, Mr. Pizer contacted the prosecutor, Mr. Pozorski, to discuss the possibility of reducing his conviction to a misdemeanor. At the time, he was mulling whether to re-enlist or perhaps seek a job as a corrections officer. But nothing changed.

"I was willing to look for a way to try to help Mr. Pizer," Mr. Pozorski wrote in an email last week. "But since Mr. Pizer was not re-enlisting, he had no need to carry a gun. Since he had no need to carry a gun, I did not need to expend the state's resources on trying find a way around the law."

Mr. Pizer pushed on. Taking classes part time, he earned an associate degree in criminal justice. He also found allies in two Madison lawyers, David D. Relles and John R. Zwieg, who agreed to help him seek a pardon.

One problem: The governor of Wisconsin is Scott Walker, a possible Republican contender for president who, since taking office in 2011, has declined to exercise his power of pardon, granted to him by the Wisconsin Constitution.

With the Pizer case emerging as a cause celebre in Wisconsin, the governor has defended his no-pardon policy, saying that he sees no reason to "undermine" the criminal justice system—no matter that pardons were frequently granted by at least the last five governors before him.

In December, Mr. Walker told a reporter from WKOW-TV in Madison that there were thousands of convicted felons "who probably have a compelling case to be made that we don't know about."

In pardon-free Wisconsin, though, "compelling" cases go unheard. The state's Pardon Advisory Board remains "inactive," according to the governor's press secretary.

Mr. Relles, a former prosecutor, and Mr. Zwieg, a former prosecutor and Vietnam-era veteran, say that Mr. Pizer has suffered from bad luck and poor timing. The initial case should have been tried as a misdemeanor, and, if it had occurred today, would most likely have been diverted to a veterans' treatment court. Lastly, Mr. Pizer's governor does not believe in pardons.

"For some reason, forgiveness is not in vogue," Mr. Relles said.

Two years ago, Mr. Relles reached out to Mr. Frazier on behalf of Mr. Pizer, but the victim did not follow up. "I wasn't quite ready," Mr. Frazier recalled.

"Broken nose" is almost too flip a term for the damage done. Mr. Frazier says that his nose had to be broken and reset twice, but it remains a bit crooked, aches in the cold and feels constantly congested. "Migraines pretty much daily," he said.

More time passed. Then, a few months ago, an organization called Ridge and Valley Restorative Justice asked Mr. Frazier whether he would meet with the man who broke his nose. After a month of "sorting it out," he says, he agreed to meet one February evening.

Now, in Boscobel's community center, next to the Art Deco movie theater, two nervous men in their early 30s talked at length about one night from their early 20s, while two representatives from Restorative Justice mediated.

Mr. Pizer explained that Iraq had probably wound him up. He said that he liked to make people laugh, and usually avoided fights at all cost—except on this one night. Mr. Frazier said that, well, this one night had affected his looks, his breathing, and even his children.

"I don't think I said sorry more times in my entire life," Mr. Pizer said. "I'm sorry. I'm sorry. It was never my intention to get into a fight that night. I never meant to." They talked some more. Then Mr. Pizer asked for forgiveness.

About 85 miles to the east, in the Capitol in Madison, the power of forgiveness goes untapped. But here in Boscobel, Mr. Frazier studied the penitent man before him, and then said it:

"I forgive you."

Mr. Pizer felt a release, and stuck out his right hand. It was received in a good, firm grip.

Finding Independence, and a Bond

A Sunday wedding that was months away, then weeks away, then days away, is now hours away, and there is so much still to do. The bride is panicking, and the groom is trying to calm her between anxious puffs of his cigarette.

Peter and Lori are on their own.

With time running out, they visit a salon to have Lori's reddish-brown hair coiled into ringlets. They pay $184 for a two-tier cake at Stop & Shop, where the checkout clerk in Lane 1 wishes them good luck. They buy 30 helium balloons, only to have Peter realize in the Party City parking lot that the bouncing bobble will never squeeze into his car.

Lori, who is feeling the time pressure, insists that she can hold the balloons out the passenger-side window. A doubtful Peter reluctantly gives in.

"I've got them," she says. "Don't worry."

Peter Maxmean, 35, and Lori Sousa, 48, met five years ago at a sheltered workshop in North Providence, where people with intellectual disabilities performed repetitive jobs for little pay, in isolation. But when a federal investigation turned that workshop upside down last year, among those tumbling into the daylight were two people who had fallen in love within its cinder block walls.

Working with the Department of Justice's civil rights division, the State of Rhode Island agreed to help the workshop's clients find employment and day services in the community—an agreement followed up this year by a landmark consent decree that requires similar integrated opportunities for 2,000 other clients around the state, completely transforming Rhode Island's sheltered-workshop system.

The decree has put the 49 other states on notice that change is coming: that in the eyes of the federal government, sheltered workshops can no longer be default employment services for people with disabilities—most of whom can, with support, thrive in the workplace.

Mr. Maxmean and Ms. Sousa are among dozens of Rhode Island residents who are seeking their place beyond the safe but stultifying island of a sheltered workshop. At the moment, though, these two are pulling away from Party City with wedding balloons bobbing out their car window.

The first balloon slips Ms. Sousa's grasp as soon as Mr. Maxmean begins to drive. Then another escapes, and another, and another, floating beyond reach. By the time they pull up to their subsidized apartment building, a deflated Lori is clutching just six balloons.

"That was a bad idea I had," Mr. Maxmean gently tells her, even as he quietly calculates the loss of 24 helium balloons at 90 cents apiece.

But the two have no time to fret over lost balloons. Invitations went out weeks ago for the wedding of Lori Sousa and Peter Maxmean at the Harbor View Manor, East Providence, Rhode Island, at 5 p.m. on Sunday, the 17th of August.

Today.

"THAT'S MY SOUL MATE"

With an hour to go, Ms. Sousa fusses into the white gown purchased for a good price at Gown Town in Warwick. But her white high heels, bought for $15.99, already hurt; she wonders about wearing socks.

Soon she is sitting with eyes closed on the couch in the couple's one-bedroom apartment, two Special Olympics medals displayed on the wall behind her, as a family friend with a cosmetics bag enhances and conceals.

"You're looking gorgeous," the friend coos, as cellphones ring, people shout and Buddy the cat hides. But in this moment, Ms. Sousa seems to have achieved inner calm.

"My day," she says to herself.

Four floors below, Mr. Maxmean is setting up in the community room, where the wedding and reception are to be held. With his sleeveless T-shirt revealing the "Lori" tattoo on his left biceps, he is a wedding-day whirligig, pushing aside the bingo machine, testing the half-frozen lasagna in the oven, unboxing the tilted wedding cake—and, most important, double-checking the D.J.'s playlist. It is vital that when Ms. Sousa makes her entrance, a particular song by Journey is playing: "Don't Stop Believin'."

Ms. Sousa remembers when this new guy at the workshop, tall, brown-haired and with glasses, joined the repackaging of remote-control devices for a contract with Cox Communications. She was removing the batteries, he was testing the remotes, and something just clicked.

"I said, 'I'm gonna marry that guy,'" she says. "That's my soul mate."

Ms. Sousa was a workshop veteran by then. Born in Portugal and raised in Providence, she had spent the 25 years after high school commuting to the Training Thru Placement workshop, a squat, ugly building hidden away in a residential neighborhood.

She and the other clients would work at their own pace to fulfill various contracts: packaging heating pads; recycling television remotes; jarring Italian specialty foods. The pay averaged about $1.57 an hour.

Federal law allows authorized agencies to pay subminimum wages to people with disabilities, based on their performance when compared with that of a nondisabled worker. But the Department of Labor later revoked the workshop's authorization after finding what it called "willful violations" of the law, including the failure to record and pay employees for all the hours they worked.

Also problematic was the general absence of encouragement to improve one's skills; to see oneself moving up, and on.

"I'd be, like, 'I want to go out,'" Ms. Sousa says. "I want to be trained for a job. Put me out there! I can do it!"

At one point the workshop did help her find a job at an Italian restaurant in Cranston. But she clashed with co-workers, stopped going to work—and back she went to that hidden-away building, packing, wrapping, answering the telephone.

Then Mr. Maxmean appeared one day, and he was different. For one thing, he listened to her.

Mr. Maxmean was raised from the age of 3 by a nurse at the Rhode Island Veterans Home who fostered several children. Although he attended a special needs school in Bristol, his true education came from the many trips and cruises taken with his foster mother. He has been to every state but Hawaii, which remains in his sights.

But Mr. Maxmean had what he calls "behavioral problems," among other issues. After spending time in and out of various hospitals and institutions, he wound up in a heavily supervised group home in Smithfield, where a van took him every morning to the workshop, and to Ms. Sousa.

"She's beautiful, she's smart," Mr. Maxmean says. "Of all the women that I used to date, which we're not getting into, I finally found the right one."

A BIT OF PANIC

An anxious Mr. Maxmean is talking to the silvery door of a rising elevator. "Open up, open up, open up," he says, sounding very much like a man getting married in a half-hour.

The door finally obeys. He sprints toward the apartment he moved into four years ago, only to stop short when his cellphone rings. The guest who has the soda for the reception is lost in Providence, and she is shouting, "Oh, my God!" over and over.

"It's O.K., it's O.K.," he says, pacing now. "You're gonna go under the bridge and take a left . . ."

Mr. Maxmean resumes his run to the small apartment, chaotic with children, relatives and a bride-to-be still being powdered and beautified.

"She looks different," a young nephew says.

"Where's your veil?" someone asks.

"Here you go," Mr. Maxmean says, veil in hand.

Dressed in a white tuxedo with a royal blue vest, Mr. Maxmean does a quick dance in his rented white shoes before hurrying to the bathroom to shave. By now, the family friend is packing up her cosmetics.

"Does she look beautiful or what?" she says. "I'm going downstairs to have a smoke." But Ms. Sousa's gauzy white veil cannot mask her look of panic. "Sit down for a minute, honey," Mr. Maxmean says. "Sit down."

Ms. Sousa regains her composure and rises to leave, but those shoes are just killing her. Then someone points out that the wedding is already 15 minutes behind schedule.

Mr. Maxmean just shrugs, and says something about life not always being on time.

DISRUPTION, THEN PLACEMENT

One morning early last year, as Ms. Sousa sat at Training Thru Placement's reception desk, armed federal law enforcement agents came through the front door. A Justice Department investigation into civil rights abuses was underway.

Everything changed. Some staff members disappeared, the piecework ended, and a nonprofit organization called Fedcap was hired to help find rewarding employment—outside the building—for as many of the 88 clients as possible.

But many parents pushed back. They argued that the workshop's established routine had provided their children with a safe place to be, among friends. How will you protect my son from being bullied again? How will you make sure that my daughter isn't ridiculed again?

The abrupt redirection infuriated a mother named Lori DiDonato. After many disappointments, she and her husband had finally found a place that their young adult son, Louis, enjoyed, and now some outsiders were taking that place apart. Her central question: "Who the hell are you?"

But Christine McMahon, Fedcap's president, challenged Ms. DiDonato with a question: How would she feel if she did the same job, with the same people, at the same place, for the same inadequate pay and with no advancement, for her entire career?

In that moment, Ms. DiDonato says, she began to understand the government's motivation. But when Ms. McMahon promised to find Mr. DiDonato a rewarding job in six months, she says, "I laughed in her face."

Within six months, Louis DiDonato III, 23, was putting on a tie and driving himself to his clerical job, recalls Ms. DiDonato. "And I became a believer."

Mr. DiDonato was among the "rock stars," as Serena Powell, the senior vice president for Fedcap's New England offices, puts it: the first 20 or so clients who easily found enjoyable, fulfilling jobs. The next 20 also did well, she says, although they needed "more hand-holding." Finding jobs for the rest will be "challenging but doable," she says.

Mr. Maxmean, who is considered a rock star, quickly got a $15-an-hour custodial job at the state psychiatric hospital in Cranston. Although he has had some difficulty adapting to the requirements of a full-time job, he is a hard, focused worker. Kellie Capobianco, the hospital's acting administrator of environmental care, has not forgotten the day she saw her new employee cleaning under the loading dock.

"He's doing well," Ms. Capobianco says.

Mr. Maxmean initially took a 10-mile bus ride to his job, adding hours to his workday and uncertainty to his weekends, when buses run sporadically. On some weekends, though, Jim Manni, a Training Thru Placement job coach, would drive 25 miles, on his own time, to deliver Mr. Maxmean to work, all the while imparting advice about expectations beyond the workshop.

You've worked too hard to get where you are. . . . One of the things that is NOT a disability is laziness. . . . Winners never quit—and you're becoming a winner.

Then Mr. Maxmean passed his driver's test. He put $800 down and drove off in a $5,000 Sonata with nine years and 156,000 miles on it. The thought of shopping for food without having to lug bags onto a bus was so exciting that when he and Ms. Sousa loaded groceries into the car trunk for the first time, they took photographs.

Now, if he has the gas money, Mr. Maxmean drives anywhere he wants: to his job, to the store, to the grave of his foster mother, who died two years ago. "If I had met you a couple of years ago and you said, 'Someday you'll have a car,' I'd say you were nuts," he says. "It's a blessing."

Mr. Maxmean often drove Ms. Sousa to her $8-an-hour job at the Hampton Inn in Warwick, which followed a brief employment at a Panera Bread. But she struggled with the expectation of cleaning a room in less than 30 minutes. After skipping two successive Sunday shifts, she was told not to come back.

This isn't unexpected, Ms. Powell says. Some people just take longer to find their niche.

Ms. Sousa is back in the job market, looking for something in food services. But right now her most pressing appointment is with a justice of the peace.

GETTING IT TOGETHER

Mr. Maxmean suddenly realizes that the marriage license is in his car and his car keys are in the apartment he has just left. Back up, back down and out the door he goes, a white-tuxedoed blur.

With the wedding nearly a half-hour late, and the hum of anticipation emanating from the common room, Mr. Maxmean presents the license to Dennis Revens, the black-robed justice of the peace, who says: "My fee. I need that. The payment before we start."

"Before you start," Mr. Maxmean repeats.

"Sure," Mr. Revens says. "Otherwise, things get busy."

At this moment, Mr. Maxmean does not have that $200. Even though he has greatly modified his once-grand wedding plans, canceling the church-hall rental and the catered meal, he is still learning to budget. The wedding dress, the tuxedo

Upon seeing his bride

rental, the cake and the shoes, among other expenses, have left him short.

"I've spent everything else on the wedding," he mutters, while a few neighbors in the lobby sit, listen and watch.

Mr. Maxmean asks a friend to check a white gift box, on prominent display in the reception hall, but there's no cash in it yet. So a couple of relatives cover the $200, including Mr. Maxmean's birth mother, who tells him not to forget that he owes her $95.

The justice of the peace counts out the $20 bills like a winner at the track. It's all there. "Ladies and gentlemen," intones the disc jockey, and guests rise to their feet in a room normally reserved for card games and bingo nights. Here are relatives, and co-workers, and people from the workshop, including Mr. Maxmean's job coach, a smiling Mr. Manni.

Mr. Maxmean walks slowly down the white-paper runner he unrolled hours earlier. He hits his mark and turns to see Ms. Sousa, resplendent in white and smiling through the pain of those shoes.

Later, Mr. Maxmean will hear the $200 justice of the peace flub the vows by referring to Lori as Lisa. Later, he will call in an order for four pizzas to supplement the lasagna. Later, he and his bride will retire to their "honeymoon suite" upstairs.

But right now, the eyes of the man in the white tuxedo are wet, as the makeshift reception hall fills with a stringed version of that song by Journey.

EPILOGUE

Peter and Lori Maxmean continue to live in East Providence. At last report, Lori was doing prep work at a Texas Roadhouse, and Peter was a delivery driver for Papa Gino's. Both have been honored in their respective places of employment as "Employee of the Month."

PART EIGHT

The Ever-Present Past

Shine little glow-worm, glimmer, glimmer

Restoring Dignity to Sitting Bull, Wherever He Is

STANDING ROCK RESERVATION, S.D. — JANUARY 28, 2007

Here, on a snow-dusted bluff overlooking the Missouri River, rests Sitting Bull. Or so it is said.

Stand before the monument and see the pocks left in the granite by bullets. Notice where the nose was replaced after vandals with chains and a truck yanked the bust from its pedestal. Spot where the headdress feather was mended after being shot off. And wonder, along with the rest of the Dakotas:

Is Sitting Bull here?

The 12-foot monument rises where Sitting Bull is supposedly buried and where he certainly once felt at home; where the steel-blue clouds of winter press down upon the hills of dormant grass; where nothing moves but a solitary bird in flight, and the whinnies of a distant horse sound almost like an old man's rueful laughter.

It all seems fitting, even the vandalism, given how this world-famous American Indian has never received the respect in death that was often denied him in life. Now two men are trying to pay that respect, in late but earnest installments.

As one of them, Rhett Albers, collects another beer bottle discarded near the base of the monument, the other, Bryan Defender, gazes up at the bust of Sitting Bull. As always, the face of stone gives away nothing.

Maybe in the end it does not matter where the holy man actually rests, says Mr. Defender, who is Hunkpapa Sioux. Like the man whose history he honors.

Sitting Bull. Distinguished as a warrior against rival tribes and American soldiers. Served as spiritual leader for the Indian victory at Little Bighorn. Refused to accept white encroachment. Surrendered. Was imprisoned. Toured briefly with

Buffalo Bill's Wild West Show. Then, at age 59, was killed during a botched arrest in 1890, an arrest rooted in the belief that he supported a growing movement of resistance among the Sioux.

The government buried him in Fort Yates, on the North Dakota side of this sprawling reservation that straddles the Dakotas. There, in what was then a predominantly white military community, his grave site became little more than a weedy lot.

Then, in 1953, some Chamber of Commerce types from the small South Dakota city of Mobridge executed a startling plan. With the blessing of a few of Sitting Bull's descendants, they crossed into North Dakota after midnight and exhumed what they believed were Sitting Bull's remains. One photograph from that strange night depicts a Mobridge mortician supervising the exhumation; he holds a cigarette in one hand and a human femur in the other.

The men raced back 55 miles to bury the remains on this bluff, across the river from Mobridge. They scoffed at North Dakota's contention that they had taken the wrong bones, and justified their actions by saying that Sitting Bull had been born near here and that the sculptor Korczak Ziolkowski would soon create a more fitting monument to him. And would having Sitting Bull's remains help tourism in Mobridge? Well, of course.

Up in Fort Yates, the state eventually unveiled a plaque that left vague the whereabouts of Sitting Bull's remains ("He was buried here but his grave has been vandalized many times"), while on this bluff across from Mobridge, the area around the monument became a place to dump used tires, to have a beer party, to shoot off a gun—sometimes into the granite.

"People would say, 'Party at Sitting Bull!'" Mr. Albers recalls. "It was a joke."

The site's poor condition vexed Mr. Albers, 45, an environmental consultant, and Mr. Defender, 35, who runs the reservation's solid-waste-removal operation. That irritation turned to embarrassment when a visiting foreign-exchange student asked Mr. Albers to see the monument dedicated to the famous Sitting Bull.

So, two years ago, the men bought the monument and its 40-acre parcel from a private owner for $55,000. They mowed the grass, trucked away 50 cubic yards of debris and established a nonprofit corporation with plans to recoup their expenses and establish a cultural and educational center.

They also came up against the still-emotional question of where the great Indian leader truly rests. Not long ago, someone scrawled a message across the granite pedestal: "Sitting Bull is not buried here!"

A drive through the reservation, from Mobridge to Fort Yates, is a drive through an undulant moonscape of stillness, disturbed only by the dance of an occasional horse. Here, unemployment among the 11,000 people is nearly 80 percent, and the challenge of restoring a sense of self-identity cannot be addressed alone by revenue from the two modest casinos.

In an office in Fort Yates sits Ron His Horse Is Thunder, the chairman of the Standing Rock Sioux Tribe and a great-great-great grandson of Sitting Bull. A lawyer by training, tall and lean, he expresses support for the Mobridge effort to honor his ancestor in a manner befitting the man. But when asked whether he believes Sitting Bull is buried on that bluff, he slowly shakes his head no.

Then where is Sitting Bull?

LaDonna Brave Bull Allard, a tribal historian and storyteller who is overseeing improvements to the Fort Yates grave site, tries to explain. "A person like Sitting Bull was never meant to just die and disappear," she says.

Yes, but where is he?

Smiling patiently, the woman opens her arms and spreads her hands.

Between Kentucky and Ohio, Hard Feelings over a Rock's Place

An eight-ton rock rested for generations at the bottom of the Ohio River, minding its own business as time and currents passed. It favored neither Ohio to the north nor Kentucky to the south. It just—was.

Occasionally, when water levels dropped, the boulder would break the surface long enough to receive the chiseled tattoos of mildly daring people seeking remembrance. But it stopped playing peek-a-boo nearly a century ago, leaving only ephemera in its wake, including a sepia photograph of a well-dressed woman in a frilly hat, standing in the middle of the Ohio, on this rock.

Now, because of one man's obsessive good intention, the fabled rock sits on old tires in the municipal garage of this river city, awaiting the outcome of a border dispute that goes something like this:

Some Ohioans say the rock is an important piece of Portsmouth history and should be put on display. Some Kentuckians say the rock is an important piece of Kentucky, period, and should be returned. And some in both states say: I've been distracted by war, recession and a presidential campaign, so forgive me. But are we fighting over a rock?

Last month the Kentucky House of Representatives passed a resolution demanding the rock's return to its watery bed, with one of its members suggesting that a raiding party to Portsmouth might be in order. Not to be outdone, the Ohio House of Representatives is considering a resolution that asserts the rock's significance to Ohio, and its speaker has said he is ready to guard the boulder with his muzzle-loading shotgun.

All this has stunned Steve Shaffer, 51, the earnest local historian who rediscovered the rock, raised the rock and anticipated a more enthusiastic celebration of the rock. But at least the rock is happy, he said. "It loves to be the center of controversy."

The boulder sat almost certainly on the Kentucky side of the river, where the shoreline remains mostly undeveloped. This is why the rock became lodged deeper in the collective consciousness of the city on the other shore: Portsmouth, now another hurting Rust Belt city, but once a center of commerce, forging steel, making shoes.

In Portsmouth and beyond, the boulder became known as Indian Head Rock, because its bottom half bore a crude etching of a round head, with two dots for eyes, another dot for a nose, and a dash for a mouth; a kind of early Charlie Brown.

The face spawned many theories of origin. An American Indian petroglyph. A river bandit's carving to mark where loot was stored. A boatman's crude measure to gauge fluctuating water levels. Or, as a 1908 newspaper article has it, the 1830s handiwork of a Portsmouth boy named John Book, who then grew up to fall at the Battle of Shiloh.

Whenever the rock emerged from the water, people would boat or swim out to read the names and initials engraved on its sandstone hide, and maybe add their own to this honor roll of stone. H.W.H. Oct. 50, and E.D.C. Sep 1856, and Luther, and F. Kinney, and D. Ford. Several of these surnames remain familiar in Portsmouth today.

But dam work in the early 20th century raised the water level several feet, and the celebrated boulder—often featured in newspapers and on postcards—vanished from view. And Portsmouth soon forgot its pet rock.

In the late 1960s, though, an Ohio Valley schoolboy read of the Indian Head Rock in a musty book of local history, and he never forgot it. That was Steve Shaffer. He grew up, studied historical interpretation at Ohio University, developed an interest in prehistoric rock carvings, and quietly resolved to find the rock.

He and some divers began the hunt in 2000, using clues in old newspaper accounts about the rock's location. He remained in the boat, though; he had lost 70 percent of his hearing to Meniere's disease, and diving could cause further damage. But when the expeditions of 2000 and 2001 found only abandoned cars and dumped refrigerators, Mr. Shaffer earned his diver's certification and joined the search—at great risk to his hearing.

The risk paid off. In September 2002, a diving buddy rose to the surface to exclaim: That's it! It's got initials all over it! Mr. Shaffer immediately went down to see for himself. There, amid the river's murk: the Indian Head Rock.

Nearly every summer after that, Mr. Shaffer dove down to pay his respects to the rock. "Just to check on it," he said.

Then, late last summer, and almost on a whim, he and some diving friends resurrected the boulder with a harness and some barrels and air bags. They soon reported to Portsmouth's mayor, James Kalb, that they had something to show him—and it's bigger than a breadbox. The stunned and grateful mayor thanked them, saying a piece of Portsmouth's past had been salvaged.

Not everyone saw it that way. Some said that once exposed to air the rock would disintegrate; it didn't. Some said that Mr. Shaffer needed a permit from the Army Corps of Engineers to remove anything from the river; he agreed, and has applied for one after the fact.

Some said the rock should not have been disturbed because that Charlie Brown-like face was an American Indian petroglyph. In November a delegation from Kentucky—with Dr. Fred E. Coy Jr., a prehistoric carvings expert, in tow—visited the Portsmouth municipal garage and waited anxiously while the doctor conducted his examination. His expert opinion: "I can't tell."

No matter. Jagged verbal stones continue to be tossed from either side of the river. Reginald Meeks, the Kentucky state representative who sponsored the resolution of condemnation, said Friday that law enforcement officials were investigating what he described as the theft of a state antiquity. He said the rock should be returned to Kentucky, where state officials could examine it and decide its future.

"I tell you, they just played cowboy," Mr. Meeks said, voice rising. "And came to Kentucky and stole this item."

But Todd Book, an Ohio legislator from Portsmouth who last week introduced the resolution praising the rock's resurrection, said Ohioans believed they were in the right.

Mr. Book—who likes to think he is related to the John Book who may have carved that face on the boulder—said the story of the rock had already become an educational tool in Ohio. Fourth graders in the region are being asked to write essays on what the state should do with the rock, he said, while high school seniors are being asked to write position papers on the following: "Why the rock should be Ohio's and not Kentucky's."

Who knows how this heavy matter will be resolved. For now, though, an eight-ton chunk of sandstone, riddled with the markings of the long-dead, sits in a municipal garage near some city trucks and a lawn mower. And every so often a well-intentioned man wearing a hearing aid stops by to check on it.

EPILOGUE

In June 2008, a Kentucky grand jury indicted Steve Shaffer on a felony charge of removing a protected archeological object without a permit. Several months later, Kentucky's attorney general sued the Ohio city of Portsmouth, demanding the return of the Indian Rock to the commonwealth.

So, yes: Things got a little silly.

The felony charge was eventually dismissed, but not before a disapproving Kentucky judge warned Mr. Shaffer "to be more careful of your actions in the future." And in 2010, as part of a resolution, the rock was taken by flatbed truck to a county maintenance garage in Greenup, Kentucky—where it sits today. Plans for public display have yet to be realized.

In the summer of 2017, Mr. Shaffer received permission to visit the rock, which he did. "Just to see how it was doing," he said.

Holding Firm Against Plots by Evildoers

GRAND CHUTE, WIS. — JUNE 26, 2009

On a buzzing boulevard in this busy shopping town, across from a supermarket and not far from a PetSmart, there sits a building that might be mistaken for a place where you can have your teeth cleaned, were it not for the name affixed to the brick: The John Birch Society.

For some, that name means nothing. Or it sparks flashbacks to the 1960s, when the John Birch Society was synonymous with seeing red here, there and everywhere. Maybe you displayed a Birch bumper sticker on your car; maybe you enjoyed the Chad Mitchell Trio song mocking the Birch obsession with communism:

You cannot trust your neighbor or even next of kin
If mommy is a commie then you gotta turn her in.

Yet for others, the John Birch Society is urgently relevant to the matters of today, in its support of secure borders and limited government, its distrust of the Federal Reserve and the United Nations, and its belief in a conspiracy to merge Mexico, Canada and the United States.

This so-called North American Union, it asserts, is part of a larger plot by an amorphous, amoral group of powerful elite—including but not limited to the Council on Foreign Relations, the Trilateral Commission and the Rockefellers—to take over planet Earth. Call it the New World Order.

Some of these theories may sound like cable television chatter, or the synopsis of a Dan Brown bestseller. But Birch leaders say this plot is real, with roots going back more than 200 years to a secret, insidious brotherhood called the Illuminati, and with most American presidents among its many dupes and abettors.

"We've always referred to it as a Satanic conspiracy," said Arthur Thompson, the society's chief executive, sitting beside an American flag.

The society, which was established in 1958, says its membership has doubled in recent years, thanks to rising interest in these beliefs and, lately, to the policies of the Obama administration. But it will not provide firm numbers, other than to say it has tens of thousands of members.

"We don't want to let our enemies know our strengths or our weaknesses," Mr. Thompson explained.

Tall, white-haired and 70, Mr. Thompson was a soldier in the ideological wars long before Lou Dobbs or Glenn Beck joined the contentious scene. He claims to have infiltrated Marxist groups in the Pacific Northwest back in the 1960s. "I would go casual," he said, laughing.

But dressed now in his preferred attire of dark blazer and red tie, he spoke earnestly of wanting to thwart the "insiders," as he calls them. "It's a war between good and evil," he said. "And sometimes it takes a strange twist."

The society is familiar with strange twists. In late 2005, for example, Mr. Thompson became chief executive after staging a coup with the help of John McManus, the society's most prominent member, its longtime president and an ultraconservative Roman Catholic. This prompted some ousted Birchers to disseminate recorded snippets of Mr. McManus lecturing to Catholic groups that Judaism became a dead and deadly religion after the establishment of the Catholic Church.

Mr. McManus is also heard to say that militant Jews have influenced the Freemasons, who are "Satan's agents," "the enemies of Christ Church"—and, in the view of the John Birch Society, part of the Illuminati conspiracy to cause world upheaval.

Mr. Thompson said that he was initially outraged by these comments, but that he now understands they were made in the context of Mr. McManus's belief in Catholicism as the one true faith. He said the John Birch Society has Jewish and black members and has never tolerated anti-Semitism or racism, notwithstanding its notorious opposition to much of the civil rights movement.

During a recent telephone interview in which he questioned the rigor of his caller's Catholic education, Mr. McManus denied being anti-Semitic and said he was highly regarded by the society's Jewish members. While they may not agree with his religious perspective, he said, he and they stand together in "working to save our country."

Toward that end, the John Birch Society—whose name honors a missionary and American intelligence officer killed by Chinese communists in 1945—still holds meetings in living rooms and public libraries. But it also maintains a handsome website that invites the curious to download literature and join a chapter. ("Click here to find like-minded people.")

A chapter usually requires at least 10 members, although Mr. Thompson said, "We'll let them start at eight." He said the mandate is to establish relationships with a community's opinion makers: "It could be a member of the city council, it could be the head of the chamber of commerce, key people in the Kiwanis."

But a request to talk to people who had recently joined the cause was met with resistance by James Fitzgerald, the national director of field activities, who began the conversation by criticizing a New York Times article about the society from 1966. The best he could do, Mr. Fitzgerald said, was to suggest a visit to a Sunday street fair in Union, N.J., where members would have a booth.

The tip was solid: there, near a funnel-cake operation, a foldout table covered with Birch Society literature.

The coordinator was Chris Nowak, 24, a substitute math teacher who said he joined after his father, a longtime Bircher, re-educated him about American history; for example, he now understood that the United Nations was founded by President Harry S. Truman "and other communists."

With Mr. Nowak were Ray Tisch, 37, an electrical engineer, and Matthew Yamakaitis, 49, a warehouse worker, who said they had joined the John Birch Society within the last two years because they shared its concerns about the North American Union, the mainstream media and the conspiracy of elite insiders.

"At the highest levels there are controls in place," Mr. Tisch said. Mr. Yamakaitis agreed, saying that if the insiders succeed in creating a new world order, "It basically means less power for us."

"And more for the elite," said Mr. Tisch.

"The Rockefellers, the Morgans, the Rothschilds," said Mr. Nowak.

"Sssssssssss," said the sausage cooking on a nearby grill.

Back in Grand Chute, a drop in donations last year—standard during a presidential election year, Mr. Thompson said—has led to a few layoffs. Still, secretaries answered phones, editors worked on another issue of The New American magazine and, in a warehouse stocked with books and society literature, Dan Shibler waited to fill orders.

Mr. Shibler, the shipping and maintenance manager, said he joined the society as a teenager in the 1970s after attending one of its summer camps, where educational sessions were mixed with fun activities like fishing and swimming. Those camps are no more; among other reasons, it became easier to reach young people on the Web.

Still, the work continues. The men and women of the society have helped to get resolutions opposed to the North American Union introduced, and occasionally passed, in state legislatures. It recently participated in many of the "tea parties" held this spring to protest government growth and spending. And, of course, every day it fights the United Nations, the Council on Foreign Relations, the elite group of insiders—evil.

It must be hard to relax. But Mr. Thompson said he draws strength from his faith, listens to music and finds other diversions. "Otherwise," he said, "it would drive you crazy."

Keeping Alive Memories
That Bedevil Him

MANCHESTER TOWNSHIP, N.J. — AUGUST 14, 2009

A retired postal worker, living not entirely at peace in an adult community called Leisure Village West, recently sent remember-the-date notes to large newspapers and television networks, then followed up with calls that often bounced to voice mail. The 14th of August; remember the date.

He was not asking so much as he was demanding.

Friday is the 14th of August: a dog day to many but always V-J Day to some, including this man, Albert Perdeck. It is the 64th anniversary of the surrender by Japan to end World War II. Attention must be paid, he says with urgency. He is 84.

"Last year, 2008, there was no mention of this on the news," reads his handwritten note to The New York Times. "I am requesting to have the day remembered by your in-depth reporting."

In addition to "V-J," as in Victory over Japan, his note contains other abbreviations, including "P.T.S.D.," as in: "The 17 months I was in combat still causes terrible flashbacks and nightmares of the mutilated bodies I helped to recover."

He does not care that some people are uncomfortable with V-J Day, given the close relationship the country now has with Japan, and given two other dates in August 1945 (the 6th: Hiroshima, and the 9th: Nagasaki). To him, the day carries its own political correctness: It celebrates the victorious end to a world-saving war in which hundreds of thousands of Americans died far from home. He saw some of them die.

Mr. Perdeck sits in a small community room at Leisure Village West, surrounded by the brittle newspapers and old photographs he carries with him. "Everyone's laughing," he says of today's world, voice rising again, tears coming again. "And I still smell it! I smell it now—beyond 60 years!"

You've seen these Al Perdecks all your life—sipping early-morning coffee, say, with buddies at McDonald's—but less so now. Stocky, not tall, with shock-white hair and a Norman Mailer look of pugnacity. Wearing shorts, dark socks and a boxy baseball cap embroidered with the name of the ship on which he served. You've seen him.

Now imagine him in June 1943, the just-drafted momma's boy from Newark. Hadn't finished high school, hadn't been with a girl. Soon he and a couple of thousand other sailors were aboard the U.S.S. Bunker Hill (CV-17), the aircraft carrier that would distinguish itself in the Pacific Theater. His job: tending to the fighter planes on the flight deck and giving the thumbs-up to the pilots before they soared into uncertainty.

He turned 19 onboard, then 20. One day he is doing Donald Duck impressions with a friend, the next he sees a crewmate killed by shrapnel from a near miss. He is boy and man, both.

On May 11, 1945, a kamikaze attack turned the flight deck of the Bunker Hill into an inferno. Pilots in the ready room died in their seats. Planes caught fire, their machine guns discharging rounds. The smoke created a black curtain that Mr. Perdeck could not quite part.

Wounded: 264. Missing: 43. Dead: 346.

V-J Day came just three months later. Mr. Perdeck remembers hearing the news while on liberty in Seattle. He ran through the streets shouting: "The war's over! The war's over!"

Discharged as a seaman first class in 1946, he returned to Newark and met a young woman named Elaine at a dance at the Y.M.H.A. They married in 1950, moved to Ocean County, raised a boy and a girl, and struggled. A wood-pattern maker by trade, Mr. Perdeck finally took a post office job; for the security, he says.

But that black curtain never quite parted. He hated Fourth of July fireworks and struggled with flashbacks, but it was more than that. Mrs. Perdeck said her husband would overreact when disciplining the children, when dealing with a conflict at work, when confronted, really, with everyday life. "He was always angry," she says, with love.

He could not shake free of the war. The burned and mutilated body parts. The rows of dead crewmates on the flight deck. That strange moment in the enveloping blackness when he stepped on a prostrate sailor, then yelled at the man to get the hell up, this is no time to sleep. The sailor, of course, could not wake.

In 1997, 51 years after his discharge, Mr. Perdeck told his wife he needed to talk to someone. She knew what he meant. It's about time, she said.

A clinical psychologist, Dr. Walter Florek, eventually gave a diagnosis of post-traumatic stress disorder. Now the rage that Mr. Perdeck felt, the isolation, the anxiety and the sadness had a name.

Mr. Perdeck spent six weeks in a veterans' hospital, where he attended lots of meetings but does not recall encountering another veteran from his war, the one a half-century past. Did his hospitalization help? He shrugs.

These days, Mr. Perdeck accompanies his wife to various social functions at Leisure Village West, and he is active with the U.S.S. Bunker Hill Association, whose annual gatherings get smaller and smaller. When he speaks of other alumni by name, he usually adds a "May he rest in peace."

He also works to keep V-J Day alive. Last year he contacted The Asbury Park Press and asked how it planned to honor the day; the paper published a story about him. This year he went national, though he says he spent most of his time talking to machines.

And every other Thursday, he drives to Dr. Florek's office on Route 70 in Lakewood for a group session with a dozen or so World War II and Korean War veterans, all of whom have P.T.S.D. A patient counselor named Olga Price guides the discussion.

The group met again Thursday. An Air Force veteran with a squawking hearing aid. An Army infantryman with a cane. A Navy flyboy, now blind, who still sees the devastated Hiroshima he flew over 64 years ago. His walking stick is adorned with a small American flag.

You've seen these men, these men who would never talk about it. But now, in the embrace of their own, they did, sometimes with sobs. One of them recalled killing an enemy soldier who was little more than a boy.

"I see him virtually every day," he said. "It just goes on and on and on and on."

The other men nodded without saying a word, including the one in shorts, dark socks and a shirt with the words "U.S.S. Bunker Hill" over his heart.

From New Deal to New Hard Times, Eleanor Endures

ELEANOR, W.VA. — DECEMBER 25, 2009

Early spring, in the Depression year of 1935. A poor girl from coal-mine country, a dark-haired girl of 4, rocks beside her mother and two sisters in a car moving through the rain-swept night. Soon they will join her father, a Great War veteran who pads his shoes with cardboard. He has been working for months on some distant government relief project.

When the car finally stops, the sleepy girl can see only a blur of mud and midnight. Not until morning does she take in this government project: a new American town, raised from a field by her father and other men with families caught in the stalled gears of a broken economy.

Marlane Crockett

The girl is told: You're home now, Marlane.

Late fall, in the Recession year of 2009. A dark-haired woman of 78 drives her Buick, a Rendezvous, slowly through the town she has always called home. "This is an Eleanor house, and this is an Eleanor house," Marlane Crockett Carr says, nodding toward oversize bungalows distinguished by the original pitched roofs. "And this, and this . . ."

The economic fallout of this annus horribilis, now drawing to a close, continues: 10 percent unemployment; tens of millions without steady access to adequate food; wholesale industry shakeouts. It takes the collective American mind to another time, an even harder time, when federal stimulus programs meant more than just bridge repairs and weatherization; when the government jump-started the economy by building highways, schools, post offices—entire towns.

Dozens of New Deal "resettlement" communities dotted the country: the Penderlea Homestead Farms in North Carolina; the Phoenix Homesteads in Arizona; the Dyess Colony in Arkansas, where Johnny Cash grew up. And here: on fertile West Virginia land beside the Kanawha River, a community named after Eleanor Roosevelt, First Lady of the New Deal.

Over the years, these New Deal towns have been praised as a sound response to paralyzing poverty and criticized as flawed, communism-tinted social experiments. But in this hard time, as half-built subdivisions stand as ghostly testaments to economic failure, a place like Eleanor reflects a government action that worked, and works.

Ms. Carr watched Eleanor grow, from a place planted in mud nearly 75 years ago—well before the Levittowns of post-World War II America—to a town that proclaims itself the cleanest in West Virginia; a town with a budget, a mayor, a library, a Dairy Queen. Its development has been bitter, sweet, messy, quiet, ugly and beautiful, not unlike the evolution of this country.

Driving her Rendezvous down roads intimately known, Ms. Carr says she fears that Eleanor's history is being pushed aside, that someday people will not know why the main street is called Roosevelt Boulevard, or even why the town is called Eleanor.

Then again, she says, maybe these are the protective fears of a woman who remembers how a dark-haired girl of 4 christened her new home long ago: by flushing the toilet in wondrous discovery, over and over, like a child of Steinbeck.

"Your eyes," she says, "look at some things through your heart."

"EVENTUAL SELF-SUPPORT"

In the desperate year of 1934, word spread through West Virginia's relief offices of another federal "subsistence homesteading" project. It would be similar to Arthurdale, a community recently created outside Morgantown for displaced mining families, many of whom had been living in shacks beside open sewers.

Detractors ridiculed Arthurdale as a wrong-headed and expensive pet project for President Franklin D. Roosevelt's activist wife. But as Blanche Wiesen Cook noted in her authoritative biography of Eleanor Roosevelt, the first lady had seen firsthand the scrawny children, eating scraps hardly worth a dog's time. She held her ground.

More than 1,000 families applied to live in this new homestead called Red House Farms, about 30 miles west of Charleston, on property once owned by George Washington. After a vetting process to identify the physically and morally strong, just 150 were accepted, including the family of Robert Crockett, who had lost his job loading coal cars in Boone County. A military veteran with three children, the youngest named Marlane, he was lucky enough to be chosen with dozens of other men on relief to build and live in the settlement.

Seventy-five years ago this month, Mrs. Roosevelt visited the nearly completed homestead with her good friend, the former journalist Lorena Hickok, whose cross-country reports as a kind of government scout had greatly influenced the first lady. "From long deprivation the health of the people is beginning to break down," Ms. Hickok had written. "Some of them have been starving for eight years. I was told there are children in West Virginia who have never tasted milk!"

Four months later, the Crocketts and dozens of other families moved into this community of opportunity, designed for "eventual self-support": 150 homes on one-acre lots, each slightly different, each with a chicken coop, a small garden and that most exotic amenity, indoor plumbing. There was a hosiery factory in the works, a dairy farm, a canning operation, a grocery store, even a pool hall. (Something it did not have: black residents.)

The families paid a modest rent to the government that could be applied to the purchase price. The government expected them to work, grow vegetables, learn home economics and engage in cultural pursuits, like joining the band. Their children were to keep clean, stay in school and take cod liver oil to ward against rickets.

If a family did not meet these expectations, it faced "house notice"—public scolding that could lead to eviction.

Not everything was idyllic. During another visit, Ms. Hickok heard complaints about cracks in the cinderblock walls, inadequate closet space, and a government that saw people as statistics. Mostly, the residents worried about finding employment beyond the homestead. A few, like Robert Crockett, worked for the community, in the dairy one day, on the farm the next.

Save for the cod liver oil, the girl named Marlane loved it all. Picking up mail from the kitchen table of the postmistress. Snapping beans with her mother to prepare them for canning. Receiving a doll with a pink bonnet from Santa, who made his rounds a few days before the first Christmas, in a government truck.

The first in the community to die was a little boy who had been struck in the head with a rock; the townspeople followed his light-colored coffin up a hill, where he was buried by the water tank. The first to be buried in the new cemetery, under some beech trees, was a woman who had cut herself while canning. Little Marlane liked to place dandelions on the sole tombstone; she would tell her mother the cemetery was so pretty that she hoped others would die.

The town called Red House Farms soon changed its name to Eleanor, after the tall, approachable first lady. During one of her visits, she gave a pack of Doublemint gum to a girl named Dymple Cockrell. "I thought I was the richest girl in town," recalls Ms. Cockrell, now 83 and living in the same homesteading house she moved into at the age of 8. "I shared it, of course."

SIDEWALKS AND MEMORIES

The Depression seeped into World War II. Three soldiers from Eleanor were killed and buried overseas. The community building called the Big Store burned down. After the war, the government got out of the controversial homesteading business, and essentially sold Eleanor to a corporation of its elders for $250,000.

One day Marlane jokingly told a friend she was going to marry that handsome sailor down the street. Two years later she did, eloping with Sandy Carr in 1947, when he was 21 and she was 16. Her father cried and said, You're going back and finishing high school. She did this, too.

Eleanor slowly evolved. Some residents complained that others had taken advantage, selling off property that had always been considered communal. One morning the town awoke to find on every doorstep an anonymous six-page letter that criticized various inside deals and concluded with several plaintive questions, including:

Why is hot-rodding allowed in Eleanor?

Marlane and Sandy, a high school teacher and coach, lived for a while above a chicken-and-gravy-style restaurant on Roosevelt Boulevard, then rented one of the original homes for about $25 a month. Finally, they built a house on the back end of his mother's property. They had three children: Sandra, Michael, and the baby, Rebekah, born with a congenital heart defect.

The communal dairy barn burned. The canning operation disappeared. Marlane's beloved Rebekah died in her arms on the first day of classes, right there in the George Washington Middle School. Just 13, she was buried in the cemetery where her mother once laid dandelions on a solitary tombstone.

To honor her daughter's memory, Marlane returned to school and became a surgical technician. All the while, little by little, Eleanor was changing: sidewalks, streetlights, a community swimming pool. A Fruth's Pharmacy where the old Big Store once stood. Even a small shopping center at the end of town.

Sensing time's fast passage, Marlane and others saw the need to celebrate Eleanor's history while some homesteaders were still alive. She helped to organize a 60th anniversary party, and a 65th, and a 70th. She began visiting classrooms, usually around Oct. 11—Eleanor Roosevelt's birthday—and talked about the disagreements over the worth of these New Deal communities, the lingering stigma of having been called welfare recipients, and the unabashed love she had for Eleanor.

She also served for a decade as a maverick member of the Town Council, one day unveiling another plan to beautify the town, and the next day tweaking the good old boys by questioning the large expenditures of the tiny police department. One thing about Marlane: she spoke her mind.

THE RUB OF TIME

Eleanor government got ugly. In 1998, the police chief and two officers accused Marlane of sexual harassment, saying she had walked into their office, raised her shirt and exposed herself. She was 67, and the kind of woman who refused to wear shorts in public. The charge was nonsense, she says: clear retaliation.

But the accusations became fodder for national late-night talk shows; Marlane wanted to hide. When she and her husband reluctantly drove up to the next council meeting, the Town Hall parking lot was packed with cars and television news trucks. She told Sandy she couldn't go in.

In the years to come, the state's Human Rights Commission would find no merit to the harassment charges. The entire police force would be dismissed, amid findings of excessive pay raises and overtime. And Marlane would feel the democratic sting of being voted out of office.

But on this night, Sandy insisted that Marlane walk into that meeting. And when she did, townspeople embraced this daughter of Eleanor with shouts of support.

Marlane Crockett Carr ends her Rendezvous drive through the evolving American town of Eleanor. Its population has grown to 1,500—a number that includes nearly 20 original homesteaders, like Marlane. Its $500,000 budget pays the salaries of a handful of employees who work in Town Hall, clean the streets, police the town. And unemployment in the county is below the national average, thanks in part to a Toyota plant and a large auto parts manufacturer, Diamond Electric.

Over all, things are good. When a business moves out, another usually moves in. When the town needed a library, students in the vocational school—based in the old hosiery factory building—did much of the labor, which helped to keep costs way down.

Still, Marlane senses the history of Eleanor being worn away by the rub of time. Original houses were knocked down for a bank, a credit union, a Rite Aid. A relative demolished the house Marlane grew up in to clear space for a more modern home.

A few months ago, town officials held a 75th anniversary celebration, even though it was only the 74th. Marlane's offer to give a historical talk was ignored, so she stayed home. In her darker moments, she wonders whether homesteaders like her parents are still seen as welfare recipients, unworthy of celebration.

But when she thinks of the struggles of Robert and Eva Crockett, both buried now in the cemetery, close to Rebekah, her eyes blur with tears. "They had come from nothing," she says. "They were told by Eleanor Roosevelt that it would be wonderful—and it was."

As for that little dark-haired girl, Marlane says: "I was so appreciative. I always loved knowing that I lived on George Washington's land."

Across from Town Hall, where portraits of Eleanor Roosevelt lie on the floor of a deserted room that is supposed to be a museum someday, the schools let out. As he does most afternoons, the police chief has parked his cruiser facing the Dairy Queen, in plain sight.

Its presence announces: Slow down for the children of Eleanor.

Dust Is Gone Above the Bar,
but a Legend Still Dangles

NEW YORK, N.Y. — APRIL 7, 2011

On Sunday morning, before the ancient doors of McSorley's Old Ale House opened once again to spill that beer-and-sawdust aroma upon an East Village sidewalk, the owner took on a sorrowful job that in good conscience he could not leave to any of his employees. Too close to tempting the fates.

But it had to be done. The New York City health department was dropping hints as loud as the clatter of mugs on a Saturday night.

So, with heavy heart, the proprietor, Matthew Maher, 70, climbed up a small ladder. With curatorial care, he took down the two-dozen dust-cocooned wishbones dangling on an old gas lamp above the storied bar counter. He removed the clouds of gray from each bone. Then he placed every one of the bones, save for those that crumbled at his touch, back onto the gas lamp—where, in the context of this dark and wonderful establishment, they are not merely the scrap remains of poultry, but holy relics.

"Reluctantly," is how Mr. Maher says he approached this task. "It's kind of— how would you put it? It's something you didn't want to touch. It's the last thing I wanted to touch or see touched."

But it had to be done.

A couple of weeks ago, another city health inspector paid another visit to McSorley's, a drinking establishment that has been around since the 1850s, and looks it.

For many, this is the charm of the place: You sip your beer, take in that portrait of Franklin Delano Roosevelt, or that wanted poster for John Wilkes Booth, or those firefighter helmets, and you can almost feel your long-dead relations beside you, waiting for a free round.

But the charm is lost upon the occasional few. They might not understand, for example, what those dust-covered wishbones above the bar have come to mean.

Joseph Mitchell, the inimitable chronicler of old New York, once wrote that the founder, John McSorley, simply liked to save things, including the wishbones of holiday turkeys. But Mr. Maher, who has worked at McSorley's since 1964—he predates some of the memorabilia—insists that the bones were hung by doughboys as wishful symbols of a safe return from the Great War. The bones left dangling came to represent those who never came back.

Over the years, Mr. Maher says, the custom continued. In fact, he says, bones representing doughboys lost in France now hang beside those representing soldiers lost in Iraq and Afghanistan. And then he adds: "Actually, it started with the Civil War."

If this is only a story, a tale embellished by time and beer, its power has resonated for generations. Thirty years ago, Mr. Maher says, he got into a tiff with a health inspector who demanded to take one of the wishbones as evidence of something. Things got physical, and the police came, and, well, he says, "all quashed, no word about it."

But times have changed: Old New York and new New York remain in conflict, and old New York is losing. For example, lounging cats had been a furry part of the McSorley fabric since Lincoln. But word recently came down from City Hall: no cats. A longtime regular, Minnie, has been barred as a result.

Then, a couple of weeks ago, a city health inspector gave the establishment a grade of A, but strongly, strongly, encouraged the removal of those wishbones above—or, at the very least, removal of the dust enveloping them.

"The chandelier had numerous strands of dust," said a health department spokeswoman.

"The inspector encouraged the operator to clean the dust, or at least avoid storing or serving open drinks directly beneath it—to avoid the dust from falling into the drinks of their bar patrons."

The way Mr. Maher heard this was with a faint touch of hope: At least the bones could stay.

So, on that sad Sunday, he climbed up on his ladder, removed the dust from the bones, and hung them back with the care you might give to heirloom Christmas ornaments. He applied the same care to the dust, which he put in a container and took home with him to Queens, because, in the context of McSorley's, it is sacred.

What We Kept

NEW YORK, N.Y. — SEPTEMBER 11, 2011

After the roar, after the first ground-trembling collapse sent clouds of pulverized matter billowing through Lower Manhattan, a man paused from his hurried retreat to take in a world now coated with the dust of uncertain gray. For reasons he still cannot explain, he bent down, scooped some of this grayness into an envelope—and kept on moving.

Meanwhile, to the south, a businessman was shredding his T-shirt and distributing strips of cloth as protection against the dust-clotted air; a bank executive accepted the stranger's gift and pressed it to her mouth. And to the north, a rattled television producer made it to the Hudson River, where someone handed her a small red ticket granting her space on a ferry bound for New Jersey, where she lived.

"Admit One," the ticket said.

In the aftermath of Sept. 11, people everywhere did what people do in disaster's fresh wake: We wept, prayed, raged, cowered, gathered, hid, drank, questioned, comforted and sought comfort. We also saved things, often little things, and often for reasons just beyond the full grasp of articulation. Now, a decade later, many of us still keep these mundane items, which timing and circumstance have forged into artifacts approaching the sacred.

They return us instantly to a moment we have no desire to revisit, but are determined not to forget. They are our Sept. 11 relics.

The footlong shred of a T-shirt that Susan Horn keeps in her bedroom drawer in Scarsdale, N.Y., as a reminder of a stranger's selflessness. The jar of multicolored wax bits, remnants of the McLaughlin family's front-porch candlelight vigil in Brewster, N.Y. The silver-framed calendar of the Rev. Paul Fromberg, an Episcopal priest in San Francisco, its page fixed on September 2001. The photo identification card kept in the wallet of Stacy Scherf Dieterlen, a temporary worker who fled the south tower's 101st floor while some of her colleagues hesitated, and died.

Living now in Kentucky, Ms. Dieterlen carries the card with her as a reminder of her good fortune, and as proof to others that she was there. That morning she was wearing a pink button-up shirt, a black skirt and comfortable loafers, and she had just bought some blueberries to eat at her desk, when . . .

The parking garage tickets never validated, the Yankees tickets never used, the airplane tickets for flights never taken. The shoes worn in panicked retreat and now tucked deep in closets, never to be worn again, never to be thrown away. The face masks and Mass cards, the children's drawings and trade center trinkets. The worthless, precious bits of paper that burst out of the twin towers, fluttered across the East River, and floated down upon the streets of Brooklyn like sorrowful confetti.

Nick Arauz, for example, who had just hurried across the Manhattan Bridge with thousands of others, found a single page, a charred piece of a Peace Corps application, on the hood of his car in Carroll Gardens. Kept in the Army chest he uses as a nightstand, this bit of paper evokes so much—from the weapon of a jetliner flying directly over him to the innocence of his infant twins—yet he rarely looks at it.

"It was just something I couldn't throw away once I picked it up," he said.

The paper saved by Amy Shigo is even smaller. It is a red ticket, the kind used at carnivals and raffles, and yet so dear now that it is kept in a jewelry box. "Admit One," the ticket says, inviting the existential question of admission to what? The refuge of New Jersey? The continuation of life?

It is Ms. Shigo's ticket to then. To having recently completed her first Ironman competition. To seeing something hit the north tower from the window of her Hoboken-bound train. To being enveloped in the gauze of denial before heeding advice to leave her Chelsea office and get on a Jersey-bound ferry. To reaching the pier, where an orderly line had formed, and where a man was dispensing tickets. To making it home some seven hours later, where poor solace was found in a container of chocolate-chocolate-chip ice cream.

"It got me home; of course I would save it," Ms. Shigo said of her ticket. "This was my Willy Wonka-esque moment. All right. I made it. Admit one."

Even the very dust.

Jean-Marie Haessle, a French-born artist with mortality on his mind—he had just discussed his will with a lawyer in Lower Manhattan—began hustling back uptown after the collapse of the first tower. But, in an action he can describe only as reflexive, he stopped long enough to scoop up dust with an envelope on Wall Street.

"I don't know why, I don't know why," Mr. Haessle, now 71, said. "As an artist, I feel this gigantic, beautiful structure, reduced to this amazingly thin powder. To me, even today, it's just. . . ."

The dust reminds him of his eventual death; of the certainty of change—"of a lot of things, not all for the best." He keeps it on his desk, encased not in a vessel of gold or silver, but in the same paper envelope he used to capture it.

"The humblest kind of thing," he said.

Mateo Taussig-Rubbo, an associate professor at the University at Buffalo School of Law, State University of New York, has studied the "sacralization" of the saved objects of Sept. 11—from the American flag raised, Iwo Jima-like, at ground zero and now missing, to the chunks of trade-center granite, marble and steel that ironworkers and law enforcement officials handed out as solemn mementos.

These objects, particularly those directly related to the catastrophe, "are no longer what they appear to be," Mr. Taussig-Rubbo said. "They are something else." The items become a condensation of many concepts: the loss of a loved one; the value of human life; the sovereignty of the United States; the exact moment of the world's alteration.

This need to possess something tangible from Sept. 11 extends beyond the individual to the communal. After the calamity, for example, the Port Authority of New York and New Jersey filled the 80,000 square feet of Hangar 17 at Kennedy International Airport with girders, vehicles and other remnants. Then, a couple of years ago, it began to grant the requests of communities around the country, and the world, for a piece of history to display in a memorial garden, or town hall, or local museum.

The Port Authority so far has granted more than 1,200 requests. There is no cost beyond transportation, and little bureaucratic hassle beyond a letter of request, an explanation of use—and the approval of a federal judge, since the steel is technically part of a crime scene.

Communities in every state have received a remnant: the fire department in Guymon, Okla., and the school district in Massapequa, N.Y.; the board of commissioners in Martin County, Fla., and the rescue squad in Crivitz, Wis.; a museum in Tunica, Miss., and the Police Department in Cambridge, Mass. Coon Rapids, Minn.; LaGrange, Ga.; on and on.

"Inevitably a handwritten note of thanks comes back from the town or fire company, or police department," Christopher O. Ward, the port authority's executive director, said. "In some ways it will allow communities and towns to touch a piece of that day. And that's important."

Not long ago, Gig Harbor Fire and Medic One, outside Seattle, learned that it had been granted a piece of girder. So, in late May, four Gig Harbor firefighters hitched an empty trailer to a fire chief's official vehicle and drove the 2,800 miles east to Hangar 17.

Dressed in formal uniforms normally reserved for funerals and ceremonial events, the four men braced themselves as they walked into the hangar early one morning. The most stoic of the four wept.

They watched a forklift lay the piece down on their trailer "like you'd lay a child on a bed," recalled Rob McCoy, a Gig Harbor paramedic. Then, just outside the hangar, they covered their 986-pound girder with an American flag, and saluted.

On the days-long ride back, the firefighters occasionally pulled over for small flag-changing ceremonies: in Shanksville, Pa., to honor the victims of Flight 93; beside a picturesque farmhouse in Iowa; in a misty shroud near Mount Rushmore. And when they returned to Gig Harbor on Memorial Day, a long motorcade provided escort, while hundreds lined the streets, waving flags and crisply saluting.

The plan in Gig Harbor is to create a memorial garden one day, but for now there is this enduring image, seen there and around the country: People lining up, as if at a church service, to place their hands upon a relic.

A Town Won't Let Go of a Coin-Drop Line to the Past

PRAIRIE GROVE, ARK. — JULY 5, 2014

As the driver of an S.U.V. drifted off to sleep one recent afternoon, her vehicle drifted across a momentarily quiet two-lane highway. It came to rest on grass, but not before hitting a utility pole, an ornamental gas lamp and an upright rectangular structure of aluminum and glass.

Yes: a telephone booth. Among the last of those once-ubiquitous confessionals of communication, and the last one operated by the family-owned Prairie Grove Telephone Company in Arkansas.

357

The 67-year-old driver, exhausted from a night spent preparing for a yard sale, was uninjured. The same could not be said of the phone booth, which had stood sentry for a half-century outside the 1930s-era Colonial Motel, where soda-bottle caps popped and dropped on lost summer days are embedded in the asphalt.

The broken booth lay on the ground, spilled of its whispered secrets and mundane mutterings, but still bearing scratched assertions of affection ("I love Teresa") and existence ("Jimmy Jones was here"). A half-dozen bystanders took pallbearer positions and carried it to a resting place behind the motel's cottage-like office.

The motel's owner, Guy Matthews, said that in his four decades at the Colonial, he had seen his share of teenagers and traveling salesmen set aglow by its interior lights, engaged in coin-drop conversation. But for many years now, he said, the booth has been little more than a photo-op curio.

"Cellphones," he explained, with forensic specificity.

The Prairie Grove Telephone Company, which serves the western half of Washington County, has known for a long while now that its last phone booth has little purpose. One employee, Wade Jones, said that he emptied the phone booth of its coins only twice a year.

"Maybe $2," he said. "Sometimes a little more. Sometimes not even $2."

So what was the Prairie Grove Telephone Company to do with this battered relic of telephony, whose semiannual return doesn't even cover the expense of sending Mr. Jones out to collect it?

This was the question facing David Parks, whose own fate was determined in 1888, when his great-grandfather, a physician named Ephraim Graham McCormick, strung a telephone wire across the main street to his brother's pharmacy—perhaps Prairie Grove's most momentous event since the quick but brutal Civil War battle that bears its name.

Because many of their neighbors also craved disembodied connection, the good doctor and his partner wound up incorporating their company in 1906. They had a switchboard and a one-page directory that listed everyone from the Prairie Grove elite to "Davis, Sam—Barber Shop."

The company grew through the years, surviving wars and the Depression in part by never disconnecting a phone for nonpayment. According to a company history, it routinely accepted payment in the form of eggs, produce and "the occasional cow."

Dr. McCormick's son-in-law, James C. Parks, took over for many years, with the phone company operating from a small office above a hardware store. An old photograph shows many wires shooting, Medusa-like, from the side of the building to link up Prairie Grove.

Jim Parks's twin sons, Barry and Donald, succeeded their father, and then Donald's son and only child, David, came on board in 1980. Although his just-earned degree from the University of Arkansas was in education, he was the logical choice to take over one day.

"To keep it in the family," Mr. Parks explained.

Tall, angular, with an easygoing way that serves him well as a community leader in a town of 4,600, Mr. Parks runs his phone company now from a renovated building across from the old Masonic Lodge. With 33 employees, 6,900 landlines and 5,800 bills sent out every month, it is no Verizon.

Rural telephone companies like his, of which there are still hundreds around the country, are often the service providers of last resort for the most remote areas. But they are part of an endangered breed in this ever-changing digital age, grappling with challenges that include the move away from landlines to cellphones, and the decline in the fees collected for long-distance calls.

After a long pause to consider a question about his company's future, Mr. Parks said that he expected his family's business to still be around in a decade—though in what shape or form, he did not know. He went on to echo a favored analyst's assessment: "We're in an in-between time."

With all this going on, Mr. Parks had not given much thought to the company's only phone booth, which he drove past at least twice a day. The morning after the accident, in fact, he passed the motel going to and from Sunday service, and never noticed anything amiss.

But the phone booth's absence became an instant Facebook cause celebre, as locals pleaded for the return of their totemic reminder of things past. Acting quickly, Susan Parks-Spencer, a telephone company board member and Mr. Parks's cousin, used a friend's trailer to move the booth to the phone company's warehouse, where several people unloaded it.

"We dragged it some," Mr. Parks acknowledged.

He previously had been inclined to disconnect the phone booth. After all, a couple of dollars every six months? But the Facebook reaction persuaded him to salvage the curio, if only to imagine a younger generation trying to decode its instructions:

1. Listen for Dial Tone
2. Deposit 25¢ in Coins
3. Dial Number Desired

The telephone booth will return to its proper place, outside the Colonial Motel, in the next few weeks. At the moment, though, it is disassembled, its four aluminum-and-glass sides propped against the warehouse walls, its black box on the concrete floor. Carved everywhere are once-urgent phone numbers, now-moot sales calculations and Alan's romantic declaration for Anna.

The employee most responsible for the booth's resuscitation is Patrick Smith, 50 years old and nearly as large as his inanimate patient, whose injuries include broken glass panes, bent supports and a battered foundation.

Mr. Smith grew up in nearby Morrow, and remembers passing the booth whenever his family trucked their cattle to the sales barn in Fayetteville. The sight of Superman's see-through closet—an arrangement that made sense only if you didn't try to make sense of it—filled the boy with wonder.

Later, as a teenager, he often stepped into the phone booth after a movie night at the 112 Drive-In theater in Fayetteville, to call as the family curfew was descending.

With the close of the phone booth's door, the teenager would glow like a firefly. A mother's reassuring voice would emanate from the receiver. And the caller from Prairie Grove would promise, promise, to be home soon.

EPILOGUE

The telephone booth has been restored and returned to its original location. In August 2017, a plaque was planted beside it that reads:

1959 Prairie Grove
TELEPHONE CO.
PHONE BOOTH

Has Been Listed In The
NATIONAL REGISTER
OF HISTORIC PLACES
By The United States
Department of the Interior

Restoring Lost Names,
Recapturing Lost Dignity

OVID, N.Y. — NOVEMBER 28, 2014

For a half-century, a slight and precise man with an Old World mustache resided as a patient at the Willard State Psychiatric Hospital, here beside spectacular Seneca Lake. You are not supposed to know his name, but it was Lawrence Mocha. He was the gravedigger.

Using a pick, a shovel, and a rectangular wooden template, he carved from the upstate loam at least 1,500 graves, 60 to a row and six feet deep. At times he even lived in the cemetery, in a small shack with a stove, beside a towering poplar.

The meticulous Mr. Mocha dug until the very end, which came at the age of 90, in 1968. Then he, too, was buried among other patients in the serene field he had so carefully tended.

But you will not find the grave of Mr. Mocha, whose name you should not know, because he was buried under a numbered marker—as were nearly 5,800 other Willard patients—and the passing years have only secured his anonymity. The hospital closed, the cemetery became an afterthought, and those markers either disappeared or were swallowed into the earth.

Now, though, this obscure gravedigger has come to represent the 55,000 other people buried on the grounds of old psychiatric hospitals across New York State—many of them identified, if that is the word for it, by numbers corresponding with names recorded in old books. This numerical system, used by other states as well, was apparently meant to spare the living and the dead from the shame of one's surname etched in stone in a psychiatric hospital cemetery.

A retired schoolteacher, Colleen Spellecy, is seeking to end the anonymity, which she says only reinforces the prejudices surrounding mental illness. One way to do this, she says, is to place a plaque bearing Mr. Mocha's name on the spot where his shack once stood.

Lawrence Mocha

"He's a symbol for what we want to do with all the rest," Ms. Spellecy said. "It's almost like if we could just do something for one, we could do it for all."

But the State Office of Mental Health, which oversees some two dozen hospital cemeteries tucked in upstate corners and along busy Long Island highways, has consistently denied her request. Its officials say that a generations-old state law protects the privacy of people who died in these institutions.

"Stigma and discrimination is alive and well, though I wish it were not," said John Allen, special assistant to the commissioner of mental health. "Outing every family, whether they want to be outed or not, does not conform with the reality."

But advocates say that other states have long since figured out how to return names to those buried under numbers—a process that the advocacy organization Mental Health America says would help to end prejudice and discrimination. In an email, its spokeswoman, Erin Wallace, wrote: "These people had names, and should never have been buried with us forgetting them."

Larry Fricks, the chairman of the National Memorial of Recovered Dignity project, an effort to create a Washington tribute to all mental patients buried without names, agreed. He suggested that the cost of memorializing so many people could be a factor in a state's reluctance—and some of those books with recorded names have been damaged and even lost over the many years.

The issue is not trivial, Mr. Fricks said. "There is something embedded deep in our belief system that when people die, you show respect."

In addition to his name and burial site, here is what else you are not supposed to know about Lawrence Mocha:

Born poor in Austro-Hungarian Galicia in 1878. Hit in the head with a rock as a young man. Drank heavily, was briefly institutionalized, and served in the Army. Emigrated, and found work at Bellevue Hospital in New York City. Caused a ruckus one day and was sent to the psychiatric unit, where he talked of guilt and depression, of hearing God and seeing angels.

Sent to Willard in 1918, never to leave.

Kept to himself for years, but eventually took an interest in tending to the graveyard. Requested freedom in 1945, but was ignored. Made an extra dollar here and there by preparing bodies for burial. Stopped having episodes, if that was what they were.

Dug, and dug, and dug.

Gunter Minges, 73, the last grounds superintendent at Willard, sat on his pickup's tailgate at the cemetery's edge and recalled Mr. Mocha in his last decade. A reclusive man, he said. Had special kitchen privileges. Smoked a pipe. Wore hip waders, because groundwater would fill his neat rectangular holes.

"He dug until he died," Mr. Minges said, and was rechristened with a number. Then, with a Catholic priest at graveside, the grounds crew used ropes to lower Mr. Mocha's coffin into a hole dug by someone else.

"But where it is," Mr. Minges said, "I don't know."

Many of the numbered metal markers, forged by hospital patients and spiked into the ground, vanished over the years, sold for scrap or tossed into a nearby gully as impediments to mowing. In the early 1990s, groundskeepers began affixing numbered plaques flat onto the ground, but the job was left incomplete when the hospital shut down in 1995.

In a last-minute search of Willard's buildings for items worthy of posterity, state workers opened an attic door to find 427 musty suitcases. Among them: a brown leather case containing two shaving mugs, two shaving brushes, suspenders, and a pair of black dress shoes that a slight and precise immigrant hadn't worn since World War I.

The discovery of the suitcases led to an exhibit at the New York State Museum in Albany, a traveling display, and a well-received book about forgotten patients called "The Lives They Left Behind: Suitcases From a State Hospital Attic." Confidentiality laws forced its authors, Darby Penney and Peter Stastny, to reluctantly use pseudonyms; Lawrence Mocha, then, became Lawrence Marek.

Ms. Penney said that for the last several decades of his life, Mr. Mocha exhibited no signs of mental illness and was not on any medication. Her guess: "There were certain people who were kept there because they were decent workers."

And Mr. Mocha was the meticulous gravedigger.

Ms. Spellecy read the book. She is a wife, a mother, and a retiree who lives in Waterloo, about a half-hour's drive from Willard. Visiting the cemetery for the first time, she "sensed the injustice immediately," she said, and quickly set about to forming the Willard Cemetery Memorial Project. Its mission: "To give these people a name and a remembrance."

Ms. Spellecy and other volunteers got on their knees to begin unearthing the numbered plaques. They searched the surrounding woods to salvage discarded metal markers. With the help of another former groundskeeper, Mike Huff, they erected signs to identify sections divided by religion—Protestant, Catholic, Jewish—and planted a small boulder where Mr. Mocha's shack stood.

They have also engaged in a contentious back and forth with the Office of Mental Health over its refusal to grant names to the dead—beginning with a plaque on that boulder to honor Mr. Mocha, and then, perhaps, a central memorial that would feature the names of all those buried anonymously or beneath numbers.

"It's as if they are saying that they own the cemetery and therefore they own the names," Ms. Spellecy said. "In so owning the names, they are owning the person—as if these people continue to be wards of the state."

State officials say that they are bound by state law to protect patient confidentiality, even after death, unless granted permission by a patient's descendants to make the name public. They also say that attempts to change the law have failed, and that, even now, some descendants express concern about prejudice.

Mr. Allen said that the state had worked with communities throughout New York to restore these cemeteries as places of reverence and contemplation, and had assisted families in locating graves. In fact, he said, "We have helped a number of families place a marker at a number."

But without some descendant's consent, Willard's dead will remain memorialized by a number, if at all.

State officials also say that at the request of the Willard Cemetery Memorial Project, they are searching for any relatives of a certain individual—they would not say "Lawrence Mocha"—who might grant permission for the public release of that individual's name. This is highly unlikely, advocates say, given that this individual never married and left Europe a century ago.

But Ms. Spellecy will not give up. She and other volunteers are developing a list of the dead through census rolls and other records, and hope to secure permission from descendants to have those names made public, perhaps even in granite.

When asked why she has committed herself to this uphill task, Ms. Spellecy paused to compose herself. With her eyes wet from tears, she said: "Every stage of life is very sacred. Life deserves to be remembered, and revered, and memorialized."

A few weeks ago, Ms. Spellecy and some others bundled up and went out again to the 29 acres of stillness that is the Willard cemetery. They removed a little brush and cleaned a little dirt from a few of the numbers in the ground.

Searching for the numbered dead

The autumn winds carved whitecaps from the steel-gray lake below, while fallen leaves skittered across a field of anonymous graves, many of them dug by a man buried here too, whose name, Lawrence Mocha, you are not supposed to know.

EPILOGUE

Colleen Spellecy and other champions of the anonymously buried have had several small successes, including a change in New York State law and a monument erected to remember, by name, 96 former residents of the Willard State Psychiatric Hospital who are buried at a nearby cemetery in Ovid, New York.

But the seminal moment came in the spring of 2015 with the unveiling of a lasting tribute to Lawrence Mocha, the gravedigger. Beside a memorial plaque affixed to a granite boulder, there is now a shovel set in concrete, poised as if in mid-dig.

Still Standing, Precariously

PITTSFIELD, MASS. — MAY 29, 2016

The world's best female duckpin bowler holds so many bowling records that she has lost count, but her game-day shirt features a star for each of her tournament wins—a sartorial requirement of the Women's National Duckpin Association. With 19 stars so far, her polyester constellation is running out of sky.

The world's best female duckpin bowler lives here in the Berkshires, where duckpin bowling is neither played nor followed. If she wants to bowl, she must drive two hours to an alley in Connecticut, where bowlers sometimes ask her for shared selfies and autographs.

The world's best female duckpin bowler is Amy Bisson Sykes, a slight woman of 37 who dominates a black-and-white pastime in a Technicolor world. Her sport is so yesterday that whenever another duckpin alley closes, the remaining alley owners descend like predatory relatives to cart off the mechanical parts of duckpin setting machines that have not been made in two generations.

But Bisson Sykes was reared in the duckpin bowling alley her father owned in Newington, Conn., amid the drone of rolling balls on pine and maple, the clatter of pins scattering like startled waterfowl. The soundtrack of her youth.

In leagues and tournaments, Bisson Sykes used to slip into an all-business cocoon that others found intimidating and even off-putting. Wearing the mask of singular purpose, she would stand with the same red-and-white ball firm in her right hand and raised close to her chest and then release it with the twinning of a ballerina's curtsy and a fencer's thrust.

"I was there to win," she said.

The cognoscenti of duckpin often pause before describing Bisson Sykes's talent and impact, as if searching for the proper superlative.

"Phenomenal," said Al Zoraian, the president of the National Duckpin Bowling Congress.

"Not unbeatable," added Lauree Schreiber, a friend and longtime opponent. "But she's about as close as it gets."

Bisson Sykes has retained much of her intense focus on the 10-pin triangle. But motherhood has taught her that the lanes of life are curlicue, with pins that can move about and refuse to fall. Now she offers high-fives to opponents who throw strikes and embraces the sense of community that has always enveloped the ancient game of bowling.

It's been an epiphany. Turns out some things in life are even more important than duckpin bowling.

IT'S NOT EASY

To all those armchair athletes rolling their eyes instead of balls, let's be clear: Odds are, you'd be lousy at duckpin.

The grapefruit-size ball weighs less than four pounds and has no finger holes, and the squat duckpins look like out-of-shape cousins to the more familiar bowling pin. And even though a turn can include throwing three balls, instead of the two in the more common game of tenpin bowling, scores are still much lower.

According to the United States Bowling Congress, there were 55,266 certified 300 games—that is, 12 consecutive strikes, for a perfect score—in the 2013-14 season of tenpin bowling. But there has never been a 300 game in duckpin bowling. As all serious duckpinners know, a Connecticut man named Pete Signore Jr. came closest in 1992, bowling a 279.

Her engraved ball

The history of duckpin is a murky pond. It was long believed that the game emerged around 1900 from a Baltimore gaming hall owned by John McGraw and Wilbert Robinson, future members of the Baseball Hall of Fame. But research has since found references to duckpin dating to the early 1890s, in New Haven, Boston and Lowell, Mass.

The sport became popular along the Eastern Seaboard, finding particular passion in Rhode Island, Connecticut and Maryland. Men now gray and halting in step will recall their glory years as pin boys, setting pins and clearing deadwood for the greats: Harry Kraus and Wolfie Wolfensberger and the singular Nick Tronsky, out of Connecticut. And don't forget the female standouts: Toots Barger and Sis Atkinson and Cathy Dyak.

Big matches drew standing-room-only crowds. Local newspapers chronicled the scores and profiled the stars ("Nick Tronsky of New Britain stole the show at the state duckpin tournament today with a nine-game total of 1,203"). Companies hired ringers for their league teams, and some stars barnstormed, taking on all local heroes. In certain American crannies, duckpin was life.

Some pastimes just fade away, to resurface only with the smirk of irony. Like so many other endeavors, duckpin has been a casualty of the fundamental change in how Americans choose to spend their leisure time. But some of the duckpin faithful will also cite what is known as the Curse of Ken Sherman.

In 1953, a submarine designer named Kenneth Sherman invented an automatic pinsetter for duckpin. It was an elaborate, Rube Goldberg-like contraption of more than 1,000 moving parts—cast-iron gears and gaskets and pin holders—that did away with the need for pin boys and made the game faster and more efficient.

But the story goes that when Sherman's company stopped operating nearly 50 years ago, he refused to sell the patent for the Sherman Pinsetter to Brunswick Equipment—some say because he feared that Brunswick would end production so that duckpin could no longer compete with tenpin.

"But we're in the same situation as if Brunswick had shut us down anyway," said Stan Kellum, 72, the executive director of the National Duckpin Bowling Congress, which is run out of a small office in a Maryland bowling alley. "Nobody is manufacturing the machines."

That is why, if you go behind the lanes at, say, Highland Bowl, in Cheshire, Conn., the back wall is lined with cardboard boxes crammed with cast-iron bits, duckpin nests and assorted other parts no longer manufactured—all scavenged and saved from closed alleys.

When all 20 lanes are operating smoothly, the deafening roar is mere background music for the owner, Todd Turcotte. But his ears are attuned to the faintest false note in the mechanical syncopation. When that happens, something is broken—off.

And what does Turcotte do then? "Pray," he said.

His situation reflects why the game of duckpin could not grow. No new automatic pinsetters means no new alleys.

Today there are 41 congress-certified duckpin bowling alleys, down from nearly 450 in 1963, Kellum said, "and we're losing houses all over the place."

In fact, he said, "We just lost T-Bowl last year." That would be T-Bowl Lanes in Newington. The alley in which Amy Bisson Sykes grew up.

WHEN DUCKPIN WAS LIFE

She was 3 years old when her father, an insurance man named Dick Bisson, bought the 48-lane alley in 1981. "His dream was to own a duckpin bowling alley," she said.

The youngest of his four children, Amy took to the game like—well, you know. "I never really found the sport to be difficult," she said.

By 12, she had her trusty red-and-white ball, engraved with her given name. By 15, she had a junior-level reputation as a fierce competitor with the exceptional hand-eye coordination required to consistently knock down a stubborn last pin 60 feet away. The junior records piled up: highest game (262); highest three-game set (567); highest average (145).

She played softball at American International College in Springfield, Mass.; graduated with a degree in elementary education; and promptly joined the professional duckpin tour. Reaching the finals of her first tournament, at Perillo's Bowl-O-Drome in Waterbury, Conn., she faced an estimable opponent, Lynne Heller, a Hall of Famer who had recently bowled a 200 game.

Into that cocoon she slipped. All business. She won the tournament and, soon, a reputation. A couple of years later, she wound up being matched with another bowler through the entirety of a weekend tournament. At the end of it, the other woman said she was glad to have spent time with her, adding, "You're not the bitch that people say you are."

Bisson Sykes remembers the moment as if it were yesterday: at Pinland Bowling Lanes, just outside Baltimore. "Back then, I probably just closed myself off to that," she said. "I was just there to bowl. But I think people took me as cocky."

The tournament wins and records kept piling up. Then, in 2007, she met Stephen Sykes, a financial adviser, through mutual friends. Coming from Pittsfield in the Berkshires, he knew little of duckpin bowling and nothing of the superstar status of the woman he was now dating.

They married and moved to Pittsfield, just 60 miles—and a duckpin chasm—away from her father's alley in Newington. "I thought I could handle it," Bisson Sykes said. "I didn't think that it would have the impact that it did."

She gave birth to her first son, Benjamin, in 2009. Returned to the tour in 2010 and was named female bowler of the year (one of at least eight such honors). Gave birth to her second, Nathan, in 2011. And was named bowler of the year in 2012.

That same year, her father died, unexpectedly, at 65. He took a cup of coffee to his work area at the back of the lanes, where all those Sherman Pinsetters were clacking and whirring, and collapsed.

And the next year, in the spring of 2013, her younger son, Nathan, was found to have a brain tumor. After two brain operations and who knows how many consultations—a neurologist, a neurosurgeon, a neuro-oncologist, a neuro-ophthalmologist—it was determined that the tumor, sitting on his brainstem, was inoperable.

These days, no news is good news. Nathan was undergoing magnetic resonance imaging every few months, but now he has yearly intervals between scans and is monitored by doctors at Boston Children's Hospital and Dana-Farber Cancer Institute. He attends preschool, sings, dances and trails after his older, protective brother.

"A goofball, a spitfire," Bisson Sykes said of Nathan. "He lights up the room."

As Nathan, 4, illuminated a room in the Sykeses' house, and as Benjamin, 6, dueled imaginary demons with his "Star Wars" saber, their mother went down to the basement. There, inside several plastic tubs stacked in a far corner, were the trophies and plaques that state her case as the world's best female duckpin bowler. Once on display upstairs, they lost out to the playthings of children.

MOURNING A FADING PASTIME

Reading through a couple of old newspaper clippings, Bisson Sykes mourned a pastime inexorably slipping into memory. Here was an article featuring T-Bowl, her father's bowling alley. Closed last year, it is now a furniture store.

"So many places are closing," Bisson Sykes said. "People just don't come out to bowl. Where is everybody going?"

Bisson Sykes knows at least where she will be for the Memorial Day weekend: at Turner's Dual Lanes, in Hagerstown, Md., for the first tour stop of the women's 2016 season. She has already paid her $115 entry fee.

She will be wearing a rubber bracelet on her right wrist that reads, "Nate the Great." And in her travel bag she will have all the essentials for a duckpin assassin:

The red-and-white ball she has carried with her since she was 12. Two other balls. A pair of Dexter bowling shoes, with the toe bottom worn away on the right shoe from so many follow-through curtsies. And a gray bowling shirt adorned with 19 stars.

It's not the same as it was, of course. When she turned professional 16 years ago, she'd see 80, maybe 100 women competing in a tour. Now, maybe half that.

But she will enjoy herself, catching up with friendly adversaries, visiting an outlet mall, going to dinner with a few close duckpin pals. And when it's time, she will lose herself in the fading, therapeutic endeavor of throwing a ball to knock things down.

EPILOGUE

As of this writing, Amy Bisson Sykes has 23 stars on her game-day shirt—one for each of her tournament wins—having added four more since this story's publication in 2016. She has also broken several more records, and has been named bowler of the year two more times. In women's duckpin bowling, she is the best there is.

More important, Ms. Sykes remains very active in raising money for A Kids' Brain Tumor Cure Foundation, a non-profit 501 (c) organization. The website is https://akidsbraintumorcure.org. The page dedicated to her son Nate is www.teamnatethegreat.org.

A Ranger, a Field and the Flight 93 Story Retold

Just another Thursday, and the morning mix includes leather-vested bikers from New Jersey, Amish visitors from Pennsylvania and a few children adjusting to a park not intended for play. They settle onto benches for the 11 o'clock retelling.

A ranger in the green and gray of the United States National Park Service tucks his peanut-butter-and-jelly lunch on a shelf and walks out to face his audience. A field of wildflowers undulates behind him; the pewter-bellied clouds seem nearly within reach. He begins:

"Remember how bad the weather was that morning?"

Hesitant nods turn quickly to head shakes. No. On that particular September morning, you could see forever.

This is just the ranger's way of buckling you in. Helping some to remember what we already know. Helping others, especially those who were not yet born, to envision a beautiful, calamitous day now nearly 15 years in the past.

His name is Robert Franz, he is 61, and his title is "interpretive park ranger," which means that his job is to tell the story of what happened in that color-dappled field behind him, again and again and again.

This is the Flight 93 National Memorial, by far the most removed of the three 9/11 crash sites. A visit requires a roller-coaster journey through the arresting Allegheny Mountains, up and down and up and down, past a Confederate flag here, a Trump sign there, to a 2,200-acre field set aside for reflection.

"Mayday! Mayday! Get out of here!" the ranger says, echoing the alarm that was heard by air traffic controllers. The words chill the late-summer air, as children fidget and bees buzz about.

He continues the story of United Airlines Flight 93, bound for San Francisco from Newark. How four hijackers redirect the jet southeast, most likely to crash into the nation's capital. How many of the 40 crew members and passengers fought back. How this hurtling jetliner nearly flipped before crashing at 563 miles an hour into the soft, strip-mined earth, killing all.

"The crew and passengers put democracy in action," Mr. Franz says. "They take a vote"—to storm the cockpit and regain control of the plane.

We connect to that day in our own way, and the storyteller in the broad-brimmed ranger's hat is no different. He was born into the military, his father an Army lifer who served in World War II's European theater, his mother a daughter of the French underground. They were married at the Cathedral of Notre-Dame in Paris, and went on a short honeymoon in an Army jeep.

Their son Rob spent the better part of two decades flying Army Hueys and Black Hawks and training other soldiers how to fly helicopters. He left the service in early 2001, and was at home on Cape Cod, Mass., that Tuesday, watching the news. He thought of those he had trained, and felt guilt for not being among them for the deployments sure to come.

Mr. Franz focused on a real estate career, volunteered with the local veterans' committee and worked briefly as a police officer. Then, in late 2011, he spotted a listing on a government website for a seasonal job as an interpretive park ranger at the Flight 93 Memorial. He quickly applied, he recalls, sensing a chance to "complete the circle."

Soon he was driving about 600 miles west to Shanksville every April, and staying until October. He proved to be such a powerful storyteller, his presentation informed by his knowledge of aeronautics, that he was recently offered permanent employment, which he accepted.

"He told this story unlike anyone I had heard," says Stephen Clark, the superintendent for the national parks in western Pennsylvania. "And, of course, being a veteran makes it all the more special."

Sometimes Mr. Franz stands at the memorial plaza, answering questions about the time of the crash and the location of the bathrooms. He commiserates as people recount their own connections to the day, and keeps his counsel as conspiracy theorists question whether such a crash even occurred. "If somebody's made up their mind, there's nothing I can do," he says.

Sometimes he distributes Flight 93 Junior Ranger handbooks, explaining to young visitors what activities they need to complete before receiving a Junior Ranger badge. The 22-page booklet is a thoughtful study in trying to find the right words: Early in the flight, their plane was hijacked by four men. To hijack a plane means to take control over it. These hijackers were angry at the United States of America . . .

But there are words, and then there are words. When children ask about the recovery of bodies, Mr. Franz redirects, ever so slightly. Since there were only remains, no bodies, he explains that a spot out there, beyond the wildflowers, is now "a final resting place."

And sometimes, Mr. Franz is standing before another 11 o'clock crowd, as he is now, telling an American epic in less than a half-hour, all the while reminding himself not to get emotional again when he comes to a certain point.

The more familiar narrative of Flight 93 focuses on those Mr. Franz calls the "big guys"—Todd Beamer, for example, the young software salesman who helped to organize the passenger revolt and whose last recorded words of "Let's roll!"

became a national rallying cry. But the park ranger makes the gentle point that the revolt was "a group effort."

"Let me tell you about Sandy Bradshaw," he says, recalling the 38-year-old flight attendant who, in a furtive call to her husband, explained how she was boiling water to hurl at the hijackers.

"Let me tell you about Honor Elizabeth Wainio," he says, recalling the up-and-coming business executive known as Lizz who, in a moment of supreme compassion, called to comfort her stepmother about what was to happen, and who was part of the revolt. She was 27.

"No, it's not looking good," Mr. Franz says. "But they weren't going to give up."

The park ranger, the father of two adult daughters, looks down and takes a long, unscripted pause. As he struggles to regain his composure, the wildflower setting becomes church-quiet, the bikers and the Amish now silent congregants in outdoor pews.

Soon these people will wander off, some over to the bone-white memorial wall, some up to the new visitors center, where Flight 93 shirts and mugs are sold, and an interactive display includes recordings from the fatal flight.

Soon, a Korean War veteran will tell Mr. Franz that he thinks the federal government "overdid it" with this park, and a 9-year-old boy in a tank top and a Penn State ball cap will ask for a Junior Ranger handbook so that he can learn about this place and earn his plastic badge.

But right now, Mr. Franz is taking a brief private moment in public that seems to him like an hour. Sandy Bradshaw. Lizz Wainio. Democracy in action . . .

His emotions in check, Mr. Franz acknowledges his awkward pause and returns seamlessly to his story. How the airplane flew right over Route 30, "the road you came in on." How this elevated ground is a place to reflect on the tragic loss of life, yes, but how it is also a place to honor the courage of the passengers and crew of Flight 93. And that, he says, "is a good story."

It's 11:30.

"Thank you," the ranger says. "Have a great day."

A Trip Down Obama Highway
in an Old Dixie Town

RIVIERA BEACH, FLA. — OCTOBER 24, 2016

The rechristened road runs beside a railroad freight line, slicing across a modest corner of Palm Beach County and a considerable section of the Southern psyche. It used to be called Old Dixie Highway.

But now this two-mile stretch, coursing through the mostly black community of Riviera Beach, goes by a new name. Now, when visitors want to eat takeout from Rodney's Crabs, or worship at the Miracle Revival Deliverance Church, they turn onto President Barack Obama Highway.

Our national journey along this highway is nearing its end, these eight years a blur and a crawl. That historic inauguration of hope. Those siren calls for change. The grand ambitions tempered or blocked by recession and time, an inflexible Congress and a man's aloofness.

War, economic recovery, Obamacare, Osama bin Laden. The mass shootings, in a nightclub, in a church—in an elementary school. The realization of so much still to overcome, given all the Fergusons; given all those who shamelessly questioned whether our first black president was even American by birth.

His towering oratory. His jump shot. His graying hair. His family. His wit. His tears.

The presidency of Mr. Obama, which ends in three months, will be memorialized in many grand ways, most notably by the planned construction of a presidential library in Chicago. But in crowded and isolated places across the country, his name has also been quietly incorporated into the everyday local patter, in ways far removed from politics and world affairs.

You can find a trapdoor spider (Aptostichus barackobamai) inching across certain parts of Northern California, or see a bright orange spangled darter (Etheostoma obama) swimming in a Tennessee river, or come upon a lichen (Caloplaca obamae) the color of gold on Santa Rosa Island, off the California coast.

You can visit the Barack Obama Academy in Plainfield, N.J., or the Barack Obama Male Leadership Academy in Dallas, or the Barack Obama Academy of International Studies in Pittsburgh. You can drive down Barack Obama Avenue in East St. Louis, or Obama Way in Seaside, Calif.—or President Barack Obama Highway here in Riviera Beach, just 10 miles and another reality from the stately pleasure-dome Mar-a-Lago.

This Obama road runs through the complex reality of America: the family-owned businesses and the ghostly vacant storefronts, a church here, a liquor store there, gas stations, convenience stores, a football field, a day care center, a medium-size manufacturing business that is expanding and hiring.

"Everything the president fought for and is fighting for—it's there," says the mayor, Thomas Masters.

Older black residents of Riviera Beach recall a time, not so long ago, when you avoided the east side of Old Dixie Highway after dusk because that was the white side of town, and no good would come from lingering.

West of the tracks was for black residents, the men who worked mackerel down at the docks, the women who worked as domestics in swanky Palm Beach homes. The only slice of white on the black side was a subdivision called Monroe Heights, which was bordered, or protected, by a high cinder block wall built in the 1940s. If your ball bounced over that wall into whiteness, you found yourself another ball.

"They put the wall up to keep us from looking at them," says Dan Calloway, 78, a former deputy sheriff and athlete revered in Riviera Beach for his half-century of mentoring and coaching local children.

The glaucoma affecting Mr. Calloway's sight has not dimmed the vividness of the Riviera Beach of his youth: the guava and mango trees, the chickens, the horse-riding lawman who would snap his whip at black people; that is, until a man named Shotgun Johnny pulled him from his horse and beat the hate out of him. Mr. Calloway remembers, too, how the "black" beach was moved up to Jupiter when Singer Island suddenly became desirable, and how the Ku Klux Klan occasionally announced itself.

"They burned those crosses," Mr. Calloway says. "We had to blow the lamps out and hide under the bed."

Dora Johnson, 88, remembers one cross that set Old Dixie Highway aglow. It was around 1948, and she was married with two babies.

"My God, it was way up in the air," she says of the symbol of her faith set aflame. "It was very upsetting. I'm a deep Christian, but seeing it, you'd break down and want to do something you shouldn't do."

With time came change. In 1962, F. Malcolm Cunningham Sr. became the first black person elected to the City Council—and, some claim, the first black elected official in the South since Reconstruction. By the end of that decade, the city was predominantly black, and by 1975, it had its first black mayor.

The notion of renaming the highway after the country's first black president popped up at a City Council meeting shortly after Mr. Obama's 2008 victory. A citizen raised the prospect before moving on to discussing a local supermarket. The suggestion went nowhere.

It was resurrected a couple of years ago by the indefatigable Mayor Masters, 64, who has followed a circuitous path to politics. A bishop in a nondenominational church, he began preaching at the age of 4—he was once known as the "Wonder Boy Preacher"—and has demonstrated a talent for publicity ever since.

Mr. Masters is not a Riviera Beach native; he moved here from California nearly 30 years ago. But as a black man, he was bothered that a constant celebration of "Old Dixie" ran through the center of his predominantly African-American city. "Dixie meant slavery, bigotry, the K.K.K.," he says.

While researching the history of his adopted city, the mayor says, he spoke with a white-haired woman in a wheelchair, Ms. Johnson, who dearly wanted to fill him in. "I wanted to tell him about the cross burnings, because there's not many of us left," she says. "So much had happened on Old Dixie."

Mr. Masters resolved to have the stretch of the highway in his city renamed, gathered community support and put it to the City Council. The vote was 4-to-1 in favor, and the sole dissenting member was also the sole white member: Dawn Pardo. But do not prejudge.

Ms. Pardo, who grew up in New York, says she voted against the plan because she envisioned a grander, more ambitious tribute, perhaps at the city's recently renovated, multimillion-dollar marina. The monument or renaming could also honor various black trailblazers in Riviera Beach's past.

"If we're going to honor him, let's make it great," she remembers arguing.

But the mayor prevailed. At a ceremony in December, residents cheered as workers in bucket trucks took down the old and put up the new. This meant, among other things, that traffic would flow through an intersection of Riviera Beach streets named after the Rev. Dr. Martin Luther King Jr. and Mr. Obama.

"It made me feel real good," Ms. Johnson, an honored guest at the event, says. "Now I don't have to think about Old Dixie."

But the reality of America again imposed. News of the name change had spread well beyond Florida, and now came the emails and telephone calls.

> If you want to honor a Black man then Honor Black Men who are fighting for our Country and Not against it . . .
>
> "This One" is lucky that I am not standing in judgment . . .
>
> Why is everyone so bent on changing this road's name? I do not get it.
>
> A lot of southern blacks are wrapped up in the past . . .

And there was much, much worse. Bad enough for Mr. Masters to alert the Secret Service.

"Hating on the president just for who he is," the mayor says. "It got so bad, they were making direct or indirect threats: 'He needs to be hung from the street sign.'"

The angry calls and emails became distant shouts, leaving Riviera Beach to incorporate into its lexicon a street name that was nearly the opposite of "Old Dixie." It has meant changes to stationery, of course, but also challenges for businesses trying to direct customers.

"Everybody from here knows Old Dixie, you feel me?" says Rodney Saunders. He owns Rodney's Crabs, a takeout restaurant on the highway, a few dozen yards from where the gray cinder block remnants of the old Monroe Heights decline in the shadows of sea grape trees.

"When people ask me for directions," Mr. Saunders continues, "I say, 'Old Dixie—but now it's President Barack Obama Highway.'"

Some along the highway call the renaming a nice but benign gesture. Some say they never took umbrage with Old Dixie; it was just a name. Some simply shrug, as if to suggest the new street name means more to out-of-towners than it does to locals.

But Mr. Calloway, the legendary coach and mentor with failing vision, says he can see into the future—20, 30, 40 years from now—when a long-ago decision will have children wanting to know the story behind the name on a sign.

In the Middle of Nowhere, a Nation's Center

BUTTE COUNTY, S.D. — JUNE 2, 2008

The mesmerizing prairie monotony along Highway 85 south is abruptly broken by a blue sign about the size of a cafeteria tray. In roadside shorthand it offers an expeditionary challenge worthy of Jules Verne: this way, 7.8 miles, to the CENTER OF THE NATION.

The unpaved road at the turnoff greets cars of the curious with growls of annoyance, and for several miles offers only sheared sheep, skittish antelope and grass. But just when suspicions of a prank begin to invade the mind, something 100 yards off the road catches the eye, something red, and white—and, yes, blue.

It is a wind-tattered American flag, flapping at the top of a silvery pole that rises from the Dakota moonscape like the claim stake of some disoriented astronaut. A hand-scrawled sign propped against a barbed-wire fence provides confirmation: Though the absence of a souvenir stand or even a snow-cone booth would suggest otherwise, this remote spot is, in fact, the declared geographic center of the United States.

Over the years this dot on the map has been treated as a holy place and as a place to share a six-pack, an inconvenient place, a nearly forgotten place, a place to reflect on something larger than one's self. Who knows why the centers of things matter—the centers of cities, of states, of countries—but they do.

No one knows this better than David Doyle, the chief geodetic surveyor for the National Geodetic Survey at the National Oceanic and Atmospheric Administration, which oversees a national coordinate system for mapping and other scientific and engineering uses. He recalls that when his mentor retired 20 years ago, the man plopped a file three inches thick on Mr. Doyle's desk and said, "Now it's yours."

The file overflowed with letters and documents, some dating back to 1925, all concerning the "center" of places American. Though the subject is hardly a government priority, Mr. Doyle says he continues to maintain the file because he now knows what his predecessor knew: "People find this to be really, really important."

For a while, this country's geographic center bounced around the heartland like the ball on an old movie-screen singalong. When Alaska joined the union nearly 50 years ago, the government determined that the center—the theoretical balance point—had moved from outside Lebanon, Kan., to some inaccessible prairie here in Butte County, 439 miles to the northwest. (Fret not, Lebanon has adapted; it now calls itself the "Historical Geographical Center of the 48 States or the Contiguous United States.")

Then, when Hawaii became a state soon after, the center moved again—just six miles to this spot, about 21 miles north of Belle Fourche, a small city of ranching and agriculture. The center of the nation was now a few dozen yards from what was then Highway 85; local officials gazed into the open pasture and saw visions of camera-wielding tourists, jammed parking lots, a Belle Fourche boom.

"Now We're Rolling," proclaimed the local newspaper, The Belle Fourche Bee.

On a windswept day in October 1959, more than 100 people gathered in the pasture for the raising of the American flag up a 40-foot pole that volunteers had set in concrete. A band played "The Star-Spangled Banner," and a visiting dignitary spoke of the many tourists surely to follow.

But in the mid-1960s the state made some road improvements just north of Belle Fourche. The new Highway 85 bypassed the center of the nation by 7.8 miles; the old Highway 85 became the road rarely traveled, the nation's center the attraction not attracting.

After a while, some road maps and guides began placing the center at a scenic rest area about 10 miles to the northeast, on a rise just off the main highway, simply because it featured a sign that essentially said the nation's center was over there somewhere.

Adding to the confusion was Belle Fourche, now billing itself as the "Center of the Nation." But the price of this boast was constantly explaining to persistent tourists that the actual center was on the other side of a barbed-wire fence, 13 miles up Highway 85 and 7.8 miles along an unpaved road. And don't expect any snow-cones.

By 1999, the year that Teresa Schanzenbach became director of the Belle Fourche Chamber of Commerce, vandalism had forced the closing of that scenic rest area; local officials had tired of replacing the "Center of the Nation" signs stolen along Highway 85; and the 40-foot flagpole had long since vanished. Only a short red fencepost marked the spot; no flag attached.

"It had lost its pizzazz," Ms. Schanzenbach says.

For years Belle Fourche struggled with how to capitalize on its nearness to the center of the nation. There were meetings, and fund-raising golf tournaments, and more meetings, and grumblings about how even Rugby, N.D., the "Geographical Center of North America," had a 15-foot stone obelisk to mark the spot.

Finally, last summer, the Chamber of Commerce unveiled a "Center of the Nation" monument planted in the grass behind its office: a massive map of the United States enclosed in a compass rose, designed by a local artist and made of 54,000 pounds of South Dakota granite. American tourists could stand on their home state and pose for photographs memorializing their visit to somewhere near the nation's center.

Ms. Schanzenbach says 2,200 tourists stopped at the Belle Fourche visitors center in September, compared with about 200 the September before—all thanks to the monument. Although staff members and handouts explain that the actual center is a good half-hour's drive away, she says 90 percent of the visitors choose to pose for photos at the monument and then carry on to Deadwood, Mount Rushmore and attractions beyond.

"We're not pretending to be the actual center," she says. "We're providing a convenience."

But Ms. Schanzenbach knows what 90 of 100 visitors do not experience. She has been to the center; in fact, she has made sure that a flag again flies there. And she encourages others to go.

You slip through the barbed wire and follow a worn path toward the flag, past dandelions and wildflowers sprouting from the scrub, with nothing before you but sky, pasture and a solitary flag, its reds and whites torn at the ends by winter's winds. And there, planted in the spring-softened ground, near pocks left by hooves and shoes, is a disc-shaped marker left in 1962 by the government's geodetic surveyors.

In the center of the disc it says: CENTER.

Hidden songbirds provide the only sound; their chatter recalls the giggles of unseen Munchkins. But then, in this remote, still place, there comes a strange sense of reassurance: that in this time of uncertain war and near-certain recession, of home foreclosures and gas at $4 a gallon, at least somewhere in this nation a center holds.

Acknowledgments

I never traveled alone. So many *New York Times* colleagues were with me in spirit that I should have been driving a Greyhound bus.

Often beside me were some of the best photographers and videographers in journalism. In addition to Ángel Franco, Nicole Bengiveno, Kassie Bracken and Todd Heisler, they included Fred Conrad, Richard Perry, and Monica Almeida, who tolerated me during a long trip through the Pacific Northwest that somehow ended inside the iconic globe of the now-defunct *Seattle Post-Intelligencer*. Among the editors providing visual guidance over the years were Jessica Dimson, Beth Flynn, Becky Lebowitz, Meaghan Looram, Michele McNally, Cornelius Schmid, David Scull, Justine Simons and John Woo.

Also along for the ride were former national editor Suzanne Daley and former deputy editor David Firestone, who helped to conceive and nurture the column; national editors Rick Berke, Sam Sifton, Alison Mitchell and Marc Lacey; and deputy editors Rick Lyman, David Halbfinger, Dean Murphy and Chuck

Strum, who recognized in my wanderings the hint of "Sullivan's Travels." Sitting in the back, occasionally giving directions, were executive editors Bill Keller, Jill Abramson, Dean Baquet, and the publisher Arthur Sulzberger Jr. (who paid for the gas). I am especially thankful to deputy managing editor Matt Purdy and senior editor Christine Kay for providing a much-needed road map—and, again, to Cate Doty, whose keen sense of what makes a good story helped to inform the This Land sensibility.

Many copy editors prevented me from veering off the road. I routinely implored them to save me from national embarrassment, and time and again they did, especially Mindy Matthews, Jen McDonald, Eric Nagourney, Joe Rogers, Karron Skog, Kaly Soto and Rory Tolan.

I am grateful to the dedicated people at Black Dog & Leventhal for hopping aboard, especially my gifted editor, Becky Koh, the champion of this collection; Frances Soo Ping Chow; Melanie Gold; Betsy Hulsebosch; Kara Thornton; Ruiko Tokunaga; and Kris Tobiassen. Also with me were Alex Ward, the editorial director for book development at the Times, and Todd Shuster, my longtime friend and agent.

Throughout my travels, I never needed a GPS or any other navigational device; I had my wife, Mary Trinity, and two daughters, Nora and Grace, to show me the way home. More than anyone, Mary made This Land possible. She provided invaluable counsel on every column I wrote—so much so that my editors at the Times would often ask: *What does Mary think?*

Lastly, I thank all those who gave their time, and more, to this gawky stranger from New York. I see us all now—the Louisiana shrimper and the Massachusetts preacher, the Connecticut stripper and the Florida Jesus, the Rhode Island wise guy, the Missouri schoolgirl, the rehabilitated Illinois drug dealer—gathered around a table at Donna's Diner in Elyria, Ohio. Donna is topping off our cups of coffee as we tell our American stories and shake our heads in wonder.

Photography Credits

Ángel Franco/*The New York Times*: 2, 8, 11, 12, 15, 16, 18, 20, 22, 23, 25, 28, 29, 40, 42, 70, 72, 74, 77, 80, 82, 112, 114, 116, 120, 124, 126, 128, 131, 133, 137, 168, 170, 172, 174, 176, 179, 200, 203, 205, 242, 244, 276, 278, 280, 284, 287, 315, 321, 322, 328, 362, 367, 386, 389

Nicole Bengiveno/*The New York Times*: 47, 51, 53, 56, 146, 209, 211, 214, 216, 218, 220, 227, 228, 247, 251, 252, 260, 263, 265, 269, 270, 288, 292, 296, 298, 301, 302, 304, 307, 333, 337, 341, 357, 359

Todd Heisler/*The New York Times*: 65, 99, 102, 104, 189, 191, 193, 375, 377, 379

Fred R. Conrad/*The New York Times*: 84, 87

Monica Almeida/*The New York Times*: 141, 223, 224

Tony Cenicola/*The New York Times*: 350

Emon Hassan for *The New York Times*: 61, 63

Frances Roberts for *The New York Times*: 33, 34

Gretchen Ertl for *The New York Times*: 59

Andrew White for *The New York Times*: 150, 161

Eric Thayer for *The New York Times*: 181

Jenn Ackerman for *The New York Times*: 310, 312

Joshua Bright for *The New York Times*: 348

Jessica Hill for *The New York Times*: 368, 370

Mary Murphy: 94

Alden Pellett/*Associated Press*: 122

Rob Godfrey/Twitter @robgodfrey: 185

Courtesy Marlane Carr: 342

New York State Archives and New York State Museum: 364